LOVE BYTES

THE ONLINE DATING HANDBOOK

DAVID FOX

PUBLISHER • Mitchell Waite
EDITOR-IN-CHIEF • Scott Calamar
EDITORIAL DIRECTOR • Joel Fugazzotto
MANAGING EDITOR • Dan Scherf
CONTENT EDITOR • Heidi Brumbaugh
COPY EDITOR • Hilary Powers
TECHNICAL REVIEWER • Harry Henderson
PRODUCTION DIRECTOR • Julianne Ososke
DESIGNER/PROJECT COORDINATOR • Kristin Peterson
PRODUCTION • Cecelia Morales
ILLUSTRATIONS • Pat Rogondino
COVER DESIGN • Cecile Kaufman

Printed in the United States of America
94 95 96 97 • 10 9 8 7 6 5 4 3 2 1
Fox, David.   Love bytes : the online dating handbook / by David Fox.
        p. cm.
    Includes index.
    ISBN 1-878739-88-3 : $18.95
      1. Dating (Social customs)–Communication systems.   2. Courtship –Communication systems.   3. Computer Networks 4. Electronic mail systems 5. Etiquite I. Title. II. Title Online datinghandbook
    HQ801.F66   1995
    646.7'7—dc20   94-40710
                                                                          CIP

DEDICATION

To Hope, the loveliest lass in cyberspace.
Or anywhere else.

ACKNOWLEDGEMENTS

Foremost, thanks to the dozens of cyberdaters who shared the juicy details of their online love stories with me, including Karen Lang and Craig Ford (and Carly D'Anne), Roberta and Paul Chesney, Mike Godwin, Ali Perry, Erin Zhu, Steven Orlin, Jan Stewart, Jill Lampi, Laura Kolb, Kate and Walt Roshon, James Herzog and Caroline Ann Murphy, Amy Guth, Robin Northup, Saundra and Kevin Brake, Kevin York, Ms. Julie, Joey Havlock, D.J. and Mary "Ruf "Armstrong, Beverly Momeault, Lisa Bishop and Steve Casey, and Mark Edwards.

I am very grateful to customer service representatives from the various BBSs and commercial services who went above and beyond their calls of duty when gabbing with me. Cyberpeople are the best!

Thanks to Mark Cirino for his pundom expertise, Shawn Klein for fashion tips, Marilyn Fox for being my "average reader," Irving Fox for being there to solder my faulty circuitry, and, of course, Jay—for his spiritual guidance.

The Waite Group Press is simply the grooviest. In particular, Dan Scherf parted seas to shepherd the project along and Heidi Brumbaugh, Hilary Powers, and Harry Henderson baked my half-baked words to perfection (talk about mixing metaphors). And, most of all, thanks to Mitch Waite, who had the vision to give *Love Bytes: The Online Dating Handbook* life, like a phoenix from digital ashes.

ABOUT THE AUTHOR

David Fox hangs his hat in New York City, freelance writing and computer consulting. He's been addicted to cyberdatin' since the good ol' days of Commodore 64 and Q*Link. David is currently cobbling together a novel about, in part, two people who fell in love online.

LOVE BYTES

TABLE OF CONTENTS

Chapter 4 The Datemobile 34

Chapter 5 Buckling Up 60

Chapter 6 Bulletin Board Systems 66

Dear Reader:

What is a book? Is it perpetually fated to be inky words on a paper page? Or can a book simply be something that inspires—feeding your head with ideas and creativity regardless of the medium? The latter, I believe. That's why I'm always pushing our books to a higher plane; using new technology to reinvent the medium.

I wrote my first book in 1973, *Projects in Sights, Sounds, and Sensations*. I like to think of it as our first multimedia book. In the years since then, I've learned that people want to experience information, not just passively absorb it—they want interactive MTV in a book. With this in mind, I started my own publishing company and published *Master C,* a book/disk package that turned the PC into a C language instructor. Then we branched out to computer graphics with *Fractal Creations*, which included a color poster, 3D glasses, and a totally rad fractal generator. Ever since, we've included disks and other goodies with most of our books. *Virtual Reality Creations* is bundled with 3D Fresnel viewing goggles and *Walkthroughs and Flybys CD* comes with a multimedia CD-ROM. We've made complex multimedia accessible for any PC user with *Ray Tracing Creations, Multimedia Creations, Making Movies on Your PC, Image Lab,* and three books on Fractals.

The Waite Group continues to publish innovative multimedia books on cutting-edge topics, and of course the programming books that make up our heritage. Being a programmer myself, I appreciate clear guidance through a tricky OS, so our books come bundled with disks and CDs loaded with code, utilities, and custom controls.

By 1995, The Waite Group will have published 135 books. Our next step is to develop a new type of book, an interactive, multimedia experience involving the reader on many levels. With this new book, you'll be trained by a computer-based instructor with infinite patience, run a simulation to visualize the topic, play a game that shows you different aspects of the subject, interact with others online, and have instant access to a large database on the subject. For traditionalists, there will be a full-color, paper-based book.

In the meantime, they've wired the White House for hi-tech; the information super highway has been proposed; and computers, communication, entertainment, and information are becoming inseparable. To travel in this Digital Age you'll need guidebooks. The Waite Group offers such guidance for the most important software—your mind.

We hope you enjoy this book. For a color catalog, just fill out and send in the Reader Report Card at the back of the book.

Mitchell Waite

Mitchell Waite
Publisher

INTRODUCTION

"I'm late, I'm late, for a very important date!"

If only Alice's white rabbit had a computer. Why, it would've taken him just an instant to plop his fluffy tail down, log on to his favorite commercial wonderland, and hook up with a bevy of bunnies.

Is online dating really that easy? Well, as a guy who's had one or two long-lasting online relationships, I can tell you: Never. I can't guarantee that, using this book, you'll find the person of your dreams and live happily ever after in a small French chateau. Trying to find a date, sharing secrets, happening onto someone you *really* like, dispensing completely with superficiality, deciding where and when to take the relationship, and then negotiating the rules of love—these are the challenges that give life its, well, *texture*.

But I *can* guarantee that the techniques, tricks, and technology in this book will painlessly pave the road for online love-seekers.

Chapters 1 through 3 introduce the ups and downs of online dating, covering all the whos, whats, wheres, whys, whens, and, of course, hows.

Chapter 4 is a crash course in telecommunications. It'll help you buy and set up your modem and communications software.

Chapter 5 introduces the various commercial services, showing you how to blast off online without being taken for a ride.

Chapters 6 through 12 cover the dating scene among the major online services. All the major ones are here, in vivid detail: bulletin board systems (BBSs), the Internet, America Online, CompuServe, PRODIGY, GEnie, and Delphi.

Lucky number Chapter 13 is a comprehensive guide showing you how to send e-mail from one online service to another.

If you already belong to an online service, its chapter will show you exactly what to do to begin dating. If not, you might want to sample *all* the commercial services, using each chapter as a guide, before you settle on one. You might as well; most services will give you free trial time.

However you decide to use this book, be sure not to skip the case examples, which are scattered throughout. They're all real, heartfelt first-person anecdotes about the online dating experience. For some people, online dating led to marriage; for others, it was the catalyst for a divorce. Interviewing the dozens of cyberdaters was one of the most fun parts of writing this book, and hopefully their stories will entertain, guide, and encourage you.

Meeting your beloved online, you will soon find out, is more than a possibility.

THE ELECTRONIC PUB

REDHEAD: HEY, YOU'RE HERE AGAIN!

Lizard of Oz: I am?

Redhead [groaning]: So what're you up to, Liz?

Lizard [holding up a wineglass]: Enjoying a fine ruby Zinfandel, a wine originally made for victorious French armies.

Redhead: Ooooh.

Lizard: What's your poison? Does red hair mean you like red wine?

Redhead [whining]: Wine? I know nothing about vino except not to go
beyond two glassfuls.

Lizard: Truth is, I know absolutely nothing about wines either. I got that
Zinfandel line from some James Bond movie.

Redhead [smirking]: Oh? So what do you know about?

Lizard: Not much, not much. I know I like redheads.

Redhead: Oh yeah? I'm into green skin myself.

Lizard [softening his voice]: You really want to know what I'm into?

Redhead: Hit me.

Lizard: No, not that! My scales extend beyond my skin. I'm somewhat of
a . . . now don't laugh . . . .

Redhead: I won't. At least, not so you'll hear me.

Lizard: A musician.

Redhead: No kidding? A rock and roller?

Lizard: Something like. A fusion guitarist for a jazz-type band. We have a gig this weekend. Ever hear of fusion?

Redhead: I always get it mixed up with fission. But, seriously . . . I'm impressed. I've seen fusion guitarists play before, and *man* do their fingers move fast. How do you find the time to practice?

Lizard: I'm on a four-year-long, all-expense-paid vacation.

Redhead: Oh yeah? *[winking]* Which college do you go to?

Lizard: Now that's privileged information, on a need-to-know basis.

Redhead: You do like James Bond, don't you? I'm a lawyer, myself, see, so I know all about privilege. Well, almost a lawyer, at least . . . . I gave up the piano when I was twelve. No time to practice. The last keys I tapped were the ones for my clunker of a car.

Lizard: Well, counselor, maybe I can teach you a few notes, or at least have you look at my briefs.

Redhead: Whoa. Maybe you can write me a note, first. My address is . . . .

Jane switched off her computer and felt a sort of tranquil wooziness, as if she'd just returned from a wild night on the town. She smiled, thinking about that Lizard guy. It was weird how *in-tune* he was with her; how he seemed to really care about what she said. This was the fourth night they'd stayed up late together, and each time Jane had felt funny and intelligent and sexy.

She drank the last of her decaf, brushed out her long, red hair, and burrowed into bed. Jane never suspected, as dreams began to engulf her, that Lizard of Oz would indeed teach her a few notes. Jane never suspected the volumes of love letters that were to come. The real-life encounter. The year and a half of longing, arguments, reconciliations, desire, and moments of absolute passion. Jane never suspected that friendly online chatter would lead to marriage.

Welcome to the Pub

If you've heard about worldwide computer networks, also called the "information super-highway," you've probably heard it compared to a vast city. A city with subways that travel at the speed of light. A city complete with millions of houses, government buildings, military bases, universities, and plenty of corporations.

You might have wondered if, anywhere in this dazzling electronic metropolis, you could find any fun spots. After all, every society has its places to unwind. In America, you can stroll into your neighborhood bar to fraternize. In Japan, you'll find *sarariman* sipping saki at karaoki bars. In France, people mingle at sidewalk cafés. In Great Britain, gentlefolk visit public houses, or pubs, to nurse pints of ale and toss darts.

Fact is, there are plenty of pubs along the information superhighway. Some pubs are huge, with rooms that cater to every interest, every hobby. Some are in strange places; in the deepest basements of military bases or beneath the boardrooms of the nation's top companies. These pubs are open 24 hours a day, always packed with colorful people, and waiting for your "digital clone" to step inside.

A Place Called Cyberspace

More than a city, though, the information superhighway is an entirely new society. It is a community built completely on words, where people are described, understood, and judged based solely on their words. Just as a book is theater of the mind, the networks are a society—a whole new world—of the mind.

Sci-fi writer/futurist William Gibson coined an apt term for this new dimension. He called it *cyberspace*. With this book in hand, you can consider yourself a cyberdater. *Love Bytes* tells you all you need to know about blasting off into cyberspace. More importantly, it will guide you through some of the world's biggest and best electronic pubs, meeting more people than you ever thought possible.

Who Is This Book For?

This book is not merely about computer dating, which attempts to match two people based on their answers to a questionnaire. Online dating is, like real-life dating, an exchange between people who want to find out more about each other. Online dating is the romantic side of the new network society. It is about human interactions in the land of bits and bytes.

If you want to meet or chat with an incredible array of people, around the clock, from the comfort of your nearest computer, you will find this book rewarding. The Internet, the largest of the telecommunication networks, connects around 15 million people from over 60 countries. The nice thing about electronic pubs is that they're a finger's distance from every corner of the world—just type a simple command and you can zoom across oceans and continents, searching for a date. Cyberspace is a never-ending party where anybody with access to a computer may show up.

> Who did I bump into today, you ask? There was the programmer from the Israeli army, who helped me figure out how to fix up the graphics in this video game I'm trying to write. I met a really weird guy who goes to college in Kansas, we talked about Scorsese movies, it turned out he's a really big fan, too. He saw *Taxi Driver* thirty-two times. He knew every line, we went through the whole "You talking to me?" monologue. Some lady from Montreal wrote a rebuttal to an editorial I'd posted about the lack of American foreign policy. And, to top it off, this struggling actress from L.A. and I had this amazing two-hour conversation about everything you could imagine. We talked about the economy, about trying to break into the art world. I even found myself telling

her about the problems I have with my parents. I suppose she just seemed honest, a good listener, so I opened up to her. She calmed me down, let me see my problems from a different angle. I've always said, friendship beats psychotherapy any day.

Some people are slick talkers. They can waltz into a room of strangers, mingle around, and soon everybody knows their names. But many others are not exactly the lifeblood of the party. Introverts, who write slicker than they talk, will appreciate the society of the mind. They may indeed become virtual party animals.

I guess you could call me introverted . . . . I mean, I always have a lot to say, but somehow I never manage to say it. And then I found bulletin boards. One day, I boldly typed a message about the ludicrous movies Hollywood tries passing off as "thought-provoking." A few people attacked my opinion, but most resounded with agreement. Soon I was an addict, logging in three or four times a day, seeing who responded to my messages and responding to them. Since then, I've calmed down a little. But I still type dozens of messages a week, on all sorts of topics. People, I feel, really know me. And like me. After all, what's not to like?

Those searching for a relationship or a deeper friendship, but who find the real-world dating scene disappointing, will enjoy having access to an entirely new world. More and more people are falling in love online.

Well, I was a woman stuck at a small Catholic university and was looking for friends. I decided to post a personal ad online. I got the predictable number of replies for a female (350+), even though I specifically said "not looking for a relationship." I replied to a few dozen who sounded somewhat interesting and not obviously looking for sex, and ended up in long conversations with a few people spread all over the world, and John was one of them. Eventually John and I were writing each other several times a day, and not just quick little one-liners either. I found him more and more fascinating, and he was dropping little hints that he felt the same way. We lived a country apart. It didn't help that I still lived with my parents, had just turned 19, and he was 33. But we tried to make plans to meet in the summer. Finally I found myself thinking about him all the time and having dreams about him (a guy I haven't even seen a picture of), so I said what the heck and wrote him a letter telling him that I think I'm on the verge of falling in love with him and he better tell me what he thinks about me so I don't go crazy reading things into his letters. Followed immediately by, "Oh I'm so silly, ignore that if you want." And because of the relatively bad connections at school and all the courses I had, I waited most of the day for his reply. His reply came, said, "Of course I love you." I almost cried in that computer room.

This Book Is for *You*

Even if your life is brimming with sparkling and diverse people, even if you are anything but shy and never fear speaking what's on your mind, even if you're madly in love with Mr. or Ms. Right and caught in a dreamworld built for two, this book will still interest you. What better or more painless way is there to take a road trip across the information superhighway than exploring some of its social rest stops?

People are joining the society of the mind at a fantastic rate. New technology is making online communication faster, friendlier, and more fun. As telephones, computers, and televisions begin to meld together, you might want to catch a glimpse of what you (or at least your children) are in for. Though the electronic pub will probably never replace the alcoholic one, it is already a viable alternative. Maybe one day you'll be able to stroll into your neighborhood tavern, sit in front of a video screen and say, "A Scotch on the rocks and an hour online, please."

What You'll Need

To launch your spaceship to this new world of the mind all you need is a computer, a modem, and communications software. The brand of home computer you have doesn't matter much. In the online dating world, all IBM couples are compatible. Whether your Macintosh seeks a mate, or your Amiga needs an amigo, cyberspace will embrace you. And inter-brand dating is easy, too.

Information on what type of modem and software you'll need is in Chapter 4, The Datemobile. Depending on your current setup and exact interests, you can be online in a matter of minutes.

How To Communicate Inside a Computer

If your experience of computers is limited, you're probably wondering how human beings can use a pile of plastic, silicon, and aluminum to interact. When a high-tech gadget known as the telephone first came out, the public was skeptical, too.

There are three basic formats for online communication:

- *Messages.* Think of an online service as a vast newspaper, published thousands of times a day. You are not just a newspaper reader, you are one of the reporters. First, you select a section of the newspaper, known as a *bulletin board, message base,* or *newsgroup.* There may be thousands of these. You can then read through a pile of public articles, which appear on your screen one at a time. The messages are written by experts and beginners, the profane and the profound, elementary school kids and senior citizens. You can publicly or privately reply to messages that interest you, or you can write and post an article of your own. On message bases you'll find gossip, debates, information, assistance, small talk, fiction, poetry, essays, and, yes, plenty of flirtation. Many places even give you the option to write personal ads, selling yourself to the highest bidder of adoration.

- *Electronic Mail.* You write a letter to a distant friend, and it appears on his or her computer screen. This is similar to the Postal Service, but with several major advantages. First of all, *e-mail* is almost instantaneous. Most mail reaches its destination mailbox

within 24 hours. Second, though some online services may charge a nominal fee for each letter you send, there is no international postage. Sending a note to a friend in China is as cheap as mailing to a pal next door. Third, you can send a message of almost any length, from a one-liner to a novel. And finally, the system is entirely electronic, saving both trees and fingers from paper cuts. E-mail may one day render standard postal "snail mail" obsolete.

Live Chat. This is the most interactive feature of all, like a telephone where you type instead of talk. A chat can be a split-screen tête-à-tête between two sweethearts. Or it can be party-like: a roomful of people talking at once, the mingled messages reading like a script. Everybody types what they want to say and their words are immediately printed on everybody else's screen. *Chat bases* are clubhouses where people sharing a special interest can meet and communicate.

Thirsty for More?

By now you might be getting enthusiastic about online dating, but are, perhaps, also a little skeptical. Let's move on to Chapter 2, where we'll discuss exactly why you might want to use a computer as the backdrop for your next date.

THE BLINDEST DATE

S O, TELL US, WHEN DID YOU KNOW YOU WERE IN LOVE?

Lizard: Know? Hard to say. I suppose it was gradual.

Redhead: It was immediate for me.

Lizard: For me, too, really. I mean, there was initial attraction, quite a bit of it. I guess though it took us a while to admit it to each other. Yeah.

Redhead: That much is true. My whole day, my whole mood, depended on whether I got e-mail from him, and how much, and its content.

Lizard: Yeah.

Okay, so when did the phrase "I love you" first come up?

Redhead: We were net-talking. I was telling him how important he was to me. I was remarking how I could tell him anything, how he was the only person in the world I was completely open and honest to. How he was the only person who I could be myself with.

Lizard: Yeah, that's right. And then I gave a speech of my own, saying pretty much the same thing. I know it sounds like romantic gobbledygook, but that's how we felt. It was amazing. For me, it was a first. But it was true. I didn't even know if her hair was even really red . . . .

Redhead: It is. And it's natural.

Lizard: . . . but she really turned me on, body, mind, and soul.

Redhead: And then I typed, "I think I love you."

Lizard: And, slowly, real slowly, I typed back: "And I love you."

Redhead: It was magic then.

Lizard: It was the early morning of February 15th, the day after Valentine's. A bit trite, I suppose, but it worked.

Redhead: Yes, it did.

Would you two ever have met if computers never existed?

Redhead: Hard to say, because it seems like we were fated to be together from the beginning of time. But . . . I don't think so, really. First of all, we lived 700 miles apart. Though there's a funny story about that. Once we were talking, and we figured out that New Year's Eve, two years ago, we were both hanging out around Times Square. There's a chance we might have bumped into each other. If we did, I probably said, "Hey, you, get outta my way."

Lizard: I never, ever, would have met her without the computer. No way. I'm a very introverted person. A social cripple, you could say. I'd been out on a few dates, but nothing much ever came about from them. I express myself in writing infinitely better than I do in person. It was only through letters that my real personality could show.

Redhead: Although I've had relationships in the past, none were as passionate, as uninhibited as this one. Over the computer you're not afraid to say what you think, what you feel. Or at least, you're much less afraid.

So would you recommend online dating?

Redhead: It's not easy, and, sure, it has its drawbacks. There were times when I got fed up, too lonely. I wanted to see this man, this man I loved. I wanted to see him in the flesh. But I guess that came about in good time. It teaches you patience.

Lizard: And the fine art of appreciating cold showers.

Redhead: But, obviously, I highly recommend it. At the very least, you would gather a whole new crowd of friends for yourself.

Lizard: As far as I'm concerned, online dating is the only way to go.

Redhead: I don't know about that, but, yes, it's certainly a viable option.

Lizard: Point is, if you must have a long-distance relationship, having it online is the closest you can get to one another.

So when did you two first meet in the flesh?

Lizard: It was about a month after that Valentine's Day. We couldn't bear it anymore. She took a train all the way out to me. It was quite an experience, seeing this woman for the first time; this woman I knew so intimately and deeply. I was waiting around the train station. All I knew was that she, of course, had red hair. And that she was tall. Naturally, that night, dozens of people matching her description wandered in. I thought it would never work. Half the crowd seemed to have red hair. Finally, I saw a slinky redhead lugging a huge bag. I knew it couldn't be her, that would've been too perfect. She was a knockout! She was standing in the middle of the terminal, seemingly searching for someone. I paced around her a few times. She stared at me, and I at her, but we didn't say anything. Finally I approached her and said, "Um, Redhead?" She lit up and said, "Lizard!" I mean, I've heard the expressions 'love is blind' and 'blind date,' but never 'blind love.' I would have hugged her then even if she wasn't beautiful.

Redhead: Aw. I don't think you want us to go into details, but that week we really got to know each other—every inch. It was surreal.

Lizard: We lived apart for about another year and a half, trying to get together every other month or so. Finally we knew we had to make it permanent or we'd go nuts. So we did. Make it permanent, that is.

So do you still use the computer?

Redhead: Sure! I use it for everything from research to word processing to e-mail. I still keep track of all my old friends using e-mail. I have quite a few of them.

Lizard [whispering]: Don't tell Redhead, but every so often, I still love meeting new people and even, well, flirting with them a tad. I suppose of all the ways of cheating, mine's the most innocent.

Redhead: Ahem. We'll discuss that topic more when we get home, Lizard.

Why in the World to Meet People Online

If Juliet had e-mail, her message would never have been delayed and she and Romeo would've lived happily ever after. And if only poor Cyrano had an Internet account, he and his big nose would easily have won the heart of many a Roxanne.

Throughout written history, loves have been sparked and maintained through correspondence. The most basic function of the paper and quill, the stamp and envelope, the telegraph, the telephone, is to bring people closer together than they would otherwise be. The computer has many amazing time-saving applications, but its most exciting and widespread impact is in how it helps connect people's minds.

Much like real-life dating, some people treat online dating as a fun way to pass time— a novelty. Some treat it as a genuine and meaningful means of socializing, leading toward a long-term relationship. Others view it in awe. Following are a few of the reasons why online dating might suit *you*.

Similarities

I build models. You might be surprised but there's a lot to know about model building, and a lot to keep up on. You have to know about new stores that open up, new glues, new dyes, new building materials, plastics, woods, new techniques. I also love hearing about other people's projects. Though there are magazines about model building, I thought I was pretty much working in a vacuum. But then someone told me about an online message base where modeling is discussed every day. If I have a problem—a glue doesn't dry properly or something—I can post it online. In a few hours, I always get advice telling me what I did wrong. It's a great feeling to know that there are so many people out there who care about the same things I do, and it's great to be able to be in continuous contact with them.

In the real world, it's often a headache for people with coinciding interests to find each other. If your pastimes are mainstream, it might not be too hard to come across others. For example, if you're crazy about cooking you can attend classes or trade recipes with your neighbors. But there are always hassles. You fall prey to scheduling problems; classes are expensive and take tons of time.

If your interests are not so mainstream, then you're pretty much stuck. It would take an inspirational amount of perseverance and luck to find others in your area who are fascinated by Japanese animation or artificial intelligence or Wicca rituals or synchronized swimming. And if you happen to have *more* than one hobby you want to share, forget it.

Online, though, it takes just a few minutes to find hobbyists who care about the same things you do. Through message bases or newsgroups, you can skim articles from people worldwide who share your pastimes, interests, religion, culture, fandom, or political orientation. It's easy to stumble onto *new* hobbies, as well. You can browse the insider news about the latest serial-killer trial, move on to read a few love poems, ask jazz experts if they'd recommend you purchase an alto sax over a tenor, and then write your opinion of the current Schwarzenegger movie.

Further, suppose you're having a sleepless night. You can't stop thinking about how The Knicks blew their playoff game and it's too late to call up any of your buddies. You switch on your computer, log in, and enter a sports discussion area. Chances are, several other insomniac fans will be online, ready to join you in a group gripe session. There may even be people who live several time-zones away, eager to hear a play-by-play review of the game.

Differences

Nancy must be the oddest friend I have. We met on an online computer service while talking about nuclear war, which we are both extremely interested in, though in very different ways. After college, Nancy worked with the Peace Corps in Africa and now works for an activist organization, staging vigils and demonstrations. She is, above all else, a pacifist. I am a career air force pilot. An officer and a gentleman. Every time we chat, Nancy types, "I can't believe I'm actually wasting my time with you." I write, "Ditto." And then we progress into a thoroughly enjoyable conversation about any and everything under the sun.

People all across the globe can be found inside the computer networks. At times, opposing cultures and beliefs cause friction, but friction often leads to tolerance. A member of the John Birch Society may find himself talking about bird watching with a Communist. Arabs and Israelis, British and Irish, all can use their computers to safely discuss or argue about any issue in the world.

There's nothing quite like chatting with some stranger from overseas. When an Italian, in broken English, describes a wild Milan fashion expo, you feel as if you're there. You'd be surprised to know what the average Turk thinks of Americans, or how a devout Buddhist spends her Saturday nights.

Weirdness and/or Stars

My name is Ambivalentia. I'm gangly, tall as an oak, but stout as bonsai. I'm very shapely, with strong shoulders. I have long, short-cropped hair, blonde and black in color, and pert breasts and football-sized biceps. I have a mixed heritage: half male and half female. I am covered with purple fur, which matches my teeth (all three of them) in the most lovely fashion. I am friendly to people, above all else. Go away.

In the real world, people often pretend to be what they're not—to a limit. Over a computer, there are no limits. You'll meet men pretending to be women, and vice versa; these cyberspace transsexuals are known as *MorFs* (Male or Female). Since faces are hidden, you'll meet aliens, werewolves, fictional characters, and green lizards.

The online world isn't limited by fashion. You'll find people and places right out of the '50s, '60s, '70s, '80s, '90s and beyond, all online. You can experience (or reexperience) free love, the trickle-down theory, peace activism, and sock hops. There are even fantasy worlds, complete with unicorns and elves. And other planets of all shapes and sizes.

You may even get to ask a true-life celebrity some questions. Many online services feature special "guest lectures" by famous writers, actors, scientists, or politicians. Rumored to frequent cyberspace are the likes of Vice President Al Gore, rock star Billy Idol (whose latest album was entitled "Cyberpunk"), members of the rock bands U2 and The Grateful Dead, and a gaggle of novelists, artists, actors, authors, and journalists.

Safety

With online dating, there is no worry about verbal sexual harassment, date-rape, or injury. You can stay up with your date all night and not worry once about getting mugged. The worst virus you can get with a computer is one that makes *it* sick.

If you run into a jerk online, you can usually get rid of him or her pretty easily. The next chapter has details on how to deal with digital harassment.

A Flexible Date

You can date online as much as you want, you can date a different person every night, you can date several people at once. There is no dressing up, driving across town and getting lost, ordering drinks, or squabbling over bills.

When dating online, you don't have to be as choosy. You can take chances. Experiment! If the person you end up with turns out to be a geek, jerk, lemon, frump, or nerd, it's easy to mumble some excuse and just hit a few keys, logging yourself off.

A Better World?

The online universe is somewhat utopian. Skin color is invisible online, as are gender, age, and physical flaws. There are no weapons, no dirty looks, no cash.

All this may sound cold and impersonal, and to an extent it is. But a world devoid of physical human contact is hardly devoid of humanity. Simple evidence is the hundreds of people worldwide, like Redhead and Lizard, who have fallen in love online.

Typing in cyberspace allows users to edit their words carefully before they speak. The discussions in cyberspace often cut through the small talk and superficiality of ordinary life. Those with access to a computer can speak their minds, often without censorship of any kind, and without the fear of facing another person. People can be intimate without being self-conscious, which is what makes cyberspace particularly suited for soul-searching.

Cyberspace is not without its dirty spots, but, just like the real world, it's an unquestionably beautiful terrain to explore.

Love Can Hurt

Naturally, the online world is not perfect. Can compu-dating compare to the uneasiness and thrill of the real thing? Isn't a future stuck in cyberspace a somewhat dehumanizing prospect? How can mere words compare to flesh and bone?

Indeed, the technology does not exist to let two lovers kiss online. Or gaze into each other's eyes. Or even see each other's hair color, hear the pitch of each other's laughter. And though such innovations are actually being researched in the field of virtual reality, no amount of gadgetry will ever replace two humans, sitting together in a small bistro, sipping red wine . . . or will it?

But for now, the online world is deaf, blind, and mute. You'll have to rely (gasp) on your imagination. However, when your compu-date is complete, you're left with more than an empty glowing monitor. You're left with fond memories and maybe, just maybe, a new reason for living.

THE MEET MARKET

TRAPPED IN THE TOXIC CAGE OF

the nuclear monitor i wish i was
electric ones and zeros,
your fingers caressing my keys.
to escape impossibility, i
screamed, for a moment your voice
vibrated upon me, you caught my
voice in yours, held it, and i heard
you,
heard you,
your breaths and pauses and little
laughs frosting each
sentence (nervous, too, huh?)
this is nuts but i've always
said i'd go insane, every
body that ever knew me always

suspected i would, and this,
my redhead, is a helluva
way

—From Lizard to Redhead upon their first telephone conversation.

Pulling Up a Stool

Whether online or in the real world, pubs can be as different as day or night (and date or naught).

Most pubs are laid-back, dimly-lit, with pop music booming from the jukebox. The environment isn't aggressive, but there are plenty of roaming eyes. The conversation is never too profound nor too suggestive. Some people are just chillin', others are on the prowl, and a few are just interested in the booze.

Friendly and busy, electronic pubs match their offline counterparts. You can find the same combination of socializers, daters, and those too drunk on the cyberbooze of news and information to be interested in other people. Some places are primarily for intellectual discussion, some are the digital equivalent of houses of ill-repute.

Within the general community of each online service, there are unique subdivisions. These cater to sexual orientation, language, geographical location, or some other broad group.

This book is a travel guide, describing the landscapes and cultures of the various regions of cyberspace, giving you exact directions to get there. Flip through Chapters 6 through 13 to get some idea of the various scenic online environments. Like the real world, love can happen anywhere, and often happens when least expected.

So Which Online Service Is Best, Dave?

Well, I couldn't begin to tell you, but I'll try. If you want to go online *only* for the sake of finding a quick date for next Saturday night, then a local adult "cybersex" BBS would probably be your best bet. To place worldwide personal ads or to correspond with the widest range of people about the widest range of subjects, use the Internet. America Online is the easiest way to strike up a friendly chat.

CompuServe is heaped full of professionals, in most every technical field. PRODIGY is home to average-Joe consumers for whom the computer is another kind of TV. The tie-dyed and bow-tied can be found lounging around the ol' GEnie commune. And the folks who hang around the Delphi neighborhood fit no mold; they just seem to have wandered there one day and gotten lost.

The online world offers more than quick and easy lovin'. Catalog home shopping, travel agencies, business advice, legal advice, medical advice, detailed databases, stock quotes, sports scores, FAX service, online magazines, museums, art galleries, encyclopedias, technical support, movie reviews, restaurant listings, road maps, libraries full of software, libraries full of information, and plain old fun 'n games are just some of the other reasons to explore cyberspace. Which features are useful to you? Each online network has its specialties.

Catching Someone's Eye

I'm no Doctor Ruth. And even she would agree, I'm sure, there is no step-by-step process to finding a perfectly matched date. However, getting social online is much like mingling in physical life. You find a group of people that vaguely interests you. Then, depending on your conversational style, you leisurely make friends. Many people are *leapers*, introducing themselves immediately, jumping right into the deep end of a discussion. And then there are *lurkers*—those who eavesdrop until they get a feel for the people and the way they talk.

As the conversation progresses, you will most likely begin to notice one or two particular people whose demeanor, opinions, or jokes particularly attract you. Let them know you've noticed. Crack a few wisecracks of your own. Begin to tell them about yourself.

If someone consistently writes sparkling messages, you may want to send that person private e-mail, complimenting the lucidity and organization in the last article he wrote. Or you could compose a message publicly lauding her for her brilliance . . . or even poking fun. Often, polite and deserved teasing is a good way to get noticed. Just be sure to let people know the difference between sarcasm and seriousness.

If you are chatting live, you can be bold and invite your potential date to a private chat room. Most people are happy to focus on a one-on-one conversation. On most systems you can also "whisper" things that only one person in a group can read.

Often, the people you meet have *handles*—descriptive pseudonyms such as Cyberdater, Lenny Lovelooker, or Lizard of Oz. Some handles—SexyGal, Stud Muffin, The Incredible Hunk—are the cyberspace equivalent of wearing a low-cut dress ("love handles?"). Other handles may be cryptic usernames, such as H737827 or 7363,234. Many people prefer such an environment because all comments are completely anonymous, like a masquerade party. When you're in a place that uses handles, try not to use your real name, or anyone else's (if you happen to know it).

Missed Manners

Although freedom of expression is of the utmost importance online, most cybercitizens live by several steadfast customs. Above all, the golden "Do unto others . . ." rule holds true. Beyond that, though, here is some more advanced *netiquette:*

EXPERT TIP

Although most online services allow you to send e-mail to people care of their handles, sometimes there are problems. If you'd like to write a letter or talk on the telephone, it's a good idea to ask your new friend to write or call you rather than prying for personal information. If you happily give Redhead your real e-mail address, for example, this symbolizes good will, and mostly likely, she will send you hers.

- Don't post anything you wouldn't put in an envelope and mail. Dealing with a glass monitor and a plastic keyboard, it's easy to forget that the words on the screen come from real people—people as sensitive, trustful, warmhearted, and open-minded as yourself. If you're rude to them, they'll shut you out.

- Attack ideas, not people. If someone praises the benefits of Communism in third-world countries, point out the problems and explain why you think the Communist system is unsavory; don't respond with, "You stink like a rotten egg you godless pinko Commie!"

- Don't fight fire with fire. Every once in a while, you'll come across a type of message known as a *flame*—a personal attack that consists of little more than a string of insults. ("You stink like a . . ." etc., running on for several lines.) When people irritate you, say by using vulgar language in G-rated conversations or posting articles in inappropriate places, correct them gently—when flame wars start, everybody gets burned.

Sending Messages

Millions of people worldwide may see what you write. This means you have more of a potential audience than the average *New York Times* reporter. Treat your words with respect. Edit your articles if you can, correct grammar and spelling. Give them a little flair, a unique voice. Be yourself.

- Avoid being wordy. Would you want to pore through a ten page dissertation—especially when you have 300 more messages to read? Only if it was consistently brilliant, witty, and clear. People have a tendency to be scared off by too many words. More users actually read a concise response, and your article has more of an impact. Try to stick to one screenful.

- Help keep cyberspace organized by staying on topic. If you're in a message base entitled "Cute, Fuzzy Animals," it's best not to discuss the latest Metallica CD. In places like the Internet, where there are thousands of message areas, only post to the appropriate places. Read a few of the messages in the areas you're interested in; this helps you decide if you're on the right track. This also prevents you from repeating something that has already been said.

- Most messages allow you to fill in a *Subject* line. Take advantage of this and be as descriptive as possible. When people browse through messages, they treat the subject lines like a table of contents to a very long book. Rather than plod through each message, one by one, they'll only read those that interest them. If you are writing a personal ad, it's better to have a subject like "BiSWF ISO bald midget MBM in SW Tulsa" than "Looking for a man."

Replying

If you reply to a message or e-mail, you should use its subject preceded by the *"Re:"* tag. Most systems do this automatically.

It's also a good idea to quote appropriate passages from previous messages. For example, if you read an article that makes ten different points, and then respond: "Your last two points are foolish because . . . ," nobody without a photographic memory will know what you're talking about. Do not, however, include the entirety of someone else's message; this wastes space and nobody wants to read through the same ideas twice. Many systems let you include the message you're replying to. If this is the case, edit the attached message down to just the germane sentences.

Sarcasm

"I'm never sarcastic," he said with an ironic leer.

In the real world, words only do half the communicating. Little giggles, smirks, hand gestures, eye squints, head tilts, foot shuffles, and millions of other nonverbal cues help explain, emphasize, and sometimes even replace our words. Words are open-ended, and the same statement can be taken many ways. Senses of humor vary as much as fashion senses (the two are often related, in fact).

Online, a remark meant to be humorous can often seem cruel. For example, Redhead may be complaining about her hair color. With a smile on your face, you might type, "Oh, yeah, that's a terrible shame. Red-haired witches should be burnt at the stake." Depending on Red's particular mood, she may laugh, punch in her monitor, or cry. The best way to avoid being misunderstood is by typing in your "facial expressions" whenever you say something doubtful. See the Mute Expression section later in this chapter.

Share and Share Alike

When you ask a question in the appropriate online area—whether it's about relationships or nuclear reactors—you're bound to get many good responses. In the spirit of sharing, lend a hand whenever you can. Everyone has an area of expertise. Keep an eye out for questions you can answer. Help out the needy and, at the same time, impress people with your encyclopedic knowledge.

Public vs. Private

Remember: e-mail is for two people to correspond, message areas are for entire communities. If you want to address comments, criticism, or gratitude to a specific person, send private e-mail unless you think everyone else would somehow benefit.

Conversely, if someone sends you something privately that you think everyone would like to hear, forward it to a message area, giving credit where it is due. Of course, you should check with the message's author first, to be sure he or she doesn't mind being published.

Digital Harassment

I hate to say it, but on certain systems it happens almost every time I log in. They see a female name and they think this gives them a license to act like pigs. They send me messages telling me how much they would love to <fill in a verb> my <fill in a body part>. If I start talking to someone, the first thing I'm asked is what my measurements are, or what kinks I'm into. Although this behavior starts off being just slightly annoying, it ends up being downright impossible to put up with. It seems like no matter where I turn, I'm being ogled and mauled. It's like a land of obscene callers, calling from every direction. Now, that's not to say there aren't good men out there. There are many classy, intelligent gentlemen. Unfortunately, though, just one persistent jerk ruins it for the whole bunch. When I get harassed, I log off. And that's that.

Even online there are hecklers, harassers, and what some people may call perverts.

Imagine this scenario: You and five new friends are having a mature, in-depth discussion about how to act on a first date. Suddenly the cyberspace equivalent of comedian Andrew Dice Clay, Putz, pops onto the scene. He swears, he insults, he singles you out, "whispering" vulgar suggestions.

- Tell Putz to stop. Perhaps the newcomer is actually a nice person, only a bit socially inept. Maybe crudity is his idea of humor. Let him know, in no uncertain terms, that he's being a pain in the ASCII, and that his tone isn't appreciated.

- Ask whoever's around whether or not Putz is bothering them, too. Maybe you're unusually sensitive, in which case *you* should find a new crowd. But in most cases, your pals will back you up. Everyone will tell Putz what a putz he (or she) is being. When a person is told off by everybody in a room, the problem usually goes away.

Putz may persist. Depending on what network you're on, you have several options. Usually there is someone in charge, a moderator, sysop (system operator), or guide. Try to contact this person and ask for help. The moderator may be able to kick Putz off the chat-channel you're on.

Most online services have an *ignore* or *squelch* command. Once you ignore people, the stuff they type doesn't show up on your screen—it's as if they didn't exist. You could also privately invite the people you like to sneak to a secretive locale:

```
"Hey this room is getting too crowded with the wrong kinda
people. Wanna meet me in the private room PUTZLESS?"
```

Always, if worst comes to worst, just log off.

Lewd Letters

If you ever get abusive or obscene e-mail, reply to it immediately, stating that you didn't find it humorous. If it continues, contact the people in charge at your system. They should set things straight. Most bulletin-board sysops and commercial online services will delete an offensive user from their systems.

Witchcraft

One renowned case of online misconduct was the LambdaMoo rape incident. One user, using some tricky programming, made *voodoo dolls*—inanimate objects in the likeness of other users. He used these dolls to make it appear as if two of Lambda's users were publicly performing lewd acts. The victims felt as though they had evil twins hiding online, slandering their good names.

A huge outcry raged; one user suggested "virtual castration." Others suggested that the voodoo man be *toaded*—locked out of all systems the way a witch might turn an annoying rival into a frog. However, there are no set laws in many areas of cyberspace, and the voodoo man is still at large.

The moral of the story is, be aware that people like this exist. There are also scammers, con-men, and snake-oil peddlers. Use common sense and don't be blinded by the medium. Stay on your virtual toes.

Security

Unfortunately, as cyberspace becomes more and more accessible, there will be those who exploit it. Though such cases are extremely rare, it's good to be wary. If your connect charges skyrocket or somebody complains about you and you haven't done anything wrong, some evildoer may have hacked your password or created a voodoo doll in your likeness.

There have been instances where people have had to relist or unpublish their e-mail addresses. Depending on which network you're on, avoiding a predator may be as simple as requesting a new address or as complex as canceling your service and enlisting someplace else.

Mute Expression

> It's amazing to me how feelings can be experienced here. We can't hear each other, can't see each other, but we do feel each other in a sense—the warmth of sincerity or lack of it. Words seem inadequate, yet this is all we have and they work. We reach out, we get angry, and we also find love.

You don't have to be the next F. Scott Fitzgerald to be able to tell someone how you feel. Cyberspace has developed its own special slang.

First, put asterisks around facial expressions and emotions. For instance, if somebody

```
*winks*
```

at you, you can

```
*blush*
```

On some systems, users prefer to surround their expressions with the less-than, more-than signs, such as <grin>, or even just <g>. Table 3-1 contains some starters.

Surrounding someone's name in curved-brackets indicates a hug. For instance, type

```
{{{{ LENNY }}}}
```

slygrin	*shysmile*	*sheepishgrin*	*giggle*	*shiver*	*sneeze*
madfrown	*sniff*	*fastnod*	*evilgrin*	*quicknod*	*groan*
pout	*growl*	*wheeze*	*tongueout*	*bitelip*	*squint*

TABLE 3-1 A few descriptive bits of body language

to give Lenny a really big squeeze. Using the underline symbol before and after words is a neat way to

```
_underline_
```

important ideas or book titles.

Typing in all capital letters is akin to shouting, and too many capitalized words SWIFTLY BECOME ANNOYING. Use caps ONLY for occasional emphasis.

A Long List of Shorthand

There are more acronyms in the online world than in any government bureau. Table 3-2 contains code words you are likely to run into in online dating and romance areas.

Table 3-3 contains a few catchphrases you may run across all over cyberspace: in messages, e-mail, and, of course, chat. Feel free to use shorthand, and don't hesitate to create your own. If you are fond of saying, "Oh, as if I really care," start typing

```
OAIIRC
```

The people you're talking to will soon catch on. You'll be amazed how much faster it is to type and read.

Personal Ads

The descriptions in personal ads usually take the format:

```
SEXUAL PREFERENCE—MARITAL STATUS—RELIGION/RACE—GENDER
```

Table 3-4 contains the symbols designating a few of the more typical characteristics. For example, a *SSBJF* is a straight, single, black, Jewish, female.

ASCII Art

The standard keyboard characters make it possible to draw simple pictures. For instance, a long-stemmed rose, for those romantic moments:

```
@>-,'-
```

or a fish, for those stinky occasions:

```
(O-<
```

BF/GF	Boyfriend/Girlfriend
B&D	Bondage And Discipline
ISO	In Search Of
ILY	I Love You
LAFS	Love At First Sight
LDR	Long Distance Relationship
LJBF	Let's Just Be Friends
LO	Love (Or Lust) Object
LTR	Long Term Relationship
MOTOS	Member Of The Opposite Sex
MOTSS	Member Of The Same Sex
NG	Nice Guy
PDA	Public Display Of Affection
POSSLQ	Person Of Opposite Sex Sharing Living Quarters
RI	Romantic Interest
RP	Romantic Partner
S&M	Sadistic And Masochistic
SNAG	Sensitive New-Age Guy
TL&EH	True Love & Eternal Happiness
(X)SO	(Ex) Significant Other

TABLE 3-2 The shorthand of love

AAMOF	As A Matter Of Fact
AFAIK	As Far As I Know
AFK	Away From Keyboard
AKA	Also Known As
ASAP	As Soon As Possible
BAC	By Any Chance
BAK	Back At Keyboard
BK	Because

continued on next page

TABLE 3-3 Some of the more common bits of cyberslang you're likely to run into

continued from previous page

BRB	Be Right Back
BTW	By The Way
CUL8TR	See You Later
EOD	End Of Discussion
F2F	Face To Face (A Real-life Meeting)
FAQ	Frequently Asked Questions
FOAF	Friend Of A Friend
FWIW	For What It's Worth
FYA(I)	For Your Amusement (Information)
GMTA	Great Minds Think Alike
IAC	In Any Case
IM(NS)HO	In My (Not So) Humble Opinion
ITRW	In The Real World
JK	Just Kidding!
KHYF	Know How You Feel
LOL	Laughing Out Loud!
NTYMI	Now That You Mention It
OIC	Oh I See
OTOH	On The Other Hand
POV	Point Of View
RL	Real Life
ROTFL	Rolling On The Floor Laughing
ROTM	Right On The Money
RSN	Real Soon Now
RTFM	Read The Freakin' Manual
TIA	Thanks In Advance
TTFN	Ta-Ta, For Now!
WTG	Way To Go
WTH	What The Heck
YMMV	Your Mileage May Vary

TABLE 3-3 *(continued)*

CATEGORY	SYMBOL	DESIGNATION
Sexual preference	Bi	Bisexual
	S	Straight
	G	Gay
Marital status	S	Single
	D	Divorced
	M	Married (not so happily)
	Cpl	Couple
Religion/race	W	White
	B	Black
	A	Asian
	L	Latin
	C	Christian
	B	Buddhist
	J	Jewish
Gender	M	Male
	F	Female
	TS	Transsexual
	TV	Transvestite

TABLE 3-4 What the funny letters in personal ads mean

Of course, as with any artistic medium, creativity is the only limit. Check out Figure 3-1.

Smileys

An entire language of pictographs has developed online. These are known as smileys. To see why, look at Table 3-5 while tilting your head to the left as far as you can (and thinking about the virtues of abstract art). Be creative; mix and match!

The winner of the most creative smiley so far has got to be the elder Elvis:

```
&B-/ - A hunka, hunka burnin' love.
```

FIGURE 3-1 A rose is not a rose is not a rose

Asking for Help

All motorists know: Sometimes stopping for directions at a roadside diner turns out to be more interesting than the final destination. In any case, all of us need a friendly hint every now and again. Some good places to look are:

- The commercial online services (Chapters 8 through 12) have free customer service numbers, online customer service representatives, and e-mail help addresses. Try searching keywords and menu entries such as *help, customer service,* and so on.

- Although experienced cyberdaters like to call the latest digital immigrants *clueless newbies*, they only mean it in jest. Trust me. Most folks are more than happy to talk you through any problem, online or off. However, if someone replies *RTFM*, it means "Read the freakin' manual," and implies that you can find the answer to your question easily in the standard user documentation.

:-)	The father of the smileys. This designates sarcasm; another way of saying, "Just kidding!" NOTE: The nose is optional, and many smilers prefer to just type :)	:-T	I'm trying hard not to laugh.
		:-{	Ohhh . . . what was in that chili?
		:-}	Mmm . . . what was in that chili?
:->	Happy, in an evil way.	:~i	Enjoying a cigarette.
:-(	I'm sad now.	:-l	Frankly, I'm not sure how to feel.
:'(	I'm so sad I'm crying.	:-|	Hmmmmm.
:-O	Ahhhhh (screaming).	:-C	I'm shocked!
:-D	That's hilarious!	:-<	You broke my heart!
;-)	Here's winkin' at you, kid.	<:-)	Dunce.
:/)	That wasn't funny!	B-)	My future's so bright, I gotta wear shades.
:-)..	I'm drooling for you.	8-)	You got me googly-eyed.
:-"	C'mere, tiger (lips puckered for kiss).	|-(	I can't keep my eyes open.
:-x :-*	Kisses (of various pucker diameters).	%-)	I'm a little drunk.
:-r	Nyeah, nyeah (sticking out tongue).	:-&	Now I'm mad.
:-,	I know something you don't know (subtle smirk).	:-<)	Yap, yap, yap . . .
:-*	Um, never mind (covering mouth with hand).	O:)	For those angelic moods.
:-#	I just put my foot in my mouth.	}:>	For those more devilish ones.

TABLE 3-5 Smileys: Have a nice day

Asking Someone Out

Are you out to meet that special someone or do you just want to speak to new people each day? If there's someone you yearn to meet again, go ahead, be bold and make a date. Ask what time tomorrow your charmer plans to be online. Ask if you can send e-mail. Perhaps agree on meeting in a more private, romantic online place. When you enter a private chat area with someone else, explain what you're looking for. Some want to find out about the interests and lifestyles of new people. Many others just want steamy (or at least foggy) net-sex (see the next section).

In other words, instead of typing, *"Hey, Lenny, would you like to retire to a private room and chat it up,"* type: *"Lenny I'd love to discuss your comedy writing style and movies in general. Would you mind joining me in a private room?"*

Sex

> Being online affected my life and marriage, and became a real problem. There are a lot of people in unhappy marriages who don't want to cheat, and so they turn to the computer. The boards can be dangerous for needy people. You tend to be very intimate. But I've also met a few very great people. Online is a good way for people to experience or explore their fantasies, by writing or sending pictures. I've even had people send me gifts, articles of clothing they thought I'd look good in, related to a fantasy we shared.

Much like any erotica, literary love-making online is only as good as the participants' imaginations and poetic skills. Online talk that is sexy yet tasteful is rare. But as far as most people are concerned, the imagery doesn't have to be deft, just plentiful. Indeed, many occupants of cyberspace are looking for a few choice words, in hopes of fueling their fantasies.

Online sex is the safest sex there is. It can be entertaining, if not arousing. There's also the possibility that it may serve as an (un)dress-rehearsal for things to come.

There are several caveats, however. Many youngsters hard-drive their puberty for a joy-ride through cyberspace. Just because "Big Bertha" tells you she's thirty-nine doesn't mean she is. In fact, she may not even be a she. In the online world, there is a vast majority of males—a ratio of nine to one according to most sources. Though this ratio grows smaller every day, it still makes cyberspace a ladies-choice paradise. To attract attention, many males disguise themselves as MorFs—they take on female names, attributes, and language.

Therefore, if online sexually-oriented typing flips your switch, be aware that what you "see" may not be what you get—though this is often part of the appeal. In addition, try not to break into sudden flagrant lewdness, as this may offend people. Be sure that, if you engage someone in online sex, it is consensual. Be slow, gentle. Try to be as good a lover online as off.

Falling In Love

Who can define love? Can what amounts to no more than piles of digital words somehow be a genuine passion?

Absolutely.

Just ask Kate "Tall Tassle" and Walt "Herr Fixit" Roshon (See Figure 3-2) or Roberta and Paul Chesney—just two of the hundreds of married couples who began their affairs online.

Indeed, a time may come when *you* feel a certain queasiness, a goofy lightheadedness that can only be the L-word. This can be a difficult moment. There are no lips to deliver that first kiss to. Instead, you might

```
*kiss*
```

or

```
:*
```

but it's hardly the same.

Even when love works, there are pitfalls. To some, falling in love with a person who lives thousands of miles away is a painful hell. Others prefer the privacy.

Since the online environment makes it easy to share intimate secrets and flattering words, what appears to be "love" can happen fast. Just remember that there's a fine line between love and infatuation. When things get heavy, you have to be careful not to rush into anything you'll later regret, though the temptation to move ahead is strong. On the other hand, nothing in the world would get accomplished if people didn't take chances.

Treat online dates the same way you would offline ones, taking things one step at a time.

The Date

If via computer is the only way you and your date can meet, the following ideas may make your invisible night-on-the-cybertown more memorable:

- If you both have VCRs, rent the same movie and watch it at the same time. Type comments to each other. Also buy the same brand of popcorn, or the same flavor of gourmet ice cream.

- In a similar vein, order in or cook the same specialty foods. Pour a little wine, light up some candles, switch on the soft-music station, power up your computer, and you're ready for a romantic dinner. You can clink your glass against the monitor after you toast. Just pretend the lights in the restaurant are dim . . . *real* dim.

- Take turns writing long, uninterrupted love letters to each other.

- Play online adventure games, card games, video games, or even something like chess, backgammon, or GO!, if you're in a cerebral mood.

- While you type your online messages, also video or audiotape messages to each other. In this way, you can live your date mentally one night, and audibly another.

FIGURE 3-2 Cybergangsters Herr Fixit and TallTassle. For their full story (which includes an online wedding), see Chapter 8, America Online

EXPERT TIP

Don't forget to capture your online trysts, love letters, and other conversations on disk. Many years from now—whether or not things works out—the pages of romance will make a heartwarming memento.

Now What?!

I met my man online and we met in person three months later. I moved across the country for him, and here we are. Things are not perfectly smooth, but we're both working hard. However much we got to "know" each other in cyberspace, we still have to start at the beginning. The sure thing is, we have a sincere wish to make our crazy relationship work. So that's what we are doing.

Online love runs the gamut. There have been couples who decided to get married before ever laying eyes on one another. Some people are lovers online but don't get along at all face to face. But almost all serious online relationships eventually progress into the offline world. Many a cyberdater eventually succumbs to the lure of the dreaded phone call.

The Dreaded Phone Call

Imagine hearing your dearest friend's voice for the very first time—will you love the tone, or hate it? Is that the laugh you want to share your life with? The thought is frightening; the reality can be surprising; the experience is always a little surreal.

It's a good idea to buffer the phone call, before and after, with online chat. A typical post-phone exchange reads something like this:

> A: Oh gee I sounded so stupid, didn't I?
>
> B: Naw, naw, I'm the one who sounded stupid.
>
> A: Oh no, no, it was me who was stupid . . . .

The Visit

Perhaps you're one of the lucky ones; your date lives close enough for an easy visit. Many neighbors have gotten a whole lot more neighborly once online. At times, a small drive brings you face to face with your soulmate.

You may even decide to fly out to your date, or to drop in if you're ever in the neighborhood. It's best not to rush things. But then again, if one of you can afford the air fare, and both of you feel it's high time, then there's no reason to stall the inevitable. But be sure you both are ready for what might be a—gulp—relationship.

If at all possible, meet in a neutral, public setting. This first *physical* meeting will be awkward; somewhere between a blind date and a reunion between two good old buddies. Next, you should . . . .

EXPERT TIP

If you get the same perma-grin, chilly sweat, and warm jitters offline that you did on, you might be onto something!

Well. Whatever happens next is offline, and beyond the scope of this book.

        it is abnormal to look
        forward to turning on a
        computer the way
        i used to look forward
        to turning on a body yet
        these days when
        a worry comes easier
        than a poem i am fortunate
        to have her help me thru love's
        sick grip—i owe her
        but what can i do but press
        my lips onto the blue
        monitor as the static plays
        with my curls and hope
        those invisible
        green eyes
        continue

THE DATEMOBILE

WHAT DOES IT MEAN, EXACTLY, TO GET ONLINE?

A computer is nothing more than a fancy manipulator of digits, hence the term *digital*. Everything you do on a computer—word processing, spreadsheets, graphics, data manipulation—is broken down into thousands of little digits (ones and zeros, to be exact). These digits can be sent to your video monitor, where they appear as graphics or text. These digits can be sent to your disk drive, where they are stored for later use. These digits can be zoomed over to your printer, where they appear as patterns of ink on paper. Last but not least, digits can be sent and received through phone lines. When you're online, all it means is that you are swapping digits, through the telephone, with another computer.

But your computer does not come with hands. It cannot just pick up the phone, dial a number, and say "Howdy." Phone lines transmit an *analog* range of sounds, not digits. To get online, you need to give your computer a special device so it can talk over the phone: a modem. Modem stands for *modulator, demodulator*—circuitry that turns the soundless bits of digital computer-talk into analog noise (modulation), and vice versa (demodulation).

Once you've installed a modem, your computer needs to be able to access it. Just as a printer needs a word processing program's printer driver, a modem needs a special communications program to tell it what to do.

This chapter leads you through buying a modem, installing it, and setting up the proper communications software. After that, you're ready to get online! Your com-

puter may already have an attached modem and communications software. If this is the case, you need only skim through this chapter for a quick idea of how everything works.

Buying a Modem

Modems come in many forms. Yours may be a small box or a thin wafer, or it may already be hidden inside your computer. Essentially, though, every modem has the same design: One end plugs into your computer, the other plugs into your phone jack. Figure 4-1 shows two types of modems.

The International Telecommunications Union (ITU) pretty much sets the standard for modems. Most modem manufacturers build their products according to ITU guidelines. This means the modem you buy can talk to anybody else's.

Although many people choose to have separate phone lines put in for their modems, this is not necessary. The modem uses your phone the same way you do, only it talks in computerese—a parakeet-like whistling (which you are not forced to hear unless you pick up your phone while the modem is in use).

You can buy modems at any computer store or through mail-order houses. Some of the commercial online services, such as PRODIGY, offer excellent prices on modems. Check out *Computer Shopper* magazine for pages and pages of ads urging you to buy all sorts of different modems with different speeds, warranties, sizes, types, and prices.

Speed: In a Rush?

Modem speed is measured in bits per second, or *bps*—more commonly called *baud*. Originally, most modems ran at 300 baud. A year later, 1200 baud was the highest-tech. Then 2400. Right now, the 9600 standard is giving way to 14,400, which is about the equivalent

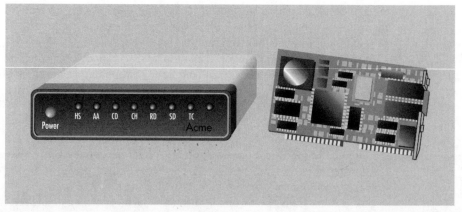

FIGURE 4-1 External modem (the box) at left, internal modem (the card) at right

of sending one short novel per minute. There are even 19,200-baud modems available, though there are very few places you can currently call to use them effectively.

The ITU, in its technical lingo, refers to 9600-baud modems as *v.32,* 14,400 bauds as *v.32bis,* and 28,800 as *v.34.* You may see modems advertised as *v.FC* or *v.Terbo,* but these do not conform to official telecommunications standards and may not provide as widespread, swift performance as you might hope.

The speed two computers communicate by depends on whichever modem is slowest. Most commercial online services, for instance, run at a maximum of 9600 baud. You may have shelled out a lot of bucks for a 19,200-baud super-modem, but if you call Delphi, you are limited to 9600 (or even 2400 in some areas)—way below your modem's potential. Many modems are built too fast for widespread use.

With online dating, high speed is not crucial. You are not dealing with pages and pages of continuous data or software. Rather, you're interacting with other multi-thumbed humans. When you're chatting with someone, how fast you get the message depends on your reading ability and your date's typing ability, not your modem speed. Occasionally, in fact, modems may be so fast that text flows by in an unreadable blur.

Most of the modems you can purchase are 14,400 baud, which run about a hundred bucks. If you can find 9600 baud for a great price, it'll do fine. You only need purchase anything *faster* than 14,400 baud if you think you'll be transferring a lot of software.

What You Speed Is Not What You Get

The faster your modem, just like the faster you talk, the more glitches there are in communication. Luckily, all modems have some form of built-in *error correction.* The modem you buy should have the ITU standard *v.42bis* or *MNP Level 5* protocol for error correction. This ensures proper data transfer, but it slows things down. A modem may actually run up to 75 percent slower than specified. This, however, is necessary and occurs no matter which brand of modem you purchase.

Also, modems may be advertised to run *faster* than their baud rates, due to crunching information via *data compression.* Compression concentrates computer files, removing blank spaces and combining popular words into a sort of shorthand. The advertised "effective throughput" speeds can be a little misleading, since data compression works only under exacting conditions.

The Fax of Life

Most every modem now comes standard with FAX capability. Naturally, only pay extra for a FAX/modem if you think you'll use it. This, along with special software (such as WinFAX, for Windows), allows your computer to send and receive FAX documents.

If a modem can FAX at 9600 baud it may not necessarily transmit data at the same rate. If a modem is listed as a 2400/9600 FAX, it is 2400-baud data and 9600 FAX.

Internal vs. External

External modems are sturdy gizmos, around the size of a cigar box, that generally plug into your computer's serial port—if you don't have a free serial port you need to buy one. Advantages of externals include

- LED lights. These indicate when you have connected to another computer, at what speed, with what specifications, and whether your modem is currently sending or receiving data. There are usually eight different lights.
- Volume control. You can make your speaker louder or turn it off altogether.
- Portability. You can switch the modem from computer to computer, in case you'd like to telecommunicate at both home and work.

You can also purchase a *pocket modem,* which is around the size of a box of cigarettes and is handy if you use a notebook or laptop computer.

Internal modems hide inside your computer. Although they are slightly more difficult to install than external modems, it's not major surgery. Some of their advantages are

- They take up no desk space.
- They usually come with their own extra serial port.
- They are cheaper than externals by anywhere from $10 to $100, depending on the brand.

Laptop and notebook computers do not have room for standard internal modems. Contact your computer's manufacturer if you're interested in an internal modem—usually there are specially-made devices available. Many notebooks come with a slot known as the *PCMCIA type 2.* Lightweight PCMCIA modems are readily available and slide right into your type 2 slot.

Also, if you have a PS/2 computer, you may not have the right type of slots needed to install a regular internal modem. Rather, you need to find a condensed version known as the *Micro Channel Architecture (MCA).* Check your computer's documentation or ask your retailer for more details.

Like Searching for a Needle in a Hayes Stack

Hayes compatibility is an absolute standard for modems. If it's not Hayes compatible, look elsewhere.

Macintosh, IBM, Etc.

External modems typically plug into most any brand of computer. You will, however, need a different connection cable for the Mac than for IBM-compatibles. See the Installing Your Modem section, later in this chapter.

Internal modems, on the other hand, are generally designed only for IBM-compatibles. The design of Mac Plus and Classic does not allow additional chips to be installed internally.

Once your modem is hooked up, however, you can call *any* other modem, whether it's attached to an IBM, a Mac, a mainframe, or whatever. The alphanumeric alphabet—called *ASCII*—is standard for all computers, so you can exchange text easily with anyone. Special software will sometimes let you trade word processor-formatted text and graphics between computer types as well. However, you probably won't be able to run any software you get from a computer of a type different from your own. The majority of BBSs cater to users of IBM-type systems, so if sharing software is important to you, remember you'll have the most choice if you get an IBM-compatible computer for yourself.

Cables

Most modems come with their own cables. For external modems, there are two important cables you need: one that plugs into your computer's serial port (the data cable) and one that plugs into your phone jack (the phone cable). Internal modems need only a phone cable.

Be sure the phone cable is long enough to reach from your computer to your phone jack. Figure 4-2 details the hookup of the data cable, which is a little trickier. One end has 25 *pins* in it, 13 in the upper row and 12 below—if you look into the cable straight on, you can count them. Since the plug has pins, and not holes, it is *male*. This end plugs into the back of your modem, which has a *female* slot with 25 holes (who ever said connecting peripherals was boring?). The other end of the data cable is typically female and

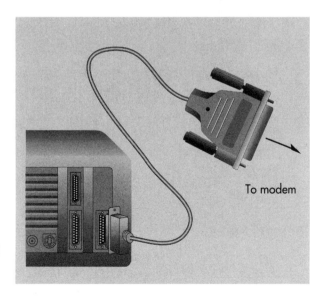

To modem

FIGURE 4-2 Connecting your modem to your computer

fits into your computer's serial port, which varies depending on the make and model of your computer. Keep the following in mind:

- IBMs and compatibles have either a 9-pin or 25-pin serial port. Look at the back of your computer to see which type you have; remember, the serial port is male, having pins, not holes. You can get special cables which fit into each, or, if your modem came with the wrong type of cable, you may purchase a cheap 25-pin to 9-pin adapter.

- Macintosh Plus, SE, II, and the Apple IIGS use a special round 8-pin female connector. Macs have a dedicated communications port, labeled with the picture of a telephone. Special communications cables are available at most any Macintosh retailer.

- Apple II, II+, IIE, III, and Macintosh XLs have female 25-pin ports.

- The serial ports on other brands of computers may vary. In some cases, such as with old IBM PCs or XTs, you may need to install an entirely new port. Check with your computer's manufacturer for more details.

Some IBMs may have two or more serial ports. If this is the case, note which port number (they are generally labeled) you've plugged your modem into. You'll need this information later when you are configuring your communications software.

Installing Your Modem

Once you get your modem out of its box, you're only a few minutes away from actually using it. Installing a modem generally requires no more than the connection of a few cables. What follows is a general guideline—always skim through your modem's documentation for the messy details.

External Affairs

Figure 4-3 shows the setup of a typical external modem; the figure is worth a thousand words.

The external modem, being the translator between your phone line and your computer, naturally plugs into both. Most modems have their own power supply. Plug this into an electrical outlet and plug the other end into your modem—the socket is usually round and labeled *V-AC*. You now need to connect the modem to your computer. If you're not sure which cable to use, see the Cables section, earlier in this chapter. Plug one end (male) into the back of your modem (female). Plug the other end into one of your computer's serial ports. Data cable connectors usually have two screws at their sides, for more permanent attachments. Make sure your connections are tight.

Internal Affairs

Figure 4-4 illustrates the installation of a typical internal modem. To begin with, you need a screwdriver. First, be sure to unplug your computer. You may now slide away your computer's casing; this usually requires the removal of a few strategically-placed screws and a few solid whacks along its sides. Be wary of static electricity, which can zap your computer chips;

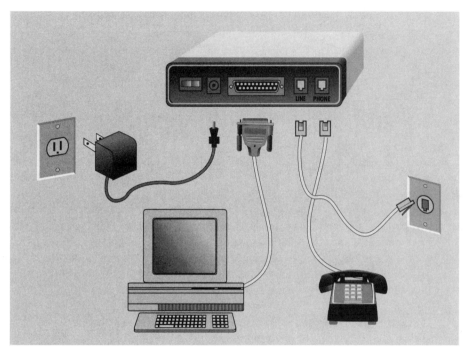

FIGURE 4-3 Setting up a typical external modem

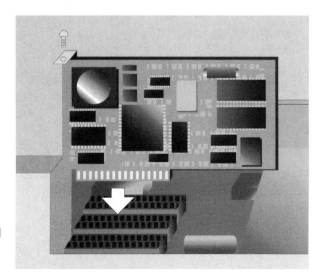

FIGURE 4-4 Inserting a typical internal modem into your computer's chassis

touch a grounded metal surface before you meddle with anything within your machine. If you've never done it before, consult your computer's documentation or manufacturer for details.

Once you've managed to pry the case off, you can see the guts of the computer. There is a landscape of green boards, spiderlike chips, snaking cables and wires, shiny metal boxes, and more. You may have noticed that the back of your computer has various slots and ports. Now, getting an inside view of the action, you can see that some of these ports are actually vertical wafer-thin boards. There should be a row of slots, some empty and some not, aligned along the rear of your computer. Tower-style cases have slots along their sides.

You can now choose any empty slot that strikes your fancy. Typically, if a slot is empty, there is a metal strip covering up the hole in the back of the computer. You need to remove the screw at the top of this strip; the metal will slide up and out. You can now plug in your modem.

One end of your modem has a thin tab, usually with gold or silver "teeth." Being sure the back of your modem (the part with all the ports and switches) is aligned with the back of your computer, slide the modem's tab firmly into the expansion slot. Once your modem is properly installed, it should completely cover the hole in the back of your computer, and its slots and controls should appear similar to Figure 4-5. You can now use the screw you previously removed to hold your new modem in place.

You may now replace your computer's casing.

Users of notebook and laptop computers need to contact the retailer or manufacturer if they're interested in an internal modem, since the shape of the modem varies with the brand of computer. If you have a credit card-sized PCMCIA slot in the back of your machine, you can easily plug in a dedicated PCMCIA modem. Simply press the wafer-thin end of the modem entirely into the slot.

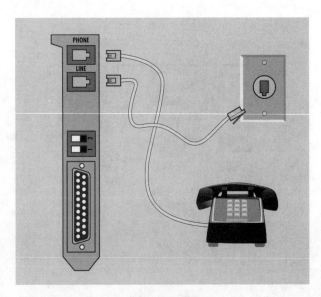

FIGURE 4-5 The rear view of a typical internal modem

Connecting to the Phone Line

The back panel of your modem—whether PCMCIA, external, or internal—contains one or two RJ-11 phone jack sockets, which should look the same as the telephone outlet on your wall. If there is already a phone or answering machine plugged into your wall outlet, unplug it. If your modem has *two* RJ-11 jacks, plug your phone into the one which is labeled *PHONE* or *EXT*. If your RJ-11 jacks are not labeled, just guess; usually, either works just fine.

Now plug one end of a standard phone cable (see the Cables section) into your wall outlet and insert the other end into the back of your modem, in the jack labeled *LINE* or *TELCO*. Pick up your phone—you should hear a dial tone. If not, try switching the plugs in the two RJ-11 jacks. Check to be sure the cables are inserted properly—you should hear a *click* once each connection is in place.

If you're using an external modem, you can now flip the power switch. A light on your modem's front panel should indicate that it is receiving power and ready to go. Internal modems automatically power-on when they're in use.

You're now just a phone call away from being online!

Communications Software

Communications software is also aptly called *terminal* (or just *term*) software because it turns your computer into a telecommunications terminal—nothing more than a screen and a keyboard. Most modems you can buy come with their own term software. This is usually no-frills and user-unfriendly, but it gets the job done. You can always use it to call a BBS (see Chapter 6) and download some better software; read on to find out how.

Front-End vs. All-Purpose

One important question is, do you even *need* communications software? Commercial online services such as PRODIGY, America Online, CompuServe, GEnie, some graphical BBSs, and even a few Internet providers require or offer their own special *front-end* software. A front-end system automatically dials its particular service, logs you on, and makes it easy for you to navigate. Each of the following chapters tells you how to obtain and install

EXPERT TIP

If your modem only has one RJ-11 phone jack, you need to plug in your phone someplace else. Most likely, you want to get a cheap doubling connector that plugs into your wall outlet and gives you two outlets for the price of one. You can now plug your modem data cable into one of the outlets and your phone into the other.

appropriate front-end software. You generally need to buy it separately, though in some cases you can call up using a standard all-purpose communications package and then download the front-end materials.

If you are using your modem *only* to call a front end-supported service, you can skip the rest of this chapter.

Wise GUIs

Those who are familiar with the Macintosh Operating System or Microsoft Windows are already masters at using a *Graphical User Interface (GUI)*. More and more term programs, online services, Internet providers, and bulletin boards are "going graphical," providing software that runs under a GUI environment. Figure 4-6 shows a screen from the MicroLink communications program for Windows, a typical GUI.

In case you don't know an icon from an ex-con, here's a little help:

Basically, you can lay your keyboard aside—except when you're actually typing messages. The mouse is the center of the action with GUIs. Use the mouse to move around the little arrow, nibbling at what you want.

Buttons are just that, rectangles on the screen that contain words or pictures; pictures, by the way, are also known as *icons*. To perform an action, you move the mouse arrow to its appropriate button and *click* (press down the left mouse button). In some cases you may need to *double-click* (quickly press the button twice) to access an option.

For example, a *list* of many options often appears. In most cases, options are preceded by a tiny icon that tells you what to expect. For example, text is preceded by the picture of a written-on page. The first option in a list is highlighted. To highlight a different option, click on it. If you double-click on an option, you access it. Alternatively, you can click on *Open* or *OK* or some such button, which opens up the currently highlighted option.

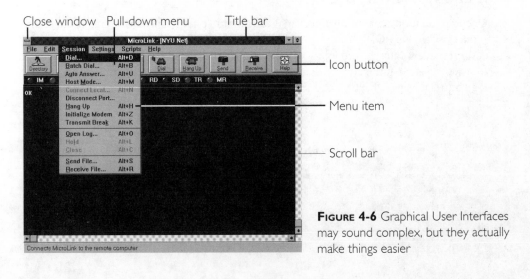

FIGURE 4-6 Graphical User Interfaces may sound complex, but they actually make things easier

Each time you open an option or click on a button a new *window* generally appears, usually overlapping the old one. This new window has all sorts of different buttons and options. Once you are done with a topic, you can return to the previous screen by clicking twice on the top left-hand corner of the window. The window disappears. This is known as *closing* the window.

You can move a window around by clicking on its top *title bar*. Without lifting the mouse button, drag the window where you will. You can change the window's size by clicking on one of its corners. Without lifting the mouse, you can stretch the window, making it larger or smaller.

The *scroll bar* (also called the *elevator*, in some circles) is the vertical bar on the right side of each window; occasionally, there may also be a horizontal scroll bar along the bottom of the window. Scroll bars allow you to scroll through text that is larger than the space provided. Click on the down arrow at the bottom of the vertical scroll bar to see the next line of information. Click on the up arrow to move back up. You can also move your mouse arrow to the little elevator and press the mouse button. Without lifting the button, *drag* the elevator down, like a thermostat control. As the elevator moves further down the shaft, you can see more and more of your text.

Lastly, the *pull-down menu* at the top of the screen is where everything you can see and do comes together. When you click on a word (such as File), a menu of various options (such as New, Open, Save, Save As) appears. Once you click on one of these options, a further *side menu* may appear, with even more options. On a Macintosh, you need to hold down the mouse button until you've highlighted the option you want. With Windows, you can just to click once on any menu item you're interested in.

Buying a Term

Many term programs are available commercially, for prices ranging from $5 to $300. Some terms are full-featured, with icons and windows, and come with an entire programming language allowing you to call hundreds of computers at pre-set times, perform thousands of tasks, and then log out, all while your flesh-and-blood self is far from your computer— say, watching a movie on the other side of town.

Unless you have some peculiar, fancy, or specific ideas on how to use your modem, most any standard communications program will do. Most of these are available as reasonably-priced shareware (see the File Transfers section, later in this chapter). Some of the most readily available terms are profiled in the Popular Communications Software section further along. In general, when buying communications software, here are the features you should look for:

Scrollback buffer (also called a *peruse buffer*). Often, text or information may appear on your screen faster than you can read it. You may wish you could go back in time and see exactly what just happened. If you have a scrollback buffer, you can. Using the scroll bar at the side of the screen, or some other handy command, you can pull down text that has disappeared past the top of your screen.

☙ *Log file* (also called a *capture file*). Many times, you want to capture the information on your screen and either use it somewhere else (such as a word processor) or save it to your hard disk for later reference. A log file lets you capture everything that appears and automatically saves it all to your disk. The easiest Windows or Macintosh software lets you mark the text you want with your mouse and then copy it directly to the clipboard.

☙ Several *File Transfer Protocols*. Any communications software you buy should have Xmodem, Ymodem, Kermit, and Zmodem already installed. See the File Transfers section of this chapter for details.

☙ *Dialing directory*. This is like an address book containing your favorite telephone numbers and each one's associated settings. To dial a service, you just select it from the directory.

One other useful feature you may find is the ability to use *macros* or *script files*. A script file allows you to write a little program to dial a number, type in your user name and password, and perform any tasks you're interested in, such as reading your mail. Macros are digital mockingbirds—they can watch you log on once and remember the steps, logging you on in the future. Some terminal programs have highly detailed script languages, allowing you full automated control.

Terminal Settings

Your software should come with documentation that tells you how to get your terminal up and running. Typically, you insert the term software's disk in the drive, access the drive, and run some sort of SETUP or INSTALL program.

Once your software is copied neatly onto your hard drive, you need to tell your software several things before it can connect to another computer. Usually, you are prompted for these settings the first time you run the program:

☙ *The* port number *of your modem*. In some cases, your communications software automatically figures out which port your modem is plugged into. However, you may need to specify a port number. If you have an external modem, look at the back of your computer; the modem port may be labeled. If not, chances are you are plugged into COM1 or COM2. If you have an internal modem, you can usually designate the modem to be any port you want (COM1 through COM4) by fiddling with the switches on its rear panel. Usually, internals are set as COM2.

☙ *The phone number you are calling*. This must belong to another modem. Most of the phone numbers in this book are *data* numbers, and dialable by modem. Standard *voice* numbers are designated as such.

☙ *Tone or pulse*. If your phone line supports tone dialing, select it—it's faster and more reliable. Otherwise, use pulse.

- *Modem speed.* Normally you set this speed to your modem's maximum baud rate. If you call a service that has a slower modem than yours, most communications packages automatically adjust.

- *Parity* (or error). This can be set to none, even, or odd (abbreviated as N, E, or O). This is an agreed-upon way of transferring data, and, as such, depends upon the service you are calling. If parity is set to even or odd, your data is automatically checked for errors. Most data numbers use no parity, though large mainframes tend to use even parity.

- *Data bits.* This can be set to 7 or 8 and depends on the service you are calling.

- *Stop bits.* This can be set to 1 or 2 and also depends on the service you're calling.

In general, always set your character format to be eight data bits, no parity, and one stop bit (8N1). If you call up a system and your screen fills with garbage, try the next-most popular setting: seven data bits, even parity, and one stop bit (7E1).

Most any terminal program allows you to adjust these settings for each number you call. If your software features a dialing directory, you can store all your favorite phone numbers and each one's associated settings.

Other file transfer settings, such as *echo, duplex, handshaking,* and *XON/XOFF,* are usually set at default values. Only change one of these settings if an online service explicitly tells you to.

You can usually change the terminal settings online, as well. There is usually a pull-down menu or command option for *device settings, port settings, modem settings,* or *format settings.*

Terminal Emulation

This is a diverse world, and there are lots of different types of terminals. Your communications software, at its heart, is actually nothing more than a big fake—pretending to be a certain type of terminal and pulling off the disguise perfectly.

To communicate effectively with another terminal, you need to match its type. Most communications packages have a *terminal emulation* menu or option. The basic terminal emulation is called *TTY,* and allows most any two computers to exchange letters, numbers, and some punctuation.

EXPERT TIP

If you are able to connect to a system and read most of the text, but some of the characters seem wrong or funny-looking, you probably are not sharing the same terminal emulation. Try changing your emulation to ANSI or VT-100. A newer emulation, called the *Remote Image Protocol (RIP),* allows graphics and mouse-maneuvering capabilities. To use RIP emulation, you need to call a RIP system and use RIP communications software, such as the shareware RIPterm.

Many systems, however, feature colorful menus, line drawings, blinking lights, underlined phrases, and full-screen text editors. This is due to the *ANSI* terminal type. When you first log in to an ANSI-supportive system you are asked:

Does your terminal support ANSI?

If your terminal emulation is set to ANSI, you can press Ⓨ and then enjoy the colors.

If a service you call requires non-standard terminal emulation (which your software may or may not support), you are generally told so as soon as you connect.

Prettier screens, such as ANSI and RIP, may take longer to draw. If you are using a relatively slow modem you may opt to use standard TTY emulation, just to speed things up.

Your First Call

It may take a little while to figure out how to make your communications software dial a number. In the meantime, if you want to make sure everything is up and running, just turn on your modem (if it's external) and start up your terminal program. You should see a blank screen, which is known as *terminal mode*.

You now want to call your first BBS, to ensure that your modem is properly connected to your phone line. To perform this test dial, you need a phone number. You can add the number to your dialing directory, in which case you generally fill in a system's name, phone number, and terminal settings. You may find a Phone Number item under one of the pull-down menus, allowing you to type it in directly. There may also be a *manual dial* option, which allows you to call up a number that isn't in your dialing directory. In any case, type

800-874-2937

in the appropriate spot. (Put in a 1 first if required in your area.) You now need to dial, either by clicking on the phone number or by selecting the Dial menu or menu item.

If you don't hear a dial tone, or if some sort of error occurs, then either your modem is not attached to your computer or your communications program is looking at the wrong serial port. See the next section, Troubleshooting, for more help

You should be able to hear your modem dialing. You can crank up the volume on your external modem by adjusting the speaker control dial. If all goes well, you should now hear a sound that will soon become as familiar to you as your own voice: the *connect tone*. This tone begins as the sound of nails scratching against a blackboard, momentarily becoming a bloodcurdling screech, and then leveling out into a long, contented squeal. Your modem speaker mutes itself as soon as you get a solid connection (thank goodness), and the following message should appear:

CONNECT 9600

Depending on the speed of your modem, the message may read *CONNECT 2400, CONNECT 14400,* and so on.

You can now turn to Chapter 6 to learn how to sign up and navigate the BBS. If you receive the

BUSY

message, then the number is currently busy. Wait a while and try your call again. Most communications programs automatically redial a busy number, again and again, until there is a connection.

Troubleshooting

Once your modem is properly attached and your terminal settings are properly defined, getting online is a snap. Sometimes, though, getting everything running can be tricky. Following are some common problems, along with their common solutions.

- None of the LEDs are lit along the front of your external modem: Check the power cord to be sure it is securely attached to the modem and plugged into your wall socket (be sure the socket has power by plugging in something else). Be sure the modem is switched on. If no lights appear, your modem may be faulty.

- Your telephone is connected to your modem, but when you lift the receiver, there's no dial tone: Be sure the phone cables are connected properly and securely.

- Your modem does not respond: Be sure all the cables are properly and securely connected. Your communications software is probably trying to access the wrong serial port. Change your terminal settings, trying COM1, COM2, COM3, and COM4, until you find the proper port.

- Your modem responds but does not dial: Be sure the phone cable is secure. Be sure you are dialing a valid number.

- Your modem dials but does not connect: Be sure your modem is plugged into your phone line. Also, be sure none of the phones that share the line are in use. If you are dialing with touch tones, be sure your phone lines support that service; otherwise dial using pulse. If everything still fails, you may be trying to dial a number that is not connected to a modem. Try calling later or cross that number off your list.

- You can't see anything you type: You need to turn on your communications software's *echo*. Search for a menu that allows you to change the Duplex, Self Echo, or Screen Echo. Set your term to Screen Echo.

- Whenever you type something, it appears twice (i.e. "help!" appears like "hheellpp!!"): Your software and your modem are both in *echo* mode. Search your terminal software's menus until you find a way to adjust the Duplex, Self Echo, or Screen Echo. Change the Duplex to half or the Echo to off.

- You connect to a service, but nothing happens: Try changing your baud rate and other terminal settings. You may be trying to connect to a modem that is faster than yours.

▓ You connect to a service, but all you see is garbage: You are using the wrong terminal settings. If you are currently set to 8N1, change it to 7E1, and vice versa. If this does not work, your line may just be noisy. Try calling a little later.

▓ Letters on the screen are readable, but not aligned properly: Your Terminal Emulation is probably off. Try changing to TTY, VT-100, or ANSI.

File Transfers

The appeal of online dating is using your modem to reach out and touch not just another computer, but another *person*. Once you're online you can join millions of people, chatting with them and exchanging all sorts of private mail or public messages.

However, the modem is also a marvel when it comes to trading files. Using a modem, you can copy software from any computer around the world onto your own. Not only is this useful for programmers, software collectors, gamers, and businesspeople, but it can add a lot of pizzazz to an online date. Daters can send each other digitized photographs, drawings, love letters, poetry, animations—anything at all that can be created or stored on a computer. Many match-making systems allow you to view pictures of prospective dates before you contact them.

This makes it useful to learn the basics of file transferring. There are a few terms you need to be familiar with. *Downloading* means copying a software program from a distant computer "down" to your own. When you send a file upstream, it's called *uploading*.

Each bulletin board and commercial online service has its own method of down- and uploading, as does each brand of communications software. There are, however, some common languages that all computers, online services, and terminals can use: *File transfer protocols*. A protocol is an agreed-upon way to send data over the phone lines. Most protocols transfer data, a little bit at a time, automatically verifying that the data received is the same as the data sent. Since phone lines are susceptible to static and other noise, a protocol knows if any data has been garbled and resends that piece of data if necessary. A typical "conversation" between two computers would be:

> *Computer A:* Okay, send me the next thousand bits of data, please.
>
> *Computer B:* Here you go, dude. Do they look okay?
>
> *Computer A:* No, you messed up somehow. Send them to me again.
>
> *Computer B:* Sure, man. How're they now?
>
> *Computer A:* Ah, now they're good. Send over the next thousand bits, if you'd be so kind.

Simply put, if you make sure that your file transfer protocol matches the distant computer's protocol, everything works out. Usually, when you opt to download a file, a list of available protocols appears. Always pick the fastest protocol available. For example, if you have a choice of Xmodem, Ymodem, and Zmodem, select Zmodem if your terminal program has the Zmodem protocol built-in.

Once the protocol is set up, you see something along the lines of:

Initiate File Transfer Now!

You must now begin the download. On most terminal programs, all you have to do is press the (PGDN) key and then select the applicable protocol. Other terminal programs require you to access the Download or Receive File option, which may be under the File Transfer or Session pull-down menu. Some terminal programs automatically begin the download for you.

The more widely used protocols, in their order of speed, are:

- *ASCII.* This is used only to send text files. ASCII (American Standard Code for Information Interchange) is the way the alphabet is stored on most computers. There is no error correction, so your text may have some flaws.

- *Xmodem.* This is one of the earliest and most popular protocols. It is also known as *Xmodem Checksum.* There are several variations to take note of: *XmodemCRC* is slower than Xmodem Checksum, but more reliable. *1K Xmodem* sends more data at a time and is thus faster than Xmodem; this is also sometimes referred to as Ymodem. *Xmodem/G* is extremely fast, but is not recommended because it aborts the file transfer if there are any errors.

- *Ymodem.* A variation of 1K Xmodem. *Ymodem Batch* has the ability for *batch* transfers, allowing you to download several files (a batch) at once. *Ymodem/G* is very fast, but like its Xmodem counterpart, it does not feature error correction, and aborts the file transfer if there are any problems.

- *Zmodem.* This protocol is both fast and reliable. Zmodem also has batch capability. In addition, Zmodem has a *resume* feature, which allows you to continue downloading a file that, for whatever reason, was only transferred half-way. For example, assume you are downloading a large picture of your online date when your computer falls prey to a power outage. You need only redial the service, initiate the download as usual, and Zmodem continues where you were interrupted.

- *HS/Link.* This is a relatively new protocol, and is difficult to find. It works only with high-speed modems and allows you to send and receive files at the same time, at great speeds.

In general, Zmodem is the protocol of choice—it is widely supported and transfers files at a fast pace. Other protocols you may come across are CompuServe B (which, as you might expect, is used on the CompuServe Information Service), Kermit (often used for downloading 7-bit files from mainframes, such as many Internet systems), and Bimodem (which allows you to download, upload, and chat, all at the same time).

Shareware

Heaps of programs, of all shapes and sizes, are available online. You may wonder why so much quality software is offered for free when similar packages are sold in stores for

hundreds of dollars. Actually, software you download may not be as free as it appears. There are two types of software legally available online:

- *Freeware.* This software is really free of charge. The author is a volunteer who is happy to share the fruits of his or her labor with you. Sometimes you're asked for a donation, but payment is optional.

- *Shareware.* Most software falls into this category. You can use the software, on a trial basis, for a certain amount of time (say, two weeks). At that point, you are honor bound to send a check to the author of the software. Once you *register*, you receive such goodies as free updates or printed documentation. When you first run this software, you may see a screen telling you how long the trial period is, how much the software costs, and where to send your money.

If commercial software is available online, it is *pirated,* and is illegal to download.

Zipping, Squashing, and Stuffing

There are a few important programs you need if you want to up- and download. These programs—called *archivers*—take many files, compress them, and bundle them into one large archive. This allows for easy organization and saves a tremendous amount of disk space. For example, 20 files taking up 10 megabytes of space may be compressed into 1 file less than a megabyte large.

For the IBM, the most popular archiver is PKWare's PKZIP. Most files you can find online end with the extension .ZIP. To use any .ZIP file, you need to PKUNZIP it. Ask your sysop for help or search for the latest PKZ204G.EXE (the version number, 2.04g, may be replaced by some higher number). Download this file and run it by typing its name. It is *self-extracting,* and automatically creates the files PKZIP.EXE, PKUNZIP.EXE, and a number of utilities. The program is shareware, and you are encouraged to register it if you find it useful.

Now, the next time you download a "zipped" file, all you have to do is, at the DOS prompt, unzip it! For example if you download a file called LOVELTR.ZIP into the *root directory,* extract it by typing

```
pkunzip loveltr.zip
```

(You'll need to specify the full path name if the file is not in the root directory.)

Other popular IBM archivers include SEA's ARC (files with the .ARC extension) and Haruyasu Yoshizaki's LZHARC (files with the .LZH extension).

PKZIP is also available for the Macintosh. The STUFFIT program, however, is probably the most popular Mac archiver. All you need to do to unstuff a file (once you have obtained the STUFFIT application) is double-click on it.

Many files stored on UNIX systems—such as those you can reach using the Internet—have the .Z extension. This requires an archiver known as COMPRESS. Versions of UNCOMPRESS are available for UNIX, IBM DOS, Macintosh, and other computers. For more tips and tricks on using UNIX archivers and the Internet, pick up a copy of The Waite Group's *Internet How-To.*

COMPUTER/PLATFORM	GIF VIEWER
IBM/Windows	PSP (Paint Shop Pro) or WinGIF
IBM/DOS	VPIC or CSHOW
Macintosh	GIFConverter
Apple IIGS	GIF 3200

TABLE 4-1 The software you need to view GIFs

If you download a file and are not sure how to extract it, contact your sysop or customer service representative.

Graphics in a GIFfy

Whether it's a photograph of your date, a reproduction of the Mona Lisa, or a close-up of Saturn's outer rings, graphics add visual light to the textual darkness of cyberspace.

Graphics files online are usually stored in the Graphics Interchange Format (GIF) which was developed by CompuServe. GIFs are viewable on most every major type of computer. To see a GIF, you need special display software. Some of the most popular GIF viewers are listed in Table 4-1.

In addition, CompuServe's front-end CIM software (for Windows and Mac) is able to show GIFs. Search for these files in the Graphics libraries of your favorite bulletin board or online service. Again, if you have trouble finding or using a GIF viewer, ask your sysop or customer service representative.

If you'd like to put your own photographs online, you must *digitize* them with a *scanner*. Scanners are similar to copy machines—they take an image and create a computer file. Since good scanners are very expensive, you may not have direct access to one. Many copy shops scan photographs for a minor fee; bring them a blank disk and a photo. Also, most of the online services give you the mailing addresses of volunteers who will scan your photo, for free, and put it online.

Be on the lookout for other graphic images called TIFs, JPGs, PICs, and MACs. Every graphic format has its own viewer, which should be available from the same place. There are also programs which convert one graphics style into another. Ask your sysop or customer service representative for details.

EXPERT TIP

Some GIFs created on Macintoshes do not appear on IBMs because they have a slightly different format. There are conversion programs available, however, to take care of this. Search the graphics libraries of your favorite bulletin board or online service for more details.

EXPERT TIP

If you have Claris Works or Microsoft Works (for either Windows or Macintosh), then you already own a full-featured terminal program. Simply select the Communications module.

Popular Communications Software

Following are basic profiles of three of the more widely-used terminal programs. Many are shareware, and are available for free trial. No matter which terminal program or computer you're using, you can skim the following profiles to learn the basics and get a feel for how telecommunications works. Naturally, the commands, menus, and features differ depending on your brand of software.

Microsoft Windows: The Terminal

If you own a copy of Windows, then you also own a no-frills terminal program. Look for the Terminal icon (a phone sitting next to a computer monitor) under your Windows Program Manager's Accessories group. To access Terminal, just double-click on it. Figure 4-7 shows a typical screen.

You need to make a new file for each number you plan to call. (Many Macintosh terminals use this same *activities* system, where each online service is treated as its own bundle of phone number, terminal settings, and file transfer settings.) Select New from the File pull-down menu. You can now enter the phone number of the service you want to call. Select Phone Number from the Settings menu. A box similar to Figure 4-8 appears. Type in the number.

Select the Terminal Emulation option from the Settings menu. You may now choose from standard TTY or VT-100 (ANSI) emulation. Click on the emulation you prefer (in most cases, this is ANSI).

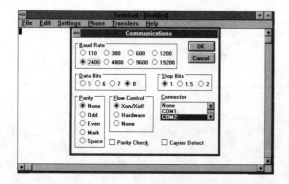

FIGURE 4-7 The Window's bones-basic Terminal: Viewing the terminal settings

Figure 4-8 Typing in your phone number

Finally, select the Communications option from the Settings pull-down menu. A screen similar to Figure 4-7 appears. You can now alter your basic terminal settings, if necessary.

Once everything is set, you can save your phone number for later use by selecting Save from the File pull-down menu. You are asked for a descriptive eight-character name, such as the name of the commercial service or BBS. Each of your Terminal files automatically gets the .TRM extension. Be sure to save all your .TRM activity files in the same directory.

In the future, you can call the service whose number and settings you've just defined by selecting Open from the File pull-down menu and then selecting the appropriate file.

Calling

You are now ready to get online. Select Dial from the Phone pull-down menu. If all the settings are correct and the service is operating, you will soon be connected online.

If text appears on the screen but then scrolls away too fast, or if you want to review something you've previously typed, you can use Terminal's scrollback buffer: Simply access the scroll bar at the right of the window.

Hanging Up

When you're ready to exit your online service, select the Hangup item from the Phones pull-down menu. You can then exit the program by selecting Exit from the File pull-down menu.

Downloading

If you come across a file you'd like to download, you can easily do so. First, you need to select a protocol by choosing the Binary Transfers item from the Settings pull-down menu. You may now click on either the Xmodem/CRC or Kermit protocol.

You may now select the file you wish to download. When the service you're calling asks you to select a protocol, choose either Xmodem/CRC or Kermit, depending on your current Binary Transfers setting. You may now begin the download by selecting the Receive Binary File option from the Transfers pull-down menu. You are asked to choose a directory and type in a file name. Once you do so, the file you requested slowly but surely is transferred onto your computer.

Procomm Plus

Procomm is a full-featured program available from Datastorm Technologies. There is a shareware version of Procomm, a commercial version, and a version for Windows. Procomm has become somewhat of a standard for terminal programs, and many other products share the same basic commands.

You can access most Procomm commands by pressing (ALT) along with another key. For instance, (ALT)+(Z) shows a help screen containing a list of all the Procomm commands. Procomm Plus and Procomm for Windows also feature sensible pull-down menus such as Dial Dir, Modes, Emulations, and File, which allow you to select each command by clicking on it, similar to Windows Terminal. You can access the pull-down menu in Procomm Plus by pressing the (~) (tilde) key.

Procomm Plus allows you to set standard *default* settings, which are the typical terminal and file transfer settings you'll be using. You can then enter up to 200 numbers in Procomm's dialing directory; each number may have its own unique settings.

To adjust Procomm's default settings, press (ALT)+(S) for setup. You can now change every bell and whistle—from where Procomm places its files to Procomm's screen colors to the modem's exact commands. Once everything is set the way you like it, press (ESC). You are asked if you want to make the changes permanent. Press (Y) for yes.

You now need to set the important terminal settings. Press (ALT)+(P) for port setup. You are able to select the baud rate, serial port, data and stop bits, and parity. Once everything is set correctly, press (ALT)+(S) to save your changes.

Calling

Press (ALT)+(D) to view the dialing directory. To add a number to the directory, use the cursor keys to highlight an empty slot and then press (R) for revise. A screen similar to Figure 4-9 appears. Prompts ask you to enter the online service's name, its number, and all of its settings. For most settings, you can just press (ENTER) to use the default value. Continue pressing (ENTER) until the system asks if you'd like to save the number. If everything seems right, press (ENTER) again. The number goes into your directory.

```
DIALING DIRECTORY: PCPLUS.DIR

      NAME                              NUMBER     BAUD PDS D P   SCRIPT
  41 Windup BBS                   1-718-428-6123   2400 N81 F D
  42 ┌─ Revise Entry 42 ─┐                         2400 N81 F D
  43 │    NAME: The GaRBage DuMP   │       -5505    2400 N81 H D
  44 │  NUMBER: 457-1111           │       -0211    2400 N81 F D
  45 │    BAUD: 2400               │       -0560    2400 N81 F D
  46 │  PARITY: NONE               │       -0159    2400 N81 F D
  47 │DATA BITS: 8                 │       -1111    2400 N81 F D
  48 │STOP BITS: 1                 │                2400 N81 F D
  49 │  DUPLEX: FULL        ┌─ UT/ANSI... ─┐        2400 N81 F D
  50 │    PORT: DEFAULT     │ IBM...       │        2400 N81 F D
     │  SCRIPT:             │ DG...        │
PgUp │PROTOCOL: ZMODEM      │ ADDS...      │ Marked    L Print Directory
PgDn │TERMINAL: ANSI        │ ADM...       │ Entry(s)  P Dialing Codes
Home │    MODE: MODEM       │ TUI...       │ ntry      X Exchange Dir
End  │PASSWORD:             │ WYSE...      │ ext       T Toggle Display
↑/↓  │META FILE:            │ MISC...      │ ntry      S Sort Directory
Esc  │ KBD FILE:            └──────────────┘ tes
     │NOTE FILE:            │
Choi └─────────────────────┘

 Alt-Z FOR HELP │  ANSI  │   FDX  │ 2400 N81 │ LOG CLOSED │ PRINT OFF │ OFF-LINE
```

FIGURE 4-9 Adding an online system to Procomm's dialing directory

To dial a number, highlight it and press (ENTER). Procomm dials the number and you are automatically connected.

If you'd like to access Procomm's scrollback buffer, press (ALT)+(F6). You can now use the (PGUP) and (PGDN) keys to review anything you've missed. You can even press (M) at this point to mark a chunk of text and save it to your hard disk.

Hanging Up

To end your call, press (ALT)+(H). Press (ALT)+(X) to exit Procomm altogether.

Downloading

Procomm has tons and tons of protocols. When it's time to download, the online service you're on asks you to select a protocol. Choose Zmodem if it is available, otherwise choose another fast protocol (see the File Transfers section). When you are told to begin downloading, simply press the (PGDN) key.

A list of protocols like the one in Figure 4-10 appears.

If you have previously selected a default download protocol, just press (ENTER) to use it. Otherwise, press the number (or letter) preceding the protocol you want. A gauge now appears, showing you the file's progress as it downloads onto your hard disk.

Smartcom for Windows LE

Hayes is the leading name in modem technology, and Smartcom is Hayes' own terminal program. There are many versions of Smartcom: the simplistic Smartcom Exec, Smartcom EZ, the handy Smartcom for Windows LE, and the power-packed Smartcom for Windows. Most Hayes modems come with an appropriate Smartcom.

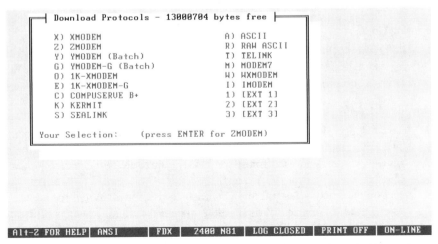

FIGURE 4-10 Procomm's plus: You need a protocol, Procomm's probably got it

When you install Smartcom, you are asked which modem type you are using. Select the Hayes option. To run Smartcom, double-click on the Smartcom for Windows LE program-group icon from the Windows Program Manager. You can now double-click on the Telephone icon. If you have already created a communications document, you can double-click on it to automatically call the associated online service.

Smartcom, like Windows Terminal, uses separate activity files (known as *communications documents*). However, it automatically organizes these files into an easy dialing directory like Procomm.

First, you need to tell the software which serial port your modem is using. Select the Choose Port item from the Connection pull-down menu. Click on Program Default so that Smartcom uses this setting for all future files. Now click on your modem's appropriate serial port (probably COM2).

You can change the rest of the terminal settings by selecting the Quick item from the Settings menu. You can alter your terminal emulation by selecting Terminal from the Settings pull-down menu. Click on the Emulator box to see a listing of many, many emulations. Most commonly, you would select ANSI.

You can now, finally, enter the phone number of the system you wish to call. Select Phone Number from the Connection menu. Type in the number and click on the OK button. You should now save your communications document. Select Save from the File pull-down menu and type in the current service's name (with the .SCW extension) and description.

Calling

To place a call, click on the *Phone Book* button (or select the Phone Book item from the Connection pull-down menu). You see a listing of each communication document's name, phone number, and description. To dial a number, select it (by clicking on it), and then click on the *Connect* button. The number is dialed and you are automatically connected.

You can also alter the current document's information by clicking on *Settings*.

Hanging Up

When you're finished with your online session, just click on the *Phone* button. To exit the program, select Exit from the File pull-down menu. If you haven't saved your current communications document, the system prompts you to do so.

Downloading

You can download files using either Xmodem or Zmodem. You can change the current protocol by selecting either the File Transfer or Quick item from the Settings menu. Click on the protocol you want (most commonly, you'd prefer the faster Zmodem, if it is available on the service you are calling).

You may now select the file you wish to download. When the service you're calling asks you to select a protocol, choose Zmodem. You may now begin the download by selecting the Download option from the Transfers pull-down menu. You are asked to choose a directory and type in a file name. Once you do so, the file you requested is transferred onto your computer.

Other IBM Terms

There are literally hundreds of different terminal programs available for the IBM. Here is a list of some full-featured, easily available software:

- Carbon Copy
- Crosstalk
- Digiterm for Windows (Shareware)
- MicroLink (Shareware)
- Microphone for Windows
- QModem (Shareware and Professional versions available)
- RIPterm (Shareware)
- SmartTerm
- SoftTerm (Shareware)

Macintosh Terms

Since all Macintosh programs make use of easy pull-down menus, icons, and mouse clicks, changing your terminal settings and dialing a number requires nothing more than finding the right command under the right menu. Typical pull-down menus include Dial, Settings, Phone, Options, Terminal, File Transfers, Session, and Connect.

Here are some popular and full-functioned Macintosh term programs:

- Microphone II
- SITComm
- White Knight (used to be Red Ryder)
- ZTerm (Shareware)

Cyberspace: The Final Frontier

You now know more than you probably need to successfully blast off into cyberspace. Like any vast unexplored territory, much of the going will be by trial and error. Changing your terminal settings or pressing your communications software to its limits can never hurt your modem. Experiment. It's that time. Time to swallow your fear. Time to switch on your modem, power up your terminal, and do what it takes to dial your way online. Time to meet some truly alien life forms. Yes, indeed. It is time to cyberdate.

BUCKLING UP

THE CHAPTERS THAT FOLLOW WILL NOT ONLY POINT YOU IN the right directions, but carry you swiftly through all the tangle; kind of like a limousine for your first date. You will soon be exploring the eclectic world of Bulletin Board Systems, the gargantuan Internet, and the United States' five largest commercial online services: America Online, CompuServe, PRODIGY, GEnie, and Delphi. Before you begin crawling through the world's telephone lines, though, there are a few basics to get down.

Putting Passwords on the Line

Your password is vital. It must be easy enough to remember, but weird enough so that nobody else can guess it. Every network or system you call will require a password, and each network's password should be different. That way, if some hacker somehow finds out *one* of your passwords, she won't be able to get too far.

Usually, you will need to type in your password each time you call a service. If somebody else gets hold of your password, he can pretend to be you, and do and say whatever he likes while you take the blame (and pick up the bill). Never tell anyone your password. Change it every few months.

Do *not* use

- Your first, last or middle name. Your maiden, company, or nickname.
- Your birthdate, phone number, or social security number.

The names of any of your family members or pets.

The name of the service you are calling.

Some systems discriminate between upper and lower case, so remember what you did and did not capitalize. Statistically, longer passwords are harder to crack, though you are usually limited to about eight letters. Adding spaces, punctuation marks, or numerals (where permitted) helps make your password completely unguessable.

One popular scheme is to come up with a personalized nonsense word. For instance, "Skooz." Then, assign a random number to each network you call and write these *code numbers* down. For instance, if you designate CompuServe to be code number 619, then compose your CompuServe password to be: "Skooz619". This is less secure, however, than having completely different passwords for each service.

Be sure to write your password somewhere where you—and only you—can easily find and remember it for next time. Many people store their passwords (or code numbers) in their terminal program's dialing directory, which is very convenient, but allows anyone with access to your computer to break into your online accounts.

Call Waiting

Imagine this scenario: You dialed up your favorite online service, bumped around a bit, and then ran into this sizzling-hot date and are having the most sultry conversation of your life. Suddenly, your screen fills with garbage characters. The connection hangs up. Your date is deeply offended and never speaks to you again.

This can happen if you have call waiting. Every time something other than modem-data comes through the phone lines, your communications program will become confused. Sometimes you'll lose your connection. (Note that this can happen even if you *don't* have call waiting, for instance if your roommate accidentally picks up the receiver.)

Dialing *70 (either with your phone touch-tone pad or your modem) before each call will disable call waiting in most areas. If you do not have touch-tone service, you can pulse dial 1170.

EXPERT TIP

If you have call waiting, precede each number in your communication program's dialing directory with:

    *70,

or, if you have to use pulse dialing:

    1170,

The comma will add an automatic pause.

Sometimes a call may have a lot of static, interspersing bits of garbage while you type, or possibly even causing disconnection. If this happens a lot, call your phone company; they may have to rewire or install another line. Often, though, you can get a clean line if you just hang up and try your call again.

Online Economics

Online prices are unpredictable, unregulated, and unsettling. Depending on the service you use, the options you choose, and times you call, online costs can run from mere pennies to hundreds of dollars.

Shop Around

Just because a price is quoted in this book, or by an online service itself, does not mean it's chiseled in stone. Flip through computer magazines, especially ones having to do with online services such as *Online Access* and *Boardwatch*. These magazines are often filled with special deals, tempting you with free software, a free month or so of use, and, sometimes, reduced rates.

When you first subscribe to an online service, it doesn't hurt to ask if they have any special deals going, either. Many services allow you to sample them for a few hours, or even a month. You should take advantage of any free offers you come across, giving you a chance to sample a service you otherwise might not try. Much like shopping for a perfect date, finding the right network is usually a matter of patience and persistence—don't expect love at first byte.

The Most Boards for Your Buck

It's very possible that you will soon become addicted to the online world, placing many calls a day. Some areas charge for each local call you make. Ask your phone company if an *unlimited local calling* option is available; it more than pays for itself.

If you live in a sparsely populated area code, the BBSs, Internet providers, and local access networks you desire may all be in a neighboring zone. Most phone companies offer a low-priced *scoping* or *circle calling* feature, which treats surrounding area codes as a local call.

Public Data Networks

Each commercial online service you'll call is actually a roomful of computers, located in some office building. In most cases, if you wanted to connect directly to the service, it would be a long-distance call.

Luckily, there are companies that have dozens of branches worldwide, all connecting to one faraway trunk. SprintNet, Tymnet, DataPac (in Canada), and CompuServe Packet

Network (CPN) are the most popular public data networks. Network charges may range from $0 to more than $30 an hour, depending on which service you use and where you're calling from. International, Canadian, Alaskan, Hawaiian, and Puerto Rican callers typically have to pay more.

The method of using these public networks varies from service to service, too. In some cases—such as with America Online, CompuServe Information Manager, and PRODIGY—the software takes care of everything for you, automatically finding the closest public network, dialing it, and connecting. In other cases, such as Delphi, you have to find the local number yourself and enter a simple series of keystrokes in order to connect. Always follow the online instructions, and call customer service if you have any difficulties.

Long Distance Bargains

If you pursue health, happiness, and the long-distance BBS way, several services are out-and-out godsends.

- *Cris* allows you to call many BBSs nationwide, without long-distance tolls. The price is about $4 an hour. Voice call 800-745-CRIS for more information.

- *Global Access* has local numbers throughout about 91 percent of the United States. You can order full long-distance service, Internet access, or direct links to America's most popular BBSs. Signing up on Global Access costs $20, with a membership of $10 a month. Hourly rates range from $3.50 to $12.50, depending on your needs. Call 800-377-DATA (3282) for details.

- *MCI PC* gives you a special long-distance rate for modem calls. Call 800-333-2511 for more information.

All Buckled Up and Plenty of Places To Go!

The technical and economic wrinkles of online dating will be ironed out in due time. As you meet new friends and read through thousands of bulletins, you'll no doubt learn hints, tricks, and ideas that will enhance the quality and quantity of your online time. For instance, you may be turned on to a new public data network that just opened in your area, or you may hear about a limited-time pricing deal. If you're careful, a night on the online town is certainly the most frugal way to date. Keep your ears perked and eyes peeled for online bargains and bonanzas, as well as, of course, beauties.

BULLETIN BOARD SYSTEMS

OUR STORY, IT'S TYPICAL.

Me and my wife-to-be met, talked, had lots in common and all, so we met again, went out on dates. One night our talk took a romantic turn and we kissed, one thing led to another, we lived together for a while, became the center of each other's lives, got married, had two girls, and we're still very much in love. But if you go back to our beginning, the way we met, it wasn't so typical. It was because of a BBS. We would call up occasionally. We knew each other's user names, though we weren't particularly attracted, yet. One day our sysop decided to throw a picnic. Expecting a bunch of teenagers, I showed up just for the heck of it, to pop by and say howdy and then drive off. But not only were there some senior citizens there and other people my age (thirtysomething), there was one particularly vibrant, flirtatious blonde hanging out by the food. After the picnic I built up my nerve and asked her out for a drink. So I didn't exactly find the love of my life online, but without being part of the BBS community we'd never have met.

What It Is

Imagine a cork bulletin board as tall as the Empire State Building, carefully subdivided into dozens of special-interest areas, each neatly labeled. One section is for notes about fine art. Another is for robotics. There's one for fishing. Jokes. Dating. Another section contains actual disks of software for you to pluck and use. Imagine people (perhaps in helicopters) flying around this bulletin board, reading whatever interests them, and posting notes and software disks of their own.

There are thousands of electronic *Bulletin Board Systems (BBSs)* around the world, ranging widely in ease of use, size, price, and focus. Quite a few exist for the express purpose of online matchmaking, socializing, and dating. America Online, CompuServe, and the other commercial online services are really nothing more than huge, fancy bulletin boards.

There is no BBS standard. Boards are eclectic, lively, and unique. The sysops for most BBSs are hobbyists who have equipped their home computers with several phone lines, fancy modems, and other high-tech equipment. They invite the computing public to call in and talk, exchange files, write messages, and discuss topics.

Be forewarned that the good BBSs are often busy; you may not be able to access them unless you try during the middle of the night or have a stroke of divine intervention. Also, new BBSs sprout up every day, while old ones, for whatever reason, die. Often the owner of a BBS moves or runs out of time, money, or patience. BBSs may also have many rules of etiquette; the sysop is Lord of the domain and may censor what he chooses.

This is not meant to shed a dismal light on the stellar BBS universe. Many BBSs are free of charge, often existing only because of donations from happy users. A BBS is much more a tight-knit community than a major online service, often having annual picnics, bar-meets, and other get-togethers. And since the people on a BBS are usually local to you, real-life dates can much more easily follow the online ones.

Naughty Bits

I've met some wild people on BBSs. A lot of times I talk to someone and we agree to meet at a local club and then take it from there—other times an online one-night stand is enough. I've had some e-mail relationships with letters you wouldn't believe. I also have a friend who's into domination who meets people almost exclusively over BBSs, all the time. It's easy and safe and it's quick. Once you get into it, it's really a whole scene in itself.

Quite a few BBSs are the cyberspace equivalent of late-night phone sex. They have adult topics and themes, with online erotic graphics, heaps of amateur and professional pornography, as well as explicit personals and topics of discussion. Some of them go so far as to hire ladies (supposedly) to type sexy to you.

These BBSs are often quite expensive and available only in certain area codes. You may be put off (or turned on) by the blatant sexual environment. If you call one of these boards, ready your libido, not your tuxedo; be prepared for come-ons from every direction. Some of these services are remarkably easy to use and are perhaps the quickest way to find other kinky (or not so) swingers, spicy pen pals, and plain ol' average people seeking new friends. If you're looking for real-life love, though, be careful to differentiate people who *enjoy* talking to you from those who are getting paid to.

There are several detailed references for these hot-boards. Many of the BBSs listed in Appendix A are date-oriented, adult-only places. If you don't find enough there, thumb through The Waite Group's *Erotic Connections*. You are warned, before you sign on, if the BBS is an "Adult Board"—that is, one that restricts access to anyone less than 18 years of age (or, in some cases, 21).

To Pay or Not to Pay: A Tough Question

Unfortunately, charging an annual subscription fee seems to be the trend among the more resplendent BBSs. Usually, you sign onto the board, get a few minutes to explore it, and then the system asks you, nicely, to leave your credit card number.

Sometimes, this fee is nominal—perhaps $15 for lifetime access. Some BBSs request a "donation"—the more you give, the more access you get. A few boards, however, are even more expensive than commercial online services such as CompuServe and PRODIGY, charging steep hourly fees.

Never leave your credit card number unless you're absolutely sure the BBS has exactly what you want, and you can't get it elsewhere for less. A good idea is to explore all the BBSs in your area. If none of the free ones appeal, you may have to flip open your wallet. Think of it this way: A typical night at a pickup bar—taxi, cover charge, mixed drinks, snacks, aspirin—probably costs as much as a year's membership to an online community.

The BBS Hunt

To connect to a BBS, you have to find one. If you have access to Internet, this is easy. Simply check the Usenet newsgroups *alt.bbs, alt.bbs.lists,* and *alt.bbs.ads* (see the section on Usenet in Chapter 7, The Internet). *Boardwatch* magazine, available at most computer stores, comes out with a monthly list of some of the best systems available. Other magazines such as *Online Access, Computer Shopper,* and *PC Magazine* often have additional listings. You can even find BBS listings in some cities' yellow pages.

Also, if you have any computer-nerd friends, ask them for their favorite BBS numbers. The people who work in computer stores are another good source to tap. To begin with, though, Appendix A lists a few of the friendliest and most romantic boards in each area code.

When you get bored with your board, it's easy to move on. Most regions in the United States are home to dozens (if not hundreds) of BBSs. With a little bit of exploring, your BBS list can grow like a virus. Once you connect to one bulletin board, it's easy to find the numbers for others in your area. Many BBSs have online listings and a BBS-ad message base where local sysops rave about their systems. You can also ask around.

EXPERT TIP

Boardwatch has its own BBS with extensive online listings at 303-973-4222. You can also try calling the Online With Hayes BBS at 800-US-HAYES (874-2937).

BBSs and the Internet

Freenets and public-access providers (see Chapter 7 and Appendix B) are BBSs and Internet doorways all in one; try one out. More and more BBSs, in addition, are beginning to offer services that let you send e-mail through the Internet, access Usenet newsgroups, and more. In addition, the last section in Chapter 7 lists a few BBSs accessible through the Internet. These provide the down-home feel of a BBS along with worldwide traffic.

"Hello? . . . Hello?!!"

If you call and a human voice answers, that means the BBS either only operates a few hours a day or has been shut down. If the person on the other end of the line has no idea what's going on, cross that number off your list. Sometimes the phone company reassigns a defunct BBS number to some poor soul. Those who suffer such a fate may get hundreds of calls a day where all they hear is the infernal high-pitched chirping of the modem.

If you call up a BBS and nothing happens, you may not have the right software. Some BBSs, attempting to follow the example of PRODIGY and America Online, use a Macintosh-like mouse/icon system. This requires you to have special software set up (usually RIPterm) before you can sign on.

However, it is also a good idea to try changing your modem settings. You can read up about parity, data bits, stop bits, and terminal emulation in Chapter 4, The Datemobile. Almost all BBSs run with eight data bits, no parity, and one stop bit (commonly referred to as 8N1). Seven data bits, even parity, and one stop bit is another popular setting (7E1). The ANSI terminal emulation mode is also standard. If the text on your screens seems strange, switch to TTY mode.

To Whet Your Appetite

What follows is a guided tour through a wide variety of systems. Some are popular, with tens of thousands of users. Others are easily reachable. Still others are just plain weird. The thing they all have in common is their atmosphere: They're all geared toward meeting others. All the phone numbers are to be dialed with your modem.

Event Horizons   800-GO-MODEM; 466-6336

Event Horizons is an innovator in the computer graphics field. "We're constantly looking for more and better ways to truly entertain our users," says sysop Jim Maxey. With 34,000 members and 128 phone lines, this megalopolis power-board features tons of adult and astronomy pictures, quality multimedia videos, sound effects, and animation. With all the pictures available online, if you can't find yourself a real date, you might want to download one—the cyberspace equivalent of a blow-up doll!

There are also 64 romantic chat lines, always buzzing. If things are going slow, there's even a live party line where you can talk to some of the Event Horizons girls. Figure 6-1 shows a typical menu.

The Singularity message area is where singles introduce themselves and talk about life. Event Horizons plans to implement the Ultra-Chat System soon, linking up BBSs from around the country and providing a gigantic forum for hundreds of users to mingle.

The price comes to $12 an hour for modems running at 2400 baud and below, $22 an hour for faster speeds. The toll-free Event Horizons number is for new users only. However, most parts of the United States can access Event Horizons through a local CompuServe number at no additional charge; you'll be given detailed information the first time you call. If you have any questions, give Event Horizons' customer service a ring at their voice number: 800-536-7700.

THe GaRBaGe DuMP
303-457-1111, 505-294-5675, 214-644-6060, or 602-331-1112

"CAUTION: ADULTS AT PLAY" taunts the opening screen in Figure 6-2. There is no emphasis on trading files here—just frolicking with lively and vibrant people who seek the

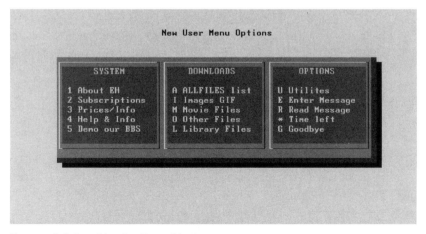

FIGURE 6-1 Reaching for Event Horizons

```
THe
   GaRBaGe
      DuMP BBS!

Albuquerque
    505-294-5675

Denver
    303-457-1111

Dallas
    214-644-6060

Phoenix
    602-331-1112

100 LINES!
    ADULTS ONLY!
Voice: 505-294-4980          (TM) DataSafe Publications, Inc. - 1991

If you are a new caller, please type NEW as your User-ID to sign-up!

User-ID:
```

FIGURE 6-2 Wading through THe GaRBaGe DuMP

same. You can chat with callers from around the country about a variety of issues. There are special adult message/chat areas where you can get down and dirty. Intriguing and spicy message areas make the DuMP an easy place to fraternize (or sororitize).

A well-stocked online dating database attracts scads of singles who are hoping to become doubles. The "Let's Get Personal" center contains thousands of eligibles. You can fill in your own profile, browse through others, and send mail to anyone who sounds interesting. Since the date-a-base is national, there are lots of choices.

Though the DuMP is probably a long distance call for you, it's one the classiest and downright friendliest date/mate BBSs around. Local access is also available in most areas for a minimal charge (typically $1.75 an hour). Call the voice line at 505-294-4980 if you have any problems or questions.

Once you log on to the BBS, you can download the validation form. Fill it out and mail it in for a free limited trial account. You can also purchase full access online (using Visa or MasterCard); $10 gets you 20 hours. When your time runs out, you can purchase more—it works kind of like a parking meter for your datemobile.

ECHO: The East Coast Hangout   212-989-8411

This is a board with a New York accent, babe. Hip and literary, sarcastic and sultry. ECHO is the East Coast condensed inside a computer. This "electronic salon," run by sysop Stacey Horn, has a nearly even male-to-female ratio—maybe because its atmosphere encourages in-depth conversation, not cheap pick-up lines. The emphasis is on lots and lots of messages. ECHO also has bimonthly F2F (face to face) events, where ECHOids can get together and smirk a lot.

On most systems, messages garner two or three replies and then fizzle out. On ECHO, each message topic is more like a never-ending dialogue, typically having hundreds of responses. Some topics, begun in the late '80s, are still hot today. The talk is mature, well-written, and very tempting to join; it's difficult to stop reading. Be forewarned: The addictive qualities of ECHO should not be underestimated.

There are nearly fifty conference areas, each containing dozens of items. Cyberia, The Jewish Conference, Lambda, The Love Conference, Off Central, Plain Wrapper, The Sex Conference, and Women's Action Coalition are just some of the possibilities. To switch to a discussion conference, type *j* (for join) followed by the name of the conference. For example,

```
j love
```

transfers you to The Love Conference. You can now type

```
new
```

to read all the latest messages, or type

```
ind
```

to view an index of available items. To read an item, just type *sh* (for show) followed by that item's number.

There is a live chat area, though it is used infrequently. You can also *yo* somebody currently online, if you'd like to hold a private conversation (type *yo* followed by a person's name). You can then send each other one-line messages.

If you get stuck at any time, a sysop is usually online, ready to guide you.

ECHO costs $19.95 a month for 30 hours ($13.75 for students and seniors); the next 30 hours are a buck each; after that, it's free. There are numerous local access numbers available to reach ECHO; call for more information. Full Internet access is also available. If you already have access to the Internet, you can telnet to ECHO at *echonyc.com*. Log on to ECHO as *newuser* for complete information.

WELL: The Whole Earth 'Lectronic Link   415-332-6106

Where hippies meet hackers. If ECHO epitomizes the East coast, the WELL captures California—the hypnotic state. The WELL features over 300 conferences, in such categories as Social Responsibility and Politics; Media and Communications; Body, Mind, and Health; Cultures and Languages; Arts and Letters; Recreation; and Entertainment.

The WELL has tremendous depth: Special topics include The Grateful Dead, computer hacking and cyberculture, cutting-edge technology like virtual reality, and New Age funkiness. Check out the Interactions category to meet people of all shapes, sizes, and lifestyles. The WELL also throws a monthly party, where you can match online users with their faces.

The WELL runs you $15 a month plus $2 per hour. A subscription to the WELL includes full Internet access. The WELL is available through the popular CompuServe Packet Network for a $4 an hour surcharge. If you already belong to the Internet you can connect to the WELL by telneting to *well.sf.ca.us*. Call the WELL, voice, at 415-332-4335 for help or more detailed information.

EXPERT TIP

To reach the WELL through CompuServe, call 800-848-8980, voice. Follow the instructions. You are given your local access number. Dial it, using your modem. You then see the prompt:

`Host Name:`

To connect, just type

`well`

If groovy discussions with intelligent people matter to you, you might very well want to throw your pennies into the WELL.

Personal Connection   708-304-9804

The emphasis, as you may guess, is on establishing that special love connection. You search through a database with real-life categories, such as physical description and tobacco and alcohol use. Many of PC's users have written out personal statements, telling you what matters most to them. Some have even uploaded digitized photographs for you to view.

Beyond matchmaking, the BBS has fun discussion areas and files. Although new users are allowed a little free time, a full subscription costs $25 for 3 months.

The Matchmaker Network

The *yenta* of the BBS universe, this network exists explicitly for online dating. Table 6-1 shows the local numbers for Matchmaker's various areas.

As soon as you sign up, you fill out a questionnaire with multiple-choice questions ranging from "What's your favorite type of food?" to "Do you have a place where you can take someone?" to "What do you consider the most romantic place in the world?" Figure 6-3 shows a typical question/answer session.

When your initial questionnaire is complete, you get a few essay questions, where you can write as much or as little as you like about your interests, goals, dreams, personality, looks, and wit.

Once your personal profile is stored online, you can browse through other people's questionnaires, searching for particular words or categories. If you like, you can have the BBS automatically compare your questionnaire to everyone else's. By designating the percentage of similarity you're interested in, you can zero in on your (theoretical) best match.

When you find someone interesting, the Matchmaker system allows you to send private e-mail. Since the matchmaker files are organized by geographical region, you can limit your search to your own area, making it easier to set up an immediate real-life date.

AREA	NUMBER	AREA	NUMBER
Alamo	(210) 337-6485	LAX	(714) 895-5862
Alaska	(907) 248-9037	New York	(516) 231-6966
Austin	(512) 458-1172	Richmond	(804) 270-0502
Bodedo	(512) 467-0197	San Diego	(619) 224-6363
Dallas	(817) 355-6600	Silicon Valley	(408) 492-9700
DC	(703) 931-4902	Southland	(818) 793-9108
Denver	(303) 232-5523	Tampa	(813) 961-8665
Houston	(713) 480-4466	Virginia Beach	(804) 547-7608

TABLE 6-1 Places where Matchmaker makes you a match

The first time you call, you may enter your profile and search for dates. If you'd like to continue calling, checking for e-mail, and reading about the latest members, you need to subscribe. Each matchmaker system has different subscription fees, ranging from a few cents to a dollar an hour, depending on the membership plan you opt for. You can send in a check or use a credit card online. There is also a dial 900 service that charges the BBS subscription to your phone bill.

```
A. I'll meet anyone, anywhere, anytime for any reason
B. I'd make a date with someone interesting
C. I'd meet someone at a party or club
D. A clandestine rendezvous might be fun
E. I'm not "available" but I might do lunch
F. It's unlikely that I'd meet someone from here
G. Pen-pals is the limit for me
H. I'm never going to meet anyone (ever again!)
=> c
You picked -> C. I'd meet someone at a party or club
Correct? => y

What style of dress do you prefer?
A. I like to get dressed up
B. I like to dress casual
C. I dress for the occasion
D. What ever is clean
E. Preppy
F. Punk
G. Nude
H. Just call me Fred Flintstone
=> c
You picked -> C. I dress for the occasion
Correct? => y
```

FIGURE 6-3 Preparing to strike up a match

Aline   212-935-8787

"Not everyone who uses a PC is a nerd," states Aline's busty poster-girl, a low-cut black dress falling off her shoulders. Aline is a 24-hour party for jet-set swingers. It features a huge number of callers—many from France—all hungrily chatting, scoping, and smooth-talkin' each other. All you have to do is sign on and type to your heart's content. Women are outnumbered by men about ten to one—on a good night.

The first thing you have to do after logging on to this place (pronounced "uh-leen") is enter your credit card number (Visa, MasterCard, or American Express). You might want to call first, voice, 212-826-3894, to get the lowdown. Typically, you can use Aline all you want for $9.50 a month.

Jezebel's Parlour   201-927-2932

This friendly New Jersey BBS is small enough to feel like a community, popular enough to attract long-distance callers, and packed with more people than you'll ever have time to meet. Figure 6-4 shows Jezebel's opening screen, which leads you into a treasury of discussion areas, file downloads, online games, chat rooms, and information files.

If you check out the adult area (by pressing (X)), you can find a number of spicy discussion and chat areas. The Connex dating area, open to all members, is a great place to learn about the other Jezebelians. To read more about Connex, see the Dating Doors section of this chapter.

Jezebel allows you 20 minutes a day of free public access. If you'd like more time, subscribe to the Parlour: $35 for 6 months, $50 annually, or $99 for a lifetime membership. Adult access is available to subscribers only.

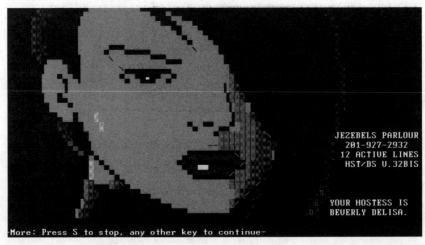

Figure 6-4 Jezebel's seductive opening screen

Real Exposure   212-691-2659

One of the features that actually made me begin the BBS itself was the fact that I had seen many friends meet some really interesting people online and then carry forward the meetings and relationships offline. I added a matchmaker to the BBS to see what happened, and it was incredible how it took off. Heather was pretty much doing what I was doing in the matchmaker—playing around to see if anyone at all would respond. And well . . . we started exchanging messages in there almost every day, and it got to be sorta-kinda like a game after a while, so we decided to talk on the phone. Anyway, we actually met the first time when we had a user-meet, party, get-together, whatever you want to call it . . . . After that night we hit it off really well (considering I had brought a date that night). Since then we have spent a lot of time together, both online and off. To sum it up, it has been one of the wildest ways I have ever met a woman/girl/chick/babe :->, and it really is one of the best relationships I have ever been involved in. I think what keeps it the most interesting is that we sorta-kinda have two relationships going on at once, which seem to criss-cross a lot. One offline, and one online, where we can really carry on some in-depth discussions, sometimes one-on-one and sometimes in the conference areas with many others participating. I guess it is one of the most interesting aspects of our "fantasy life," you might say.

—Joey Havlock, Co-Sysop of Real Exposure

Expose yourself on this mega-board, newcomer (see Figure 6-5). See Figure 6-6 for a sample list of Real Exposure's conferences. If you're interested in files, Real Exposure has tons of them. If you're interested in chatting, Real Exposure is always full of a variety of folks looking for fun and adventure (especially at night).

If you'd like access to the adult area, you can send in (or FAX) a copy of your driver's license. You can then use the "Let's Get Personal" matchmaker to find pals, lovers, or something in-between. The adult chat areas steam up your monitor while introducing you to a bevy of, well, uh, *interesting* people. Definitely interesting.

Real exposure has limited free access, allowing you about 45 minutes of time per day. If you'd like more time or access, you can also subscribe. Real Exposure plans to be reachable though the Internet by telneting to *rex.com*.

Figure 6-5 Indecent exposure?

```
                    Local Conferences on Real Exposure

Personal E-Mail         LO - # 000   NYC General Chit Chat  LO - # 001
Political Discussion    LO - # 002   Films & Videos Forum   LO - # 003
Adults Only - General   LO - # 004   Photographers Forum    LO - # 005
Literary Library        LO - # 006   European Community     LO - # 007
Entrepreneurial Forum   LO - # 008   Micro Ingenuity        LO - # 009
Travel & Vacation       LO - # 010   Fine Art/Artist Forum  LO - # 011
Real Exposure Wishes    LO - # 012   Screenwriters Forum    LO - # 013
Classified Advertising  LO - # 014   GP & Environment       LO - # 015
Sports & Sports Fans    LO - # 016   Teen Talk              LO - # 017
Student Bar             LO - # 018   Classic Cars & Bikes   LO - # 019
BBS Sysops Conference   LO - # 020   Performing Artists     LO - # 021
New York at Night       LO - # 022   Sysop Notes    *PRIVATE* - # 023
Virtual Reality         LO - # 024   On-Line Magazines      LO - # 025
On-Line Communications  LO - # 026   Psychology             LO - # 027
UNREAL NY Stories       LO - # 028   Transit & Subway Talk  LO - # 029
New York Crime          LO - # 030   New Jersey Getaways    LO - # 031
Connecticut Getaways    LO - # 032   New York Bars & Clubs  LO - # 033
New York Holidays       LO - # 034   InterNet Discussion    LO - # 035
New York Restaurants    LO - # 036   Theatre & Stage        LO - # 037
Wired Magazine          LO - # 038   Opera & Classical      LO - # 039
```

Figure 6-6 Topics, topics, and more topics. And this is only page 1!

Logging On: Your First Call

Once you dial up a BBS, your terminal program gives you the message:

CONNECT 2400

Of course, *2400* may be replaced by *1200, 9600, 19200*, etc., depending on how fast your modem and the modem you're calling are. Wait a few moments for the BBS software to set itself up. You may have to press (ENTER) a couple of times to kick the board into action. Other systems ask you to press the (ESC) key twice. You then get a message greeting you, something like:

```
Welcome to fictional DATES-R-US BBS in Loveland, Colorado
                    (303)111-2222

We have more nets than your average fisherman, namely:
                FIDOnet and EROSnet

/2400/9600/14,400 Baud         Your Friendly Sysop: Allen Love
```

Every BBS has its own approach, but all are friendly and at least try to be self-explanatory. Sysops are beginning to use more standardized software, which means many BBSs you call will have similar commands. Most BBSs begin by asking you:

Would you like ANSI graphics? (Enter)=no?

ANSI (which, for the record, stands for American National Standards Institute) allows your screen to display simple graphics and colors; however, it takes longer to draw each screen. If you have a fast modem (over 9600 baud), and are using software that offers ANSI emulation (almost every program on the market does), press Ⓨ for yes. Otherwise, just press (ENTER) or Ⓝ for no. Try using ANSI; you need it to play most online games and it makes the screens easier to read. If your screen fills with garbage, or things are moving too slowly, hang up and call again, without selecting ANSI emulation.

You are then asked a few self-explanatory questions, such as:

`What is your real first name (handles are not permitted!)?`

Type in a name and press (ENTER). Remember, a *handle* is a pseudonym or nickname you can go by, such as Lizard Of Oz, Redhead, or Lenny Lovelooker. Some systems, especially the adult ones, require these pseudonyms. Next, predictably, you see:

`What is your last name?`

The BBS may then ask you for your city and state, in case there is more than one Lenny Lovelooker. You are then told, ever so politely:

`Looking up "LENNY LOVELOOKER". Please wait . . .`

If you've never called before, you need to register. This process varies from board to board. On some, you just have to answer a few basic questions. On others, you have to fill out a form and mail it in, sometimes with a check or credit card number attached. Often, adult-topic BBSs are required by law to have proof that you are over 18 or 21 (depending on local laws), so they ask for a photocopy of your driver's license. A typical online registration session looks like:

`Your name "LENNY LOVELOOKER" wasn't found in the user data base.`
`Is your name spelled correctly?? [N]`

If you spelled your name wrong, here's your chance to fix it. Otherwise, press (ENTER), and the BBS assumes you're a new user. You may now get to choose your own password, though some BBSs assign one to you. Choose wisely! As you type it in, you won't see anything. This is for security, in case an evil hacker is peeking over your shoulder. You then verify your password; carefully re-enter the word. *Remember this password;* you'll need to know it the next time you call. If you forget your password, many sysops will refuse to tell it to you, no matter how much you beg and plead. If that happens, you will need to re-register.

EXPERT TIP

A new terminal emulation, called RIP, allows fancy graphics, mouse-clicks, and extra colors. You may be asked if you'd like to use RIP graphics. To use this dazzling and easy-to-use emulation, you need to have a copy of RIPterm or any other RIP-compatible communications software. RIPterm is shareware and available on many BBSs.

Registering

```
DATES-R-US BBS

Hello! You are a new caller to this system, so welcome. There
are many features to discover, so please read the HELP files
and experiment with new choices. As a new user, your access is
limited. After I get a chance to verify you, I'll upgrade you.
Check the Bulletins Menu and Newsletters for additional
information.
```

Some BBSs let you try sample areas without registering, but most require registration for access to the interesting stuff (i.e., dating). If you decide to register, you are asked a variety of questions, such as your address, home/business phone number, computer and modem type, gender, and birthdate. Answer these truthfully and completely. You're calling into someone else's home or business—it's only fair they know a little about you. The registration information is always confidential and for the sysop's use only.

Often, you are asked how many characters per line your screen can display. Unless you have a very old computer, type

```
80
```

If the BBS's lines of text don't fit on your screen, count how many characters across your screen can hold. Later, you can re-configure the display options.

You are also asked how many rows your screen contains. Almost all computers can display 25 rows, but most communications programs have a *status line* of information on the bottom most row of the screen. To be safe, the best answer is

```
24
```

You may get another chance to choose ANSI or RIP; if you're not sure, use ANSI. You may also be asked which "default download protocol" you want. A *protocol* is a language that sends and receives software over the modem, checking to be sure everything is transferred safe and sound. If your terminal software offers Zmodem, choose it. Zmodem is among the fastest of protocols and it includes a feature that lets you continue transferring a file in case you somehow get cut off from the BBS. Xmodem is one of the original protocols, and though it is slow, it can be found on almost every BBS and communications software package. See the section on File Transfers in Chapter 4, The Datemobile, for more information.

You may be asked if you'd like to use *hot keys*. This means you need only type a single letter, instead of the letter followed by (ENTER). For instance, on most BBSs, typing (B) and then pressing (ENTER) allows you to view the latest informative bulletins. If hot keys are effective, you need only press (B).

One important question is:

```
Do you want to pause after every page? (Y/N)?
```

It's a good idea to press Ⓨ. This way, a long article won't scroll past and beyond the top of your screen, before you get a chance to read it. At the end of every page there will be a prompt like:

```
More? <y/n>
```

This gives you a chance to press Ⓔ Ⓝ Ⓣ Ⓔ Ⓡ or Ⓨ for yes to continue, or Ⓝ for no to skip the rest of the article.

Last, the BBS may inquire:

```
Do you want to use a full screen editor? (Y/N)?
```

If your communications software can use ANSI, then it can use a full-screen editor. Go for it! Then, when you type a letter or an article, you can do it using a low-frills word processor, instead of line by line.

If you don't know the answer to a technical question, just press (ENTER), and the system uses the most sensible choice automatically. You can always consult your sysop and change your settings later.

You generally don't get much access to the BBS the first time you call. Try again in 24 hours. If you're still given the cold shoulder, leave feedback asking the sysop if there's a problem (see the section on e-mail).

Call Me Back!

Sysops want to make sure you actually exist. You may be asked for a convenient time when you can be *voice verified*. Sysops may call you at home and ask you a few questions. Be friendly!

Many BBSs are equipped with a fancy gizmo known as the *Automatic Call-Back Verification System*. This handy system allows you immediate access to the board, and allows the sysop to know where you are dialing from.

You are told, after registering, if the BBS offers call-back. Remember the instructions you're given, and follow them carefully. Usually, pressing Ⓡ for register starts the call-back procedure.

You are asked to verify your phone number. The BBS then hangs up on you. This may seem rude, but don't get steamed. In less than a minute, the BBS courteously calls you back! Most every terminal program has not only the ability to call, but to pick up the phone, too.

Within a minute, your phone should ring. Do *not* pick up the receiver. Your communications software typically tells you that it hears the phone:

```
RING
```

Simply type:

```
ATA
```

and press (ENTER). This is a modem code that automatically picks up the phone and begins talking computerese. In a moment, you are back in the BBS. You get a welcome message and a request for your password. If all goes well, you are now an official member of a BBS. If you have any problems, send e-mail to the sysop. Describe your problem and call back the next day for an answer.

Logging Off

Theoretically, all you have to do to leave a BBS is hang up. However, the BBS does not know you have left until it notices you haven't typed anything for a while—this may take ten or fifteen minutes. Also, if you suddenly hang up on some BBSs, the software becomes confused and refuses to let anyone else log on. Thus, it's always a good idea to tell your BBS when you're finished.

Like any other menu command, the log-off varies from BBS to BBS. In some cases, all you have to do is press Ⓖ for good-bye. Other BBSs require you to type

```
quit
```

or *exit* or *logoff* or *leave* or even *bye*.

Always check your BBS's main menu for the exact command.

Getting Around

There are many brands of BBSs. Depending on what software a sysop chooses, signing up, navigating, and executing commands all look a little different.

However, most BBSs focus on two things: messages and files. In addition, there may be areas for chatting, online games, online dating, news, or informative databases.

The Main Menu and the Prompt

Once you type in a correct user name and password, the BBS's virtual doors open wide. You are usually told if you have any new mail. There may be a few screens listing the latest statistics, weather, horoscopes, quotes, or news. Continue through these screens until you reach the *top* or *main menu*.

Pressing the question mark Ⓠ, Ⓗ for help, or typing

```
HELP
```

usually gives you a descriptive list of available commands.

All BBSs use menus, in one form or another. A menu is nothing more than a list of all the things you can do or the places you can go. Most menus require you to tap one letter or number to navigate. These special characters or words are typically highlighted in bold or different-color print or bracketed by parentheses, such as:

```
(F)iles
```

The menu in Figure 6-1 is another good example.

Just like a restaurant menu, a BBS menu is usually organized into sections. And just as some restaurants offer "Tuna Melt" and others have "Cheese and Charlie" or even something like "Tuna Nicois en Fromage a la Baguette," different BBSs offer the same general things using different menu commands or terminology. The only way to learn a BBS in and out is to explore it, through trial and error.

Some BBSs are set up so that every possible command is available from the main menu. You can read messages, download, chat, and use a door, simply by selecting the appropriate command. For instance, the following is a typical PCBoard menu:

```
                     Dates-R-US BBS
  M*A*I*N    M*E*N*U                          [H] for help


  Messages and Mail      File Operations     Miscellaneous

  [A]bandon conference   [D]ownload a file   [B]ulletins
  [C]omment to sysop     [F]ile directories  [G]oodbye (logoff)
  [E]nter a message      [FLAG] downloads    [I]nitial welcome
  [J]oin a conference    [L]ocate filenames  [M] ANSI toggle
  [K]ill a message       [N]ew files scan    [O] Chat
  [Q]uick message scan   [T]ransfer protocol [OPEN] a [DOOR]
  [R]ead messages        [U]pload a file     [S] News
  [REPLY] to a message   [Z]ippy file scan   [USERS] listing
  [Y]our mail scan                           [V]iew Config
  [SE]lect conferences                       [W] Change Config
                                             [X]pert Mode


(1 min. used; 29 min. left) Main Board Command?
```

Most main menus, though, reroute you to specific submenus the way this one does:

```
Dates-R-Us BBS
M*A*I*N    M*E*N*U


L..Library of Files
T..Talk Live With Other Users
F..Forums (Message Areas)
E..Electronic Mail
D..Doors
B..Bulletins
A..Account Display and Edit
G..Goodbye
P..Polls and Questionairres
R..Registry of Users


Make your selection (L,T,F,E,D,B,A,G,P,R, ? for help, or X to exit):
```

For example, to enter the message forums, you'd press Ⓕ, and then to read the messages you'd press Ⓡ. To download a file, you'd enter the library by pressing Ⓛ and then pressing Ⓓ for download.

The line that says *Main Board Command?* or *F,M,E,D,B,C,G, or H?* is known as the *prompt*. It usually tells you how much time you have remaining. BBSs—especially the free ones—limit your time so others also get a chance to call.

Some BBSs have *hot keys,* allowing you to press just the first letter of the command you're interested in. Other BBSs require you to type an appropriate letter, number, or word and then press (ENTER). In the above menu, for example, you'd simply press Ⓑ to view the latest bulletins.

As you progress deeper through the jungles of menu hierarchy, you will probably need to back out to a previous menu. On many systems, pressing Ⓧ (for eXit), Ⓠ (for quit), or Ⓑ (for back) returns you to the menu you just came from. Some BBSs require you to press the minus sign ⊝. On other systems, you need only press (ENTER) to back out. Experiment and read your menu options carefully.

Most systems also have a command that takes you directly to the main menu, such as pressing Ⓜ for main, pressing the asterisk ⊛, or typing

TOP

Paging

Most BBSs allow you to summon the sysop. By pressing Ⓟ (for page) or some equivalent command, you cause your sysop's computer to beep. If the sysop is around, he or she may suddenly break in and begin typing.

You can page sysops whenever you have an immediate question, are utterly lost and confused, or if you just want to talk. Most sysops are happy to meet their users: That's why they began their BBSs in the first place.

If your sysop is not available, you are generally given the option to send him or her e-mail, typically known as *feedback*. Next time you log in, there may be an answer waiting in your mailbox.

Sub-Menus

Think of cities. The street names from city to city differ (though there is almost always a Main Street). However, at the heart of things, each city is laid out similarly. There's a downtown business district, a suburban residential district, an industrial area, an entertainment area, and so on. Most BBSs, like most cities, share the same general structure. Once you know what BBSs usually offer, all you have to do is look at each one's road map (the menus) to find what you need.

Branching from the main menu of a BBS you can typically find:

- *Bulletins/News/Information Files.* This section contains informative text. Look here for BBS etiquette and rules. Sometimes you can find lengthy BBS listings. Also, BBSs that require a fee often discuss their subscription terms in this area: what they offer, how to register for it, and for how much.

- *User's List/Member Listing.* If you're interested in seeing the names and locales of your BBS's fellow users, you can check this out. You might just spot somebody you already know. A few BBSs also tell you each user's home phone number, though you can usually decide whether or not you want yours listed.

- *Config/Change Options/Your Stats.* Remember all those nasty questions the BBS asked you the first day you called? If you want to change anything, whether it be ANSI mode emulation, full screen editor, page length, line length, address, password, or your phone number, this is the place to do it.

- *File Areas.* This is where you can obtain tons of the latest software. See the next section, Downloading.

- *User Profiles.* Information about fellow BBS users. See the Profiles in Courage section later in this chapter.

- *Message Areas.* Here is where the BBS's own bulletin boards lurk. See the Messages section, later in this chapter.

- *Doors.* BBS extras such as games, databases, or online dating software. See the section on Doors.

- *E-mail.* See the Mail section for details.

- *Chatting.* A few BBSs have several phone lines, allowing you to chat with other callers. See the Chat section for details.

- *Goodbye/Logoff.* Sayonara, and happy trails.

Downloading

Files are generally not important to online dating. However, there may be exceptions. For instance, you may want to retrieve a digitized photograph of a potential date. Some BBSs require you to electronically receive, fill out, and then send a form of personal information for use in their date-a-bases. In some cases, you mail in a picture of yourself. The sysop scans it for you and places this digitized image onto the BBS for others to view.

In addition, huge lists of other BBSs worldwide can be found in the file areas. Since BBS lists are typically stored as *text files*—directly readable files containing only the standard letters of the alphabet plus regular numbers, punctuation marks, and so on—both Macintosh and IBM users can download them.

Usually pressing Ⓕ allows you to enter the File Bases. Alternatively, some BBSs require you to press Ⓣ for Transfer Area, or just Ⓓ for Downloads or Database.

Once you've entered the file area, ⓁL usually lists the files available to you. Usually a command such as ⓐA shows the available file areas. The subjects in a typical file directory may be:

```
1.  New Uploads
2.  Archivers
3.  BBS Lists
4.  Business and Financial Files
5.  Communications
6.  Database Programs & Files
7.  Word Processing Files
8.  Food and Drink
9.  Games
10. Graphics and Pictures
11. Programming Languages & Utilities
12. System Utilities
Area Number? [Area #, '?'=Re-List]:
```

Some BBSs have thousands of detailed file areas. Select the area you're interested in by typing its number. A list of files, along with their sizes and descriptions, should then scroll down your screen. When you see one that catches your eye, remember its name. You can then typically type ⓓD to download it. See Chapter 4, The Datemobile, for the lowdown on file transfers.

You may also want to search for a certain file or category. On some BBSs, pressing ⓕF or ⓢS allows you to search for a particular filename. Other BBSs require you to press ⓀK to search for a keyword or ⓏZ for "zippy file scan"—a fast search for relevant files. Again, these are only guidelines. The process may be a little daunting at first, but selecting what you want from a BBS menu is certainly easier than ordering in French!

To be fair about things, many BBSs make use of *file ratios*. These ratios are usually 3:1 or some such number. This means for every three files you download you must upload one; not a bad deal. Sometimes ratios are based on the lengths of the files, so for every

EXPERT TIP

You may come across the term *batch*. This is a group of files you designate to be downloaded or uploaded all at once. A few popular protocols that allow you to transfer batches of files are: Y-Modem Batch, Zmodem, and Bimodem. See the section on protocols in Chapter 4. When transferring a batch, you either mark each file you're interested in (typically by pressing ⓂM for mark or ⓉT for tag and then typing the filename) or you can type in several filenames, when asked, separated by commas or spaces.

30,000 bytes you download, you have to send up 10,000. Obviously, you must send software the BBS doesn't already have, which you can get from other BBSs. Don't send commercial or copyrighted material.

Profiles in Courage

Most every BBS has a listing of all its members. This listing may be accessible by a command on the main menu or it may be offered under the Doors menu. Typically, this listing tells you the user name or handle, real name, and home town of everyone on file.

If you'd like to find out more about someone, there may be an Adult Profiles or Member Profiles option. Typically, you need to fill out your own profile first. This is a simple online questionnaire; answer as many of the detailed and personal questions as you'd like. Questions range from physical features to fantasies. Once the BBS stores your form, you can then browse through other people's forms until you find someone who interests you. You may usually search for a keyword, such as "jogging." Don't be shy. If someone seems enticing, mail a letter, strike up a conversation.

Doors

The *doors* on BBSs have nothing to do with Jim Morrison; rather, they are portals that can lead to games, online newspapers, special features, or areas specifically suited for cyberdaters. A door actually runs a separate program. Your sysop can install as few or as many doors as she wishes. Several doors particular to dating are:

- Match Maker
- The Personal Connection
- Date-A-Base
- Profman
- Heartthrob
- Connex
- Let's Get Personal

All these doors lead to similar locales: Computer dating at its finest and fastest. You answer a long list of questions about yourself, usually multiple choice. There may be an essay question or two. If you have a digitized photograph of yourself, you may even be able to upload it here (sometimes with the ability to protect it with a password, which you can give away to potential dates).

You can then browse through the profiles—either manually, or, more easily, by telling the computer what you expect out of your ideal mate. Typically the computer asks what gender, age, and sexual preference you are looking for. Or it asks for particular descriptive *keywords*, such as "atheist" or "communist," "brunette" or "skinny," "dominant" or "transvestite," "modest" or "genius." You may be asked what percentage of perfection you desire. For

instance, finding someone who fits 100 percent of your expectations is rare—in life and on BBSs. Be a little flexible. After all, opposites attract, too (within limits). The computer instantly gives you the name, or names, of the hunks or enchantresses most suited for you. You can then e-mail them a vibrant and brilliantly seductive letter reminiscent of Shakespearean love sonnets, telling your potential date where you found his or her name.

```
Dear Redhead:

I came across your name in the Online Dating area. I hope you
don't think me too forward, but I felt compelled to write you.
What do I like about you? Everything, from what I can tell so
far. Really. I like the fact that we share the same musical and
literary interests (how many other people like both Hip Hop and
Shakespeare?). I also liked the way you described yourself as,
"Easy to please on Tuesdays, impossible to appease on Wednes-
days." You sound like you'd be a lot of fun to hang out with. You
sound like an adventure. You also sound romantic. And, if I may
say, beautiful.

I'd love to tell you a little about myself, but, hoping not to
seem too egotistical, I'll end the letter now. Let's just say you
piqued (and peaked) my interest. I truly hope to hear from you.

Until them, I remain yours,

Lizard of Oz
```

Don't be too surprised if you receive e-mail from a secret admirer one day, too. It's the cyberspace equivalent of being "picked up."

Some of the more popular online dating software is:

Let's Get Personal

The Let's Get Personal door is typical of an online dating session. Let's Get Personal is quick and easy, acting like a supercharged personal ads page. Press Ⓒ the first time you use LGP to create your own entry. You are asked a number of multiple-choice questions, some of them silly, some of them downright personal.

The LGP menu looks like this:

```
<G> General information
<E> Edit your registry entry
<L> Look-up another user's entry
<M> Match yourself against other user's entries
<P> Profile for searching
<Q> Questionnaire essays, enter/edit
<R> Redo your summary line
<S> Summary
<X> Exit to main menu
```

If you're serious about meeting people online, it's a good idea to tell as much about yourself, honestly, as you can. After all, you don't want somebody to fall in love with your description and then be disappointed by the real thing. To fill out an additional questionnaire, press (Q). You can type essay-like answers to these questions, showing off your wit and letting people know what makes you tick (or what ticks you off). It's also a good idea to press (R) and redo your summary line every so often. When people are casually browsing through the profiles, this summary line appears foremost. A catchy summary catches more dates.

Press (L) to look up another user in the LGP database. Suppose, while reading messages and chatting, you notice that Lenny Lovelooker has a great sense of humor. You can come to LGP to find out more. Is he married or single? How old is he? Press (L) and then type in his name. You are given a quick synopsis of Lenny, such as his real name, height, weight, age, location, and sexual preference. You are then asked if you want to view Lenny's entire questionnaire.

If you're bold, you can match yourself with other BBS users. First, press (P) to set up the profile of the type of person you're looking for. You can specify sex, sexual preference, and a minimum and maximum age, height, and weight.

You can now press (M) to automatically read all about anyone who fits your given profile. You can also press (S) to view a quick bit of information about the eligible users in the LGP database.

Match Maker

Match Maker is useful because it often works anonymously; you can use your own special handle and send and receive mail through MM's own e-mail system. Match Maker also allows you to specify exactly what you're looking for in your ideal mate; all eligible people are then shown. The main menu looks something like

```
(R) Register
(Q) Questionnaires
(S) Search Registry
(V) View The Responses Of A User
(B) Browse Registry
(E) Read Match Mail
(W) Write Match Mail
(?) Instructions

(X) .. Return to Previous Menu
```

The first thing you need to do is fill out your own registry. Many BBSs have multiple Match Maker questionnaires: One for swinging couples, one for straight singles, one for those interested in bondage, and so on. Each questionnaire acts autonomously; you can usually only browse through questionnaires of a type you have filled out on yourself.

You are asked for all sorts of personal information, starting with your age, sex, and a brief physical description. You are then asked more detailed items, including strange questions you may never have thought about before. Most questions are multiple choice, in which case you need only type in the letter that corresponds to the appropriate answer. There may be an Other option, which allows you to fill in your own response. Some multiple-choice questions allow you to select several answers. Simply separate the answers by a space. For example, if the question is

```
Name your favorite hobby (more than one answer is allowed):
A. Video Games
B. Reading
C. Sports
D. Sleeping
E. Mirror-Gazing
F. Cooking
G. Gardening
H. Gambling
```

and you are interested in both video games and gambling, type

```
A H
```

Some questions are *short answer,* in which case you are allowed to type one line of text. Type your answer and press (ENTER). There may also be essay questions, which you can use the editor to answer. Write as long an answer as you wish. You are told how to exit the editor once your answer is complete. Usually, this requires typing

```
/S
```

on a blank line.

You are now ready to make your match. Press Ⓢ. You are given a short questionnaire. Fill in the attributes you are most looking for in your Mr. or Ms. Right. You can select as few or as many qualities as are relevant. A list of everyone who meets your criteria is shown.

You may also browse through the registry casually by pressing Ⓑ. Press Ⓥ to find the registry of a specific user.

Once you've found the man or woman of your dreams, you can send that person some fan mail by pressing Ⓦ (see the e-mail section, later in this chapter). Some BBSs allow you to send your mail anonymously, others send the message through ordinary e-mail. You can read any of your own mail by pressing Ⓡ.

Connex

Connex, written by Gary H. Grosse, is a unique dating program that asks insightful psychological questions, giving you a strikingly accurate personality profile. You're also told which personality type would best complement your own.

Once you've added your profile, you can search for a potential friend or lover by such criteria as sex, personality type, age, religion, sexual orientation, and more. This allows you to home in on exactly the type of person you're interested in. All the while, Connex displays inspiring quotes at the bottom of the screen, from people who know all about love—like Chico Marx, Zsa Zsa Gabor, and Shakespeare.

It takes a little while to complete your Connex profile, but the end product is a well-rounded self-portrait. First you are asked to specify your personal attributes. You are then asked to answer a series of questions to determine your personality profile. Lastly, there is a free-form interview session where you can type long answers to a number of personal questions. You are asked if you'd like to upload a digitized photograph of yourself. If you have one, select this option.

You can now meet others. Highlight the SELECT option and press (ENTER) to describe the type of person you'd be most attracted to. You are given a list of attributes such as sex, age, personality type, sexual preference, and so on. Highlight the attributes you care about and then, using the arrow keys, highlight the parameters you hope to match. You may highlight more than one parameter per attribute. For instance, you may be interested in introverted creative people as well as extroverted creative people. You may select the SAVE PROFILE command if you want to use the same matchmaking guidelines in the future.

Once you've selected a personality type, select the MATCH command. You are shown the profiles of everybody who fits within your specified attributes. If no profiles appear, you need to broaden your search. Next time, don't be so picky!

If you'd like to browse through every user's profile, highlight the ALL command and press (ENTER). To search for a specific person's profile, select the USER command and then type in that person's user name.

If a list appears, type the number preceding the name you're interested in. That person's entire biography is shown. Press (ENTER) to read through the profile. You may now read about that person's personality type and communication style or view his or her interview session. You can even download the entire profile, by selecting the Download option. The user may also have a digitized photograph online, which you can download and view. Users who have an online photo have an asterisk (*) preceding their profile number.

EXPERT TIP

If you are using Connex at more than one BBS, you need only fill in your profile one time. Call up a BBS where you have a Connex profile already filled out, and download your *own* profile, selecting the "Connex Data File" option when prompted. You may now call up another BBS. When you begin answering the questionnaire, you are asked if you'd like to upload a data file. Select this option. You can now upload your previously saved data file.

Game Doors

Behind BBS doors you can find a variety of strategy, adventure, and shoot-'em-up games. Many BBSs have interactive tournaments, allowing you to chat with fellow players. Games such as MUDs can also be found on many BBSs. MUDs are discussed in more detail in Chapter 7, because the Internet is the easiest way to reach them. If you're looking to play in the MUD, ask around once you're online.

Messages

Messaging goes by many names in the land of BBSs. Check your menu for words like: Message Bases, Conferences, Special Interest Groups (SIGs), Newsgroups, Forums, Echos, or, naturally, Bulletin Boards.

Each message area you can read and write to is either *local* or an *echo*. Local messages can be seen only by those who call the current BBS. Echoed messages, however, can be seen nationwide and sometimes even worldwide. As a result, local messages are always much less formal.

Echos: How Does a Net Work?

Online, there are valleys where you can shout whatever you like, and your words echo to hundreds of other valleys. Many BBSs are members of an echoing network. Whatever articles you type are automatically traded, every night, with a BBS called the hub. This hub then shoots copies of all the messages to other hubs. Soon every affiliated BBS has a copy of your words of wisdom. You can also easily and cheaply send e-mail to distant users.

Echos are nice for meeting people in other states and countries, and for getting a wide range of opinions on any given subject. There are many small networks; some of the major ones particular to online dating are discussed below.

Boning Up on Fidonet

The first and largest of the echoed networks, Fido has 500 topics open for discussion. Each Fido-affiliated BBS carries only a few of the possible topics, but you can usually request others if you ask nicely. A few doggone message areas you might want to check out are:

- *FLIRTS_NOOK.* Flirtation, teasing, introductions, descriptions, and every nuance of human courtship behavior.
- *LOVELINE.* A place where you can seek new loves and complain about old ones.
- *PEN_PALS.* Meet friends who want to correspond through e-mail or even regular United States snail mail.
- *PP.* Monthly pizza party, where you can imbibe in grease and cholesterol while meeting new folk.
- *PURSUIT.* A place to unwind for those tangled in the pursuit of love.

≋ *NA-ADULT.* North American adult discussion of all genres.

≋ *NA-CRS-ADULT.* More of the same.

Specialty Networks

There are far too many networks to list. There are networks especially for environmentalists, educators, Californians, and so on. Some of the more popular networks with areas useful in online dating are:

≋ *EROSnet.* A subnetwork of Fido, featuring adult messages and files. Areas include Personal (personal ads), ASK (ask other adults advice), and Swing (talk about the swinging lifestyle).

≋ *Lion Net.* An adult-only network; profanity is allowed. Most people here use handles, or anonymous aliases.

≋ *ThrobNet.* Another adult-oriented network.

≋ *AdultNet.* Yet another one.

≋ *KinkNet.* A network devoted to those whose sexual tastes are anything but vanilla.

≋ *ProW.L.* Prowl cyberspace looking for adventure and fun times.

≋ *RIME* (RelayNet International Message Exchange). A standard echo on a number of topics found on BBSs the world over.

≋ *Majornet.* Found on systems using the Major BBS software, this network is eclectic and far reaching.

≋ *Usenet.* This is the world's largest network, containing over 5000 worldwide message areas. See Chapter 7, The Internet, for more details.

≋ *WWIV.* Found on the WWIV brand of BBSs, this network has a number of standard discussion areas.

≋ *Citadel.* Found on Citadel BBSs, this network has various "rooms," organized by "floors," where individual topics are discussed. Both messages and files are stored in each room.

Joining a Discussion Group

While some BBSs have only two or three areas of discussion, others have a seemingly interminable list of thousands of topics. To see a list of topics you can typically press Ⓛ (for listing) or Ⓐ (for areas) or some such command. Other BBSs require you to press Ⓙ, to *join* a topic. You may then press ⑦ or Ⓛ to list the available choices. Each topic is preceded by a number. To move to a particular topic, or to join it, just type in that number.

Figure 6-6 (see page 78) shows just a little bit of the list of bulletin boards from Manhattan's Real Exposure BBS (profiled earlier). Each topic is designated by a code, telling you which echo it's from.

Some BBSs allow you to set up a list of your favorite forums. Each time you log on, you get a note about any new messages in your listed forums. Check your messaging menus or consult your sysop for help.

Reading

Once you've joined or selected the area you're interested in, you typically press Ⓡ to read the messages. You may be asked whether you want to read only the new messages; if you have previously pored through many of the messages in the current group, this is a good way to avoid reading something you've already seen. You may also be asked whether you'd like to read the messages forward or backward. Reading them backward shows you the latest talk, but makes it difficult to follow the flow of the conversation.

Often, you have the option to browse through the messages. You get a list of each message's subject and can then choose only those which sound interesting. You can search all messages in all groups, new messages only, messages addressed specifically to you, or you can search for a particular word or phrase.

On most BBSs, you can continue reading the messages in a group by pressing Ⓔⁿᵗᵉʳ (ENTER) or Ⓝ for next. You can also usually press Ⓡ to reply to a message you've just read. Pressing Ⓟ usually re-displays the previous message.

Each brand of BBS software has its own special way of storing messages. Some BBSs have *threads*, which allow you to read a message and all its responses at once. Other BBSs store and display the messages chronologically. Depending upon the style of BBS, reading through messages may be similar to listening to a conversation, flipping through a newspaper, or standing in the middle of a room full of screaming people.

Writing a Message

You can enter a message of your own either by replying to an earlier message or by starting a new subject of your own. Typically, you can post a message by pressing Ⓐ for add or Ⓟ for post or another applicable command. If you opt to post a new message, the BBS may ask for the name of the addressee. Unless you want to direct your message to one particular person, type

ALL

EXPERT TIP

Full-screen editors often have commands that let you move around your message, insert missing words, delete whole lines of text, and even mark areas to cut and paste. Typically, pressing (CTRL)+Ⓗ or some other key combination displays a screen of help. If you need help, ask your sysop to tell you the available commands. The top of the screen typically tells you the basic commands you need to know, such as (CTRL)+Ⓢ to save the message, once you're done typing.

The BBS then asks for the message's topic or subject: a one-line summary of your article. If you are replying to a message, you generally inherit that message's subject.

You may now type in your message. If you are using ANSI or RIP emulation, you can usually use a full-screen editor. Otherwise, you need to type in your message one line at a time, pressing (ENTER) at the end of each line and pressing (CTRL)+(S) for save or some other key combination when you're finished. Some line editors require you to type

OK

or

/S

or just a period (.) when done. Carefully read the instructions on your screen to learn how to use your BBSs editor.

You may be asked if you'd like to attach a file. This allows you to upload a previously typed text file as part of your message.

Mail

Many BBSs make little distinction between e-mail and public messages. Each user's e-mail box is often treated like a bulletin board area of its own: an area with a readership of one. To enter e-mail on most BBSs you need only press (E) at the main menu.

Reading New Mail

Almost all BBSs tell you if you have new mail each time you log on. If so, you can generally read it then and there. If you see something along the lines of

You have 3 letters in your mail box. Read them now? (Y/N)

just press (Y).

You can also read new mail on most BBSs by entering the e-mail area and pressing (R). You are often shown a list of all your mail, new and old. You can then type the numbers preceding the messages you're interested in reading.

After you read a message, you generally get the option to delete it. Do so; it unclutters your mailbox and saves space on the BBS. Some systems will delete your mail automatically.

EXPERT TIP

If you're a pack rat, you can save your mail on your hard disk by turning on your communication software's *log file* or *capture to disk* feature before you begin reading mail. Anything that scrolls down your screen is captured. Many programs also allow you to use your mouse to paint text, which you can then copy to the clipboard and paste in your favorite word processor.

EXPERT TIP

Many matchmaking programs have their own e-mail systems, which automatically send e-mail to the person you're interested in. Be sure to check the menu.

Replying

When you read a letter, you may get the option to reply. Typically, you need only press Ⓡ. The system then automatically addresses a new letter to the appropriate person.

Alternatively, you may have responded to a bulletin board message (see the Messages section), and opted to send a *private* reply. Whenever you reply—whether it is to a letter or a message—the appropriate e-mail address and subject are already filled in. All you have to do is type in the letter.

Writing a Letter

Suppose you're browsing through one of the BBS's matchmaking doors and you find the name of a person who sounds just groovy. If you'd like to send a private letter, access the e-mail area and then compose your letter. Typically, this involves pressing Ⓦ for write.

You usually have to type the name of the person to whom you want to write. Some BBSs require a real name, others allow you to send to a user name or handle. Often, if you're not sure of the exact spelling of a name, you can type in your best guess and then look over a list of possibilities. So, for example, if you'd like to send a letter to Lizard, just type

```
Lizard
```

You may be told:

```
There is no user Lizard, however Lenny Lovelooker goes by that
name.
```

If you still have difficulties sending mail to someone, search the BBS member directory for clues.

When you get the query:

```
Who do you wish to send this message to?
```

EXPERT TIP

Since your friendly neighborhood sysop is the Supreme Being of the BBS, he or she can read anything you write. Most, however, have the decency to allow you your privacy. Just in case, though, don't say anything that you wouldn't want overheard.

you can often press (ENTER) to send a letter to the sysop. Other BBSs require you to type

```
Sysop
```

The BBS will also ask for the subject or topic of your letter. Type in a descriptive one-line summary of what you're about to write.

Depending on which BBS and terminal program you're using, you now enter your message either one line at a time or with the full-screen editor. The editor is handy, like a word processor, allowing you to use the arrow keys to edit your letter as you write it. There are often commands that let you insert and delete lines. Typically, pressing (CTRL)+(H) displays the help screen. When you're done entering your text, you can usually press (CTRL)+(S) to save the message. Different BBSs have different editor commands.

If you must enter your letter one line at a time, do so carefully—it's a pain to line-edit your text. Press (ENTER) at the end of each line. To send your letter, you typically press (ENTER) at the beginning of a blank line, or type

```
/S
```

or

```
.S
```

or some other command. You are usually told how to complete your letter when you first begin typing.

Often, you get a chance to edit your letter before you send it off. A menu similar to

```
(A)bort, (S)ave, (R)e-type a line, (L)ist, (I)nsert line, (D)elete line
Select (A,S,R,L,I,D, or ? for menu):
```

appears. You can press (L) to see how your letter will look to the recipient. You can then change, delete, or insert lines until everything looks fine. Finally, press (S) to send your letter away.

You may get a chance to attach a file to the message. Some BBSs allow you to upload a text or data file (such as a digitized photograph of yourself) along with your letter. You may also be able to request a *return receipt*. The receipt is a handy feature that automatically notifies you, through e-mail, once your message has been read. Last, you may be asked if you'd like to send a copy of the letter to anyone else. If so, just press (Y) and type in that person's user name.

Chat

Chat areas are where it all happens. People will start talking and have some mutual interest. People are a lot more open online because they're anonymous. I don't have an agenda when I meet someone, I just like to talk and see where it goes. A lot of times, I have to turn away online friendships because there are just too many people! I like to make that first phone call, it makes whoever I'm talking to seem more like a real person.

Once upon a time, BBSs only had one line. A few users would call, fighting each other and fighting fate, hoping to be the lucky one who wouldn't get a busy signal. But thanks to new technology, such as high-volume phone lines, multitasking computers, and inexpensive modems, the multiline BBS was born. Not only could more callers reach a BBS at once, they could interact with each other. They could chat.

Depending on which BBS you call, no one may be chatting—or everyone may. Talking live with other BBS users is an optimum way to make good friends, and to let your own personality shine. Discussions are sometimes insightful, sometimes silly, often raunchy. Since many BBSs do not charge by the hour, you may find yourself caught up in an all-night chatting spree. There's nothing quite like sharing a sunrise with people who live miles, cities, or even states away.

To see who else is online you can generally press Ⓦ or type

WHO

If you'd like to chat, you may have to enter a special chat room. Some BBSs have one huge chat conference, where everyone gathers and gabs. Other boards have various chat channels, where users can pair off. Still other systems have a separate chat area for each and every bulletin board topic. Many BBSs have a special adult chat area, where four-letter words are allowed. Explore your BBS's menus. You may need to ask your sysop for permission to access certain chat areas.

When you enter a chat area, you are typically told who else is currently there. The names also appear before each statement, so the conversation looks like a play script. For example:

LENNY: Hi there folks, what's shaking besides your cellulite?

If you'd like to say anything, you can usually type it and press (ENTER). Everyone in the current chat area sees what you just typed. For instance, if your user name is Cyber Dater and you type

Hi, I'm brand spanking new to this system. How's everyone doing! I look forward to meeting you all.

Then everyone present sees:

CYBER DATER: Hi, I'm brand spanking new to this system. How's everyone doing! I look forward to meeting you all.

In this way, you can hold extended conversations. When you first enter a chat room, don't expect to understand what's happening. It takes a while to catch the flow of the talk, learn about the speakers, and gain your bearings.

Often, typing

/H

or

/HELP

shows a list of available commands. Some useful commands you may want to look out for are

- *Message/Whisper.* This allows you to send a short, private message to another user. Whispering is useful if you'd like to invite someone to join you in a different chat area or channel.

- *Send/Page/Notify/Call.* This allows you to send a message to a user who is currently logged on to the BBS but is not in the chat area. This is a good way to invite someone to join you for a pleasant chat.

- *Change Channels/Areas.* This allows you to switch from channel to channel, if available. There may also be a command that can *list* all the channels, telling you how many people are on each one and what its topic is.

- *Who/List Names.* This shows you the names of the people you're talking to.

- *Private/Unlist.* This allows you to create a private chat area where you and a date can have a one-on-one conversation, without fear of intrusion.

- *Squelch/Ignore.* This allows you to ignore pages or whispers from an annoying or harassing user. It often suppresses public messages as well, so that no matter what that person types, you never see it.

Some chat systems have specialty verb commands for you to use. For example, if you typed

```
kiss redhead
```

everybody in the room would see

```
Lenny plants a firm, wet smackeroo on Redhead's lips.
```

Remember: You're in a chat area. If you get confused or want to learn about more advanced commands, just ask straight out. Most people are more than glad to help. Chat the night away!

Nailing Down the Board

BBSs have it all. On BBSs you can find the best intellects and the worst sleaze that cyberspace has to offer. You can find colorful graphical boards that are easy to use and convoluted, suffocating menus. You can log on to places that ask outrageous hourly fees and you can find feature-packed systems that are absolutely free.

When it comes to making contacts with real people, for real-life dates, real relationships, and real commitments, it's tough to beat a good ol' local BBS. A BBS is like a social club, singles bar, office building, and software store all in one. Though each BBS requires you to learn a new set of commands, menus, and terms, you will also get to meet a whole new set of people. The more BBSs you call, the easier it'll get. Soon you'll be zipping through a dozen BBSs a day, sending mail to old friends, bumping into new ones, and, all in all, having the time of your life. It may sound farfetched, but to thousands (perhaps millions) of people around the world, it's a part of life—if not a way of life.

THE INTERNET

I STARTED READING REC.SKYDIVING TWO SUMMERS AGO.

There was a guy who kept posting things that absolutely fascinated me. He seemed to feel about skydiving and free fall like I did. We started an e-mail relationship. We found out that we were both born in the same year, but he had started jumping in the '60s and had pretty much stopped, while I had only started a couple years before. He asked me for my phone number, but I was hesitant to get in deeper. I live in Colorado and he lived in California. This meant long-distance calls! Eventually, however, he sent me so much mail that I acquiesced. We started a phone relationship, which continued to the tune of $400 a month! So we started visiting each other. He then made a decision to quit his job and move out to me. The very best part is that he is jumping again, and we spend our weekends having good jumps together and sharing this very important part of our lives. I am very, very grateful for having met him, under any circumstances, but the fact is that the Internet gave us a chance to meet, something that could have happened no other way. We have already, in one short year, changed each other's lives totally, and we're just getting started!

What It Is

The interconnected, international, interesting network, the Internet, is nothing short of grandiose. It is the world's largest conglomeration of computers; a network connecting hundreds of thousands of smaller networks. The Internet is so vast and intricate that it can be thought of as a new dimension.

At last estimate, fifteen million or so users from over sixty countries belonged to the Internet. That's more than a lot of keyboards, it's a lot of prospective dates. It is also one of the cheapest and most easily-reached networks, functioning thanks to the cooperation of hundreds of volunteers.

Because of its size, the Internet is the best way to meet the greatest assortment of new people. It has thousands of discussion groups and live chat areas, as well as the widest-ranging mail system. However, the Internet is also unregulated, making it one of the most cumbersome networks to navigate. This chapter will give you the basics, but it will take time and effort before you become a full-fledged cybernaut. Take the time. Make the effort. It will be well worth it.

After figuring out the most convenient way for you to hook up to the Internet, you'll be whisked on a tour through the basic Internet commands: *telnet, gopher* and *ftp*. You'll then read about the arsenal of more sophisticated Internet resources such as Usenet, e-mail, and RTC.

How to Connect

Internet is not a company. Part of the Internet's charm is that there are no authorities or police. It is a free-for-all of information. There are literally millions of ways to connect to the Internet. But this also complicates things. Each type of Internet access has its own set of rules, commands, and menus. Some services charge mindbogglingly more than others. What is the best way to join the Internet? Here are some of the easiest and cheapest options:

Your Own Backyard

Chances are, you may already belong to the Internet and not know it. Almost every major corporation, university, government office, and military base has access to the Internet. Find someone, such as a systems manager or computer geek (er, I mean, *whiz*), who knows a lot about the computer network where you work or study. Ask that person if local computers are connected to the Internet and if there's any way to snag an account. Universities usually offer their staff and students free access for the asking, or for a small one-time fee. Companies generally set up Internet accounts for their employees if they can be convinced that it would be good business.

Once you have an account, you may have to access the Internet from your office or university computer network. However, you can usually use your home computer to call a *dial-in*. Ask your systems manager for details.

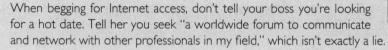

Universities and the Internet

Universities are the widest supporters of the Internet. Check your local university's computing facility to see if they allow public Internet access. You may be charged, but the price should be nominal. If you know someone at a university, you may be able to get your friend to create or sponsor an extra Internet account for you.

Are Freenets Worth the Price?

The next option is to try to join a free network, or *Freenet*. Freenets usually allow you to send and receive mail and to participate in a few news groups; however, most Freenets do not have full Internet access. Freenets may also have a limited number of phone lines, limiting you to an hour or so a day of connect time. Try using a Freenet. If it doesn't live up to your expectations, you may have to use a not-so-free network.

The closest Freenet to you may be a long-distance call, which can wind up being quite costly. Table 7-1 lists America's most popular Freenets:

FREENET NAME	PHONE NUMBER	LOG ON INSTRUCTIONS
CapAccess	202-785-1523	Log on as *guest;* password is *visitor.*
Seanews	206-747-6397 (voice)	
Marob	212-675-7059	
SDF	214-248-9811	When it asks you to log on, type *info.*
Cleveland	216-368-3888	Select *2* (or *fnguest*) from the first menu.
Lorain County	216-366-9721	When it asks you to log on, type *guest.*
	216-774-3025	
Akron	216-972-6352 (voice)	
Medina County	216-723-6732	

continued on next page

TABLE 7-1 The people who run Freenets are a friendly bunch, volunteering their time and facilities to allow the public to enter cyberspace. They'll tell you exactly how to connect up and access the Internet.

continued from previous page

FREENET NAME	PHONE NUMBER	LOG ON INSTRUCTIONS
Youngstown	216-742-3072	When it asks you to log on, type *visitor*.
NCoast	216-582-2460	When it asks you to log on, type *makeuser*.
Prairienet	217-244-1962 (voice)	
	217-255-9000	When it asks you to log on, type *visitor*.
Denver	303-270-4300 (voice)	
	303-270-4865	When it asks you to log on, type *guest*.
Nyx	303-871-3324	When it asks you to log on, type *new*.
Heartland	309-677-2544 (voice)	
	309-674-1100	When it asks you to log on, type *bbguest*.
Big Sky Telegraph	406-683-7680	When it asks you to log on, type *bbs*.
Dark Side of the Moon	408-245-7726	
M2 Xenix	503-297-3211	
Genesis	508-664-0149	
Bigtex	512-346-2339	When it asks you to log on, type *guest*.
Victoria	604-727-7057	When it asks you to log on, type *guest*.
Madnix	608-273-2657	
Pnet51	612-473-2295	
National Capital	613-788-3947 (voice)	
	613-564-0808	When it asks you to log on, type *guest*.
Medsys	615-288-3957	When it asks you to log on, type *bbs*; password *bbs*.
BCA	616-961-3676 (voice)	
Orange County	714-762-8551 (voice)	
Buffalo	716-645-6128	When it asks you to log on, type *freeport*.
Chippewa Valley	715-836-3715 (voice)	
Aquila	812-476-7564	
Suncoast	813-273-3714 (voice)	
Tallahassee	904-488-5056	When it asks you to log on, type *visitor*.
Amaranth	904-456-2003	

TABLE 7-1 (*continued*)

Nationwide Services

The commercial services detailed in the next few chapters allow you to send and receive e-mail through the Internet—see Chapter 13, Shouting Over the Wall, to find out how. In addition, most of the services are in the process of upgrading, hoping to eventually feature full Internet pathways.

Local Networks

Many BBSs act as Internet providers, offering their services via an *800* or local access number. Try: Cr Laboratories, CRIS, CSN, Dial 'n Cerf, HoloNet, Hookup (Canadian), Michnet, Millennium, Novalink, OARnet, Portal System, PSILink, The WELL, and The World. Information on each of these systems can be found in Appendix B.

Be wary of 800 numbers since they tend to be more expensive than a mere long-distance call, once surcharges are tacked onto your bill.

Delphi

Delphi is a feature-packed network in itself, detailed in Chapter 12. For a flat monthly cost of $3 (waived the first month you join) above and beyond the standard Delphi fee, you are given full access to the Internet. Once you are connected to Delphi, simply type

```
go internet register
```

to sign up. Follow the instructions. All the Internet functions are available from easy-to-use menus, and Delphi's Usenet reader is especially thorough and uncomplicated.

America Online

Right now, AOL offers near-complete Internet access. You can send e-mail, read most newsgroups, and explore Gopher. All these features are available through AOL's easy push-button environment. AOL may very well be the easiest way to fly through the Internet. Use the *internet* keyword to begin exploring.

Other Nets to Catch

If you can't find free access, there are a few surefire, though more expensive, alternatives—*public access providers*. Most of these services require you to pay a monthly fee of around $20 or a connect toll of about $2 per hour. Some systems require a startup fee and come with additional surcharges. It usually pays to subscribe within your area code, but check out all nearby areas too. Table 7-2 lists each area code and its best systems. The details are in Appendix A. Most listings include a modem number. Dial it up and log on as instructed for information and guest access. Call the voice number if you have any problems.

201 PSILink	415 a2i, Class, CRL, IGC, Portal, WELL
202 ClarkNet, Express	416 Hookup, UUnet
203 PSILink	419 OARnet
204 MBNet	503 Agora, Netcom, Teleport
205 Nuance	504 NeoSoft
206 Eskimo, Glaids, Halcyon	505 Elnet
212 MindVOX, Panix, Echo, Maestro	506 NBnet
213 Crl, Dial n' Cerf, Kaiwan, Netcom	508 Anomaly, Nearnet, Northshore, Novalink
214 Metronet, Netcom	510 Class, Crl, Dial n' Cerf, Holonet, Netcom
215 PREPnet	512 Realtime
216 OARnet315, Wariat	513 Fsp, OARnet
217 Prairienet	514 Cam, UUnet
301 Capcon, Express, ClarkNet, Tmn	515 Eskimo, netIOWA
302 SSnet	516 Dial n' Cerf
303 CSN, CNS, Netcom	517 Michnet
305 Gateway	519 Hookup, UUnet
310 Class, Crl, Dial n' Cerf, Kaiwan, Netcom	602 Crl, Evergreen, Indirect
312 InterAccess, MCSnet, Netcom, Xnet	603 MV, Nearnet
313 Michnet, MSen	604 UUnet
314 CRL	606 IAC
319 netIOWA	612 MRnet, Winternet, SkyPoint
401 Anomaly, IDS	613 UUnet
403 PUCnet, UUnet	614 OARnet
404 CRL, Netcom	616 Michnet
407 Gateway	617 Nearnet, Netcom, Northshore, World
408 a2i, Netcom, Portal	619 Cyber, Cg57, Class, Crash, Netcom
410 Express, ClarkNet	703 Capcon, ClarkNet, Express, Netcom, Tmn
412 PREPnet, Telerama	704 Rock-Concert, Vnet

continued on next page

TABLE 7-2 Internet public access providers, listed by area code

continued from previous page

707 Crl	816 Tyrell
708 InterAccess, MCSnet, Xnet	817 MetroNet
712 NetIOWA	818 Class, Dial n' Cerf, Netcom
713 Black Box, Nuchat, NeoSoft	819 Achilles, Resudox
714 Class, Express, Kaiwan, Netcom	902 NSTN, PEInet
718 MindVOX, Panix, Maestro, Pipeline,	905 UUnet
719 CNS, CSN, Old Colorado	906 Michnet
801 XMission	907 Alaska
804 Wyvern	908 Express
810 Michnet, MSen	910 Rock-Concert
812 IAC	916 Netcom
814 PREPnet	919 Rock-Concert, Vnet
815 InterAccess, MCSnet, Xnet	

TABLE 7-2 (continued)

Logging On

Once you access an Internet provider, you are asked to select a user name and a password. These are important. Other people will know you by your user name (also called user ID). Many times, however, you are automatically assigned a user name and have no say in the matter.

Registering with an Internet provider is usually similar to signing onto a BBS; see Chapter 6's Logging On section for more help.

Once you are connected, all Internet services are free of international data transfer surcharges, whether you are downloading files from Switzerland or sending mail to a Pakistani pal.

Your Address

When somebody in cyberspace asks for your address, answer with your Internet address. This is your user name plus the "at" sign (@) plus the name of your system. For example, if Lenny Lovelooker got his Internet access through a little-known company called Banana Cybersystems, Inc., his address would be something like *lenny@banana.com* (his user name *lenny* at a computer called *banana*, which is a *com*mercial organization). Addresses

can get weird, involving initials, social security numbers, and more. If your name is Molly Bloom and you attend the University of Chicago, for instance, your username may be something along the lines of *mb123@midway.uchicago.edu*.

There is a whole art and science to Internet addresses. For instance, an address ending in *.mil* is a military base, an address ending in *.nl* is in the Netherlands. You don't have to worry about the particulars. The important thing is to know your own address. You should also be able to spot other people's addresses in letters and in messages, which is easy. Just look for the @—every address has one.

Many other online services can receive mail from the Internet, as long as you specify the correct address. See Chapter 13, Shouting Over the Wall, for more information.

Stick Shift or Automatic?

Okay. You now have access to the Internet. You've called up where you're supposed to call, you've logged on the way you're supposed to log on. What do you see? There are, in general, two ways of getting around the Internet: *Menus* and *Unix commands*. A menu is a list of choices, each one usually preceded by a letter or number. If you are working with menus, your screen should look something like this:

```
HELLO. PLEASE CHOOSE ONE OF THE FOLLOWING:

1. File Transfer
2. Internet
3. Utilities
4. Messages and Bulletin Boards
5. Local Mail
X. Exit
```

To select a menu item, type the letter or number preceding it. For example, in the above menu you would access the Internet resources by typing

```
2
```

and then pressing (ENTER).

Explore your menus until you find something that has to do with the Internet. You may have to look under Communications or Remote Networks. You may not see the word "Internet" at all. Menuing systems may not list a command by its actual name, in which case you should look for items which describe what the command does. For instance, the *telnet* command may be listed under Connect to a remote host. Menus automatically prompt you to type in any needed information once a command is selected.

If you get stuck, you can always try typing *HELP* or press the question mark (?). You can also call up the company or try sending e-mail to the sysop.

On the other hand, some systems don't have menus at all, in which case they are probably using Unix. Unix is an operating system popular with networked computers. If all you see is a

```
%
```

then you are working in a Unix system. This can be baffling, because there are no menus or help screens pointing you in the right direction. All you have to know, though, is a few simple commands. To access an Internet command, you have to type it in and press the (ENTER) key.

Getting Around

If a piece of information is hiding somewhere on the Internet (as almost *everything* within cyberspace is), you can bet your gigabytes that there are dozens of different ways to locate it. Table 7-3 lists the basic Internet navigation commands.

Telnet

Telnet zooms you across the Internet. If you're interested in online dating, you don't want to sit around in your home system, twiddling your thumbs. You want to get out into the world and explore thousands of other Internet sites. Once you know the name of the system you want to reach, type

```
telnet <systemname>
```

or select *telnet* from your menu and then type the <systemname> when asked.
For example, to telnet to the Banana company, all you have to do is type

```
telnet banana.com
```

If the company does not exist you receive a message like:

```
DOMAIN lookup failed for: banana.com
```

COMMAND	DESCRIPTION
telnet *<systemname>*	Transports you to the given *<systemname>* network.
gopher	Provides an easy menu for navigation of the Internet.
ftp *<systemname>*	Transfers computer files between your system and *<systemname>*.

TABLE 7-3 The standard Internet resources

EXPERT TIP

If you cannot find Gopher, or if your Gopher seems too complex, you can teleport to a different system to find another. To do so, you would use the telnet command, along with one of the systems in Table 7-4. For example, try typing

```
telnet gopher.ohiolink.edu
```

and then, when it asks you to LOGIN, type

```
gopher
```

Voilà! You are in Gopherspace.

If you telnet to a valid computer, you may be asked for a password. If a system asks you to

```
LOGIN:
```

you can often type *visitor* or *guest* or, most likely, *anonymous* and be allowed access.

Go Far with Gopher

Gopher is the simplest way to navigate the Internet. Gopher is a system of menus, as in Figure 7-1. You move an arrow to where you want to go or type a menu item's number and you're there. If you want to move back to a previous menu, press Ⓤ for up. Press Ⓠ to quit. Simple as pie. (You can easily find the recipe for almost any flavor of pie, by the way, by searching the Usenet recipe list on Gopher.)

```
            Internet Gopher Information Client v2.0.14

               Columbia University Experimental Gopher

         1.  Help & Info/
         2.  ColumbiaNet/
   -->   3.  Scan the ColumbiaNet Menus <?>
         4.  ColumbiaNet Full Text Searches/
         5.  Gophers & Internet Resources/
         6.  WAIS Databases/
         7.  NetNews and AP Newswire /
         8.  Software Download Area/
         9.  Sounds & Graphics (exp)/
        10.  AcIS Logo <Picture>




Press ? for Help, q to Quit, u to go up a menu          Page: 1/1
```

FIGURE 7-1 Burrowing through Gopher

gopher.ohiolink.edu	gopher.uiuc.edu	gopher.uv.es	gopher.denet.dk
gopher.unc.edu	gopher.sunet.se	gopher.th-darmstadt.de	gopher.puc.cl
gopher.msu.edu	gopher.chalmers.se	gopher.brad.ac.uk	

TABLE 7-4 Gopher holes

Gopher provides easy access to telnet, FTP files, and many other Internet resources. Start out by trying to find Gopher on your system (Freenets may not have it). Type

gopher

No two Gopher screens look alike, but they all act alike. To navigate, use the ⊙ and ⊙ cursor keys to move the little arrow to a desired number. Alternatively, Ⓚ moves up; Ⓙ moves down. If you move the arrow beyond the bottom of the page, a new page (if there is one) appears.

The bottom line of the Gopher screen tells you how many pages the menu has. Most Gopher pages can display about 15 items. If you continue on to the next page, items numbered 16 through 30 are displayed. You can move to a new page quickly by pressing the plus key ⊕ or the more-than sign ⊙. Return to a previous page with minus ⊝ or less-than ⊙.

Once you reach an item you want, press (**ENTER**). You can also just type its number. In the above example screen, to access Gopher and Internet Resources, type

5

The slash Ⓞ allows you to search a Gopher menu for a particular item. This is useful because some menus scroll on for many, many pages. For instance, if you were viewing a list of every Gopher in the world, and wanted to find New York University's, you'd type the least common word:

/york

and the menu scrolls to the next item with "york" in it. Upper and lower case does not matter. Once you've found an item, you can continue the search by pressing Ⓝ for next.

The question mark ⊙ provides a quick list of other useful commands, many of which are summarized in Table 7-5.

Finally, pressing the letter Ⓠ quits Gopher.

EXPERT TIP

You can customize your favorite Gopher lists by placing *bookmarks*. To add the current item to your bookmark list, type Ⓐ. (**SHIFT**)+Ⓐ adds the entire menu to your list. Use Ⓥ to view your bookmarks list and Ⓓ to delete a bookmark you no longer need.

COMMAND	FUNCTION
U	Moves up to the previous menu.
Q	Quits Gopher.
‹	Moves to the previous page in the current menu.
› or SPACEBAR	Moves to the next page in the current menu.
/	Searches for a word in the current menu.
N	Searches for the next occurrence of the word.
A	Adds the current menu item to your bookmark list.
SHIFT + A	Adds the entire current menu to your bookmark list.
V	Views your bookmark list.
D	Deletes a bookmark you no longer need.
<number>	Moves to item number <number>.
SHIFT + D	Downloads the current item's file.

TABLE 7-5 An overview of basic Gopher commands

Veronica

You might already have noticed that there are reams of information available through the Gopher. Where does one begin?

You're interested, foremost, in finding people. A computer program called Veronica can help you. Veronica is a great private investigator. You can ask her to look for anything, and if it's somewhere in the land of Gophers, she finds it. You need to find a menu item that looks like

```
XX.  Search titles in Gopherspace using veronica/
```

Once you select this item, you should see another menu that looks something like this:

```
Search titles in Gopherspace using veronica

--> 1. Search Gopherspace using veronica at CNIDR <?>
    2. Search Gopherspace using veronica at NYSERNET <?>
    3. Search Gopherspace using veronica at PSI <?>
    4. Search Gopherspace using veronica at Pisa <?>
    5. Search Gopherspace using veronica at UNR <?>
    6. Search Gopherspace for GOPHER DIRECTORIES (PSINet) <?>
    7. Search Gopherspace for GOPHER DIRECTORIES (Pisa) <?>
    8. How to compose veronica queries.
    9. FAQ: Frequently asked questions about veronica.
```

You want to select any number between 1 and 5—a search of the entire known Gopherspace. Later, once you are familiar with Internet and Gopher, you can search for particular directories you might have seen before. Some Veronica menus allow you to search specifically for phone lists, telnet sites, or software areas.

Press (ENTER). You then see a box that looks like this:

```
+------Search Gopherspace using veronica at CNIDR-------+
|                                                       |
| Words to search for  _____            |
|                                                       |
|                          [Cancel ^G]  [Accept - Enter]  |
|                                                       |
+-------------------------------------------------------+
```

You can type as many words as you want, separated by a space. Try typing

```
date
```

(upper or lower case doesn't matter) and pressing (ENTER). The search may take a while. Be patient. If something is wrong (networks shut down or change names every day), Gopher tells you. One message to watch out for is

```
--> 1. *** Too many connections - try again soon ***/
```

This means Veronica is too busy to do your dirty work. Press (U) to return to the Veronica menu, and try her at a different location (the one at University of Pisa, maybe), or wait and try again a little later.

If all goes well, you get a screen with listings such as:

```
1. excel-date-formulas
2. a summary or RPA process and implementation to date.
3. the up-to-date forest resources of the USSR.
4. date of ear tag application and control of face flies.
5. Re: timezone in Date: line
6. .......
```

You don't have to read much further to realize that the search was too broad. What's a face fly anyway? The word "date" can apply to more information than you'd ever care to look at. Press (U) to back up to the previous menu, and then run Veronica again by pressing (ENTER).

Now try the word

```
dating
```

This time you get a menu listing of items that are more relevant, shown in Figure 7-2. You can now read any of these articles as you'll see in the next section.

You can make your search even narrower. Suppose you are interested in stories about dating. Access Veronica, and when asked for the word to search for, type

```
dating story
```

A list of articles and letters about this subject appears. You can also search for two subjects at once. To find any information with the word "dating" or "story" in it, type

```
dating or story
```

```
            Internet Gopher Information Client v2.0.14

            Veronica at NYSERNet (affiliates only): dating

-->   1.  The Origin of Modern Humans and the Impact of Chronometric Dating.  .
      2.  Dating and relating across ages
      3.  Dating and relating across ages
      4.  Re: Dating younger nen
      5.  Re: Dating younger nen
      6.  dating older and younger people
      7.  dating older and younger people
      8.  Domestic Abuse & Dating Violenc
      9.  Dating Violence
     10.  Facts About Domestic Abuse and Dating Violence
     11.  POLACH - "RADIOCARBON DATING L" (ISBN: 0-12-559290-6)
     12.  RAPE AWARENESS WEEK: Dating Violence
     13.  NEWS - Inproved dating life
     14.  Symposium on Archaeological Dating
     15.  nagna-chamber-dating
     16.  Dating in the '90s
     17.  The Fed: OPINIONS: Grading and Dating
     18.  barry.dating

Press ? for Help, q to Quit, u to go up a nenu           Page: 1/9
```

FIGURE 7-2 Gopher dating

Finally, if you want to search for part of a word, you can use the wildcard asterisk (*). For example, if you want any word that begins with "love" (lovers, lovely, loves, Lovecraft), type

    `love*`

You can combine multiple words, wildcards, and ORs to create complex queries, searching for exactly what you want. You are now a Veronica master-sleuth.

Ordering from Gopher's Menu

You might notice that each line of the Gopher menu ends in a strange symbol. This tells you what to expect if you select the item. The main symbols Gopher uses are shown in Table 7-6.

With Veronica's help, you can use Gopher to find everything from MOOs to Bulletin Boards to Usenet articles—all described later in their own sections. Gophers are the best

---

EXPERT TIP

If you understand how to use the download features of your communications program, you can use Gopher to retrieve an article directly to your home computer. Simply point to the article in question and hit (SHIFT)+(D). You are then able to choose from Zmodem, Ymodem, Xmodem, Kermit, and Text protocols. In this way, you can even download pictures and sounds, if you have the proper hardware and software.

SYMBOL	DESIGNATES
.	A text file: a printout of information you can read, download, or even mail to yourself.
/	Another Gopher menu.
<?>	Search for something. You type a word (or words), and Gopher hunts for it.
<CSO>	Computing service office. A special type of directory listing where you type in whatever you know about a person (parts of his or her name, ID number, phone number), and the system shows you whatever it can find about that person.
<TEL>	Telnet. A different system is called. Gopher will usually tell you what to do once you are connected.
<BIN>	A binary file (a piece of software) you can download.
<Picture>	Display a picture. This only works on computers with special hardware and software.
<)	Play a sound. Again, only specially-equipped computers have this ability.

TABLE 7-6 Gopher shorthand

way to stumble into a corner of the Internet that interests you. The people at that corner may be just the ones you've been hunting for.

Every time you select an *article* (a menu item that ends in a period) it is displayed, page by page. Press (SPACEBAR) to continue reading. You may press (U) to quit back to the Gopher menu. There are a number of article commands. Press (?) to see them, as shown in Figure 7-3. For instance, pressing (B) takes you back to the previous page. Pressing (S) saves the

```
Dating in the 90's (0k)                                              100%
+----------------------------------------------------------------------+
|      Title: Dating in the 90's
|     Series: Non Series
|   Contents: UHS, +---------------Pager Help----------------+
|   Run time: 30:00!
|   Producer: Canbr!  u, ^G, left : Return to menu             !
|  Placed by: Human!  space, down : Move to the next page      !
|                  !  b, up       : Move to the previous page  !
| Focuses on the is!  /           : Search for text            !
| dating.  Deals wi!  n           : nail current document      !
| friends to be sex!  s           : save current document      !
| importance of the!  p           : print current document     !
| values as a means!  D           : download current document  !
| Terrific program !
| peer pressure, se!              [Cancel: ^G] [OK: Enter]      !
|                  +---------------------------------------------+
|
+----------------------------------------------------------------------+
[Help: ?] [Exit: u]
```

FIGURE 7-3 Commands you can use while reading a Gopher article

article; Ⓟ prints. If you save or print the article, it is stored on your system's network, not on your home computer. Ask your system operator how to retrieve printouts or files.

You can, however, easily mail the file to yourself. Press Ⓜ and enter your e-mail address. Within a few minutes you will get the full article text in your mailbox.

Teleporting

If you use Gopher to access another network, you select an item that ends with the <TEL> logo. You then see the message:

```
+---------------------<system name>---------------------+
|                                                       |
| Warning!!!!!, you are about to leave the Internet     |
| Gopher program and connect to another host. If        |
| you get stuck press the control key and the ] key,    |
| and then type quit                                    |
|                                                       |
|                          [Cancel - ^G] [OK - Enter]   |
|                                                       |
+-------------------------------------------------------+
```

Simply press (ENTER). As the box says, if you get into any trouble or if nothing seems to be happening, hold down the (CTRL) key and press the right bracket (]), then type

```
quit
```

Each system you connect to has its own syntax and rules. Always read instructions carefully. You can usually type ⓘ or

```
help
```

for a brief description of available commands.

Geographical Gophers

Later in this chapter, you'll find out about interesting systems to explore within Internet. If you know the address of a particular Gopher you want to access, you can start Gopher by typing

```
gopher <address>
```

If you're not sure of the Gopher's exact system-name, you can browse Gopherspace geographically or alphabetically. One item every Gopher menu should share is something similar to

```
X. Other Gopher Servers Around the World.
```

Select this. You should see, at the bottom of your screen

```
Retrieving Directory...
```

This could take a while. There are many Gophers. Often, the menu that appears is organized geographically. You can then select the continent, country, and state of the Gopher you're interested in. You can then use the slash (/) command to search for the particular Gopher's name.

Most worldwide menus also come equipped with a search utility—a menu item that ends with (?). Select this and then type the name of the Gopher you are looking for.

Downloading: FTP

The File Transfer Protocol (FTP) is a way to exchange software and text-files over the Internet. In your exploration of cyberspace, you may come across a person or an article that discusses an interesting piece of software and tells you where to FTP it from.

Using archie (see the Expert Tip below) you can find online magazines, articles, and letters about dating; there are also several computer-dating services, programs, and even WEDPLAN—a program which helps you plan every facet of a wedding—in case your online dating is more successful than you bargain for! Some people even post digitized photographs of themselves, allowing you to download them and see who you're dealing with. Table 7-7 lists the common FTP commands you need to know.

EXPERT TIP

Look for a command called *archie*, which searches FTP directories around the world and finds a particular program for you. After typing

```
archie
```

you get a prompt asking for the word you're looking for. For instance, you can type

```
dating
```

You may be asked if you'd like the result mailed to you. If so, type

```
y
```

You then get a list of various system names where dating files or directories were found, and are told which directory to switch to. For instance, you may get a listing that looks like:

```
Host think.com
    Location:/mail/joy-abuse/rochester
      FILE -r--r--r--
 1 1295    staff      626 Oct 22 1990 dating
```

This lets you know that you must access the *think.com* FTP, and switch to the */mail/ joy-abuse/rochester* directory. Read on to find out how.

COMMAND	FUNCTION
ftp <systemname>	Logs on to the FTP library at <systemname>.
cd <directoryname>	Changes to the <directoryname> directory.
dir	Shows the current directory listing.
get <filename>	Downloads the file <filename>.
exit	Quits the FTP library.

TABLE 7-7 Important FTP commands

To access an FTP library, type

```
ftp <systemname>
```

and then log on as *anonymous*. For example, to access an essay about dating, type

```
ftp think.com
```

and then when it asks you for your *user name*, type

```
anonymous
```

For the *password*, just type your Internet address. If you're not asked to log on, you have to do it manually. Type

```
login
```

and then type in *anonymous* as the user name and your e-mail address as the password.

To change to the proper directory, you use the *cd* command

```
cd /mail/joy-abuse/rochester
```

paying special attention to upper and lower case. Then type

```
dir
```

to see a directory listing of all the files, which, in this case, appears something like

```
<ASCII data connection for /bin/ls (128.122.128.16,4043) (0 bytes).
total 153
-r--r--r-- 1 1295    staff     441 Oct 22 1990 Asimov
-r--r--r-- 1 1295    staff    2178 Oct 22 1990 README
-r--r--r-- 1 1295    staff     411 Oct 22 1990 challenge
-r--r--r-- 1 1295    staff    5523 Oct 22 1990 chocolate
-r--r--r-- 1 1295    staff    7487 Oct 22 1990 cops
-r--r--r-- 1 1295    staff    1228 Oct 22 1990 dark
-r--r--r-- 1 1295    staff     626 Oct 22 1990 dating
....
```

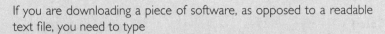

EXPERT TIP

If you are downloading a piece of software, as opposed to a readable text file, you need to type

`binary`

before you *get* the file.

The last word in each line is either the name of a directory or a file; the first letter of the line tells you which. If it is *d* then you are looking at a directory, and must access it using the *cd* command. Otherwise, you are looking at a file and may download it by typing *get* followed by the name of the file exactly as it appears. To retrieve the "dating" file, you simply type

`get dating`

The way FTP works, the files you retrieve go to your Internet provider's computer, not your own. The procedure to load the file from the system computer down to your own varies from system to system. See the Downloading section in Chapter 6, Bulletin Board Systems, for further information.

The (Wo)Manhunt

The time will come when you have friends scattered all over the Internet. You may even start an e-mail affair, trading daily letters with your special someone. You don't have to wait till your sweetie is logged on; Internet users all have mailboxes to hold e-mail. But perhaps you want to talk live with your date. To chat with someone, you do have to find out if he or she is available. How can you tell if someone halfway across the world is logged on to the Internet?

Fingering a Suspect

If you know a person's address (user name plus system), you can *finger* them. When you finger a person, it may tell you nothing, a little, or a lot, depending on the person's system. For example, our pal Lenny Lovelooker's imaginary mailing address is *lenny@banana.com*. You type

`finger lenny@banana.com`

If there is no such system as *banana.com,* then the following message notifies you

`connect: Connection refused`

If there is a banana company, but there is no *lenny* with an Internet account there, then the following screen appears:

```
[banana.com]
Login Name: lenny          In real life: ???
```

If Lenny exists where you finger him, you see

```
[bananas.com]
Login name: lenny          In real life: Lenny Lovelooker
Phone: 111-222-3333
Directory: /usr/lenny
On since Jan 1 15:01 on ttyp1
No unread mail
Project: One-liners.
Plan:
You call those shoes? It looks like fungus with buttons.
```

Alternatively, you could have fingered *lovelooker@banana.com*. If there were multiple Lennys or Lovelookers, a screen of information about each one would appear.

So you have a screenload of information. What does it all mean? Most of the text is either self-explanatory or unimportant technical detail. You have Lenny's user name, his real name, his phone number, the name of his personal Unix directory, and then a line that tells you about his Internet usage. If the line says

```
On since Jan 1 15:01 on ttyp1
```

Then Lenny is currently logged onto the Internet. Thus, Lenny has been working (or playing) around the Internet since about three P.M.

On the other hand, you may see the line:

```
Last login Sat Dec 31 16:46 on ttyp1
```

This means Lenny last used the Internet at a quarter till five on New Year's Eve.

The next line tells you Lenny's mail status. If he already read and deleted all his latest mail, you see

```
No unread mail
```

EXPERT TIP

If you are having a problem fingering someone, check your spelling and be sure you are typing in lower case. It is also possible that your friend's system does not allow itself to be fingered.

EXPERT TIP

If you are using a Unix system, try typing

    chfn

This is the *change finger* command. This allows you to change your name, phone number, and miscellaneous other information. If you want, you can trick people who finger you into thinking you're Michael Jackson or Saddam Hussein, though this makes it more difficult for people to find the real you.

If, on the other hand, Lenny has mail but hasn't looked at it yet, you'd see exactly when it arrived:

    Unread mail since Sat Dec 31 19:33:01 1993

These messages can come in very useful. Suppose you send the most exciting, sparkling, intelligent woman you ever met an e-mail invitation to dinner. As suppertime approaches, there's no response. You sweat, you bite your fingernails, you feel put down, you feel stood up. Then you get an idea: Finger her! You do so and notice that she hasn't yet read her latest mail. Your pride, at least, is saved!

The remainder of the finger information is a fun or informative message of the user's choice, called a *plan* and a *project*. Some people have their home addresses here. Others have famous quotations. Lenny has a few insults.

Finding Someone

You are interested in finding a date. This usually means you know no particular names or addresses—you are just on the hunt for interesting and fun places and people.

But sometimes you meet someone you'd like to meet again and forget to ask for an e-mail address. Perhaps you know the name but nothing else. There are many methods to track someone down in cyberspace. Two of the best are:

The White Pages

If you know *where* a person is, but little else, you can use Gopher to access the university or company (as described earlier in the section on Geographical Gophers). Many organizations

---

EXPERT TIP

If you know how to use a Unix text editor such as *vi*, you can create or change your *.PLAN* and *.PROJECT* files so that when you are fingered, your personalized message is displayed.

have a directory or mailing list on their Gopher menu. You can then search for your friend. Some directories not only tell you the person's e-mail address, but his or her real address, phone number, and some personal details.

Suppose you're chatting one day with a man named "Mr. Jones," and you think he's the best thing since sliced bread. You say good-bye and all you recall is that he works as a secretary in the psychology department of Smartpants University. You access the Smartpants University Gopher (via the Geographical Gopher search commands) and see an option

7. Information Sources: Phones, Places, and Publications/

All you have to do is enter the name Jones into the phone directory search. The names of several Mr. Joneses are printed out, along with each one's department, phone number, and e-mail address.

The Gopher at Notre Dame University (in Indiana), has a special phone book that contains a listing of almost every university and company directory. Select

Non-Notre Dame Information Sources/

from the first menu, and then select

Phone Books--Other Institutions/

Author Search

If the person you are looking for has ever posted an article on Usenet you can search a handy list at the Massachusetts Institute of Technology that has the name and e-mail address of every Usenet writer. You do this either by using Gopher's Veronica to

SEARCH USENET

Alternatively, there's a nice service that searches for someone on your behalf. Simply send mail to

mail server@rtfm.mit.edu

Leave the *SUBJECT:* line blank. Your mail message should be one line long:

send usenet-addresses/<*username*>

In place of <*username*> type the name of the person you are looking for. See the Mail section below for more information.

Be careful. If all you search for is John you will get a monstrous list returned to you. There are many Johns who use Usenet. Do *not* search by first name unless it is rare.

So, if you met a lady named Mary Ziggernaught and are dying to send her a letter, you would send mail to the server at MIT, the body of which would say

send usenet-addresses/ziggernaught

You would then, automatically, get a letter telling you if she was found, and, if so, what her address is.

WAIS and The Web

The Internet is constantly evolving, becoming even larger, even more information-packed, but also even easier to use. Some of the latest Internet resources you may want to keep an eye out for are

- *Wide Area Information Service (WAIS).* You might come across this term while using Gopher or reading Usenet articles. WAIS is an easy-to-use database of databases. You select from a huge list of reference books and can search for the definition of the word "loquacious," census information during the Ford administration, mailing lists that have something to do with martial arts, the chief export of Botswana . . . almost anything. This can help you find areas, on and offline, where you can run into people who share your interests. Again, the easiest way to access WAIS is to use Veronica and the Gopher and search for it. WAIS is intricate, but menu-driven. Play around with it; you'll be amazed how much information is a keystroke away.

- *World Wide Web (WWW or W3).* The "Web," along with special Mosaic software, allows you to jump around the Internet. When you come across a word, icon, or concept you're interested in, you can click on it with your mouse (or type it in) and receive deeper and deeper levels of information. This system—known as *hypertext*—makes full Internet navigation as easy as any other commercial online service. Several companies have developed Mosaics which allow you to easily access not only text, but sound, video, and high-resolution graphics. This means online art galleries, photographic databases, and multimedia.

Your Internet provider may give you a copy of Mosaic or other Web-browsing software. If not, many Unix systems have text-based commands called *lynx* or *www,* which allow you to begin exploring The Web. Type *lynx* followed by an address to access a part of the Internet directly. Try Web address *http://wwa.com:1111/* to check out The Virtual Meet Market, an online personal ads area complete with pages of detailed info and photographs. Eventually, this service might even support sound and video clips. *Wired Magazine*'s HotWired service at *http://www.hotwired.com/* also has a comprehensive personal ads section in the Coin department.

Messages

My husband and I met over the net—alt.personals, actually. He was an American on a contract in Germany and I was in California. He was looking for people to write to since he was having English withdrawals. I figured that nothing could happen if I responded to his plea for mail. Now look at me! We are married and have a beautiful baby. My family didn't understand how we met, and I was nervous about marrying him since we had only been together physically for a total of a month before (he ended his contract and returned to the States to be with me . . . sigh). However, it was the best decision I ever made. He is a wonderful husband, father, and best friend.

User's Network (Usenet)

This is the Internet's claim to fame. It is a collection of over 5000 different discussion areas, also called newsgroups. Usenet is the world's fastest way, period, to meet people interested in the same things you are. Every topic is covered, from computers to religion to education to music to sports to cooking to the paranormal to politics to nature to—this sentence could go on for a few more pages. There are also interactive fiction newsgroups, where one person starts a novel or poem, and another continues it. The list of newsgroups grows every day. More importantly, there are areas particularly suited for online dating.

Becoming a regular on a Usenet newsgroup is like joining a club or being a barfly. Soon you know all the people, and they all know you. However, many systems don't try to carry all newsgroups, due to the tremendous amount of space required to store all the messages. Freenets especially may have a limited number of groups to choose from.

Remember, there is no additional fee to access Usenet. If you are not happy with the types of newsgroups available to you, ask whoever is in charge of your system if they can sign on to more areas. You can also use telnet or Gopher to connect to a system that has better Usenet resources.

Subscribing to a Usenet Newsgroup or Two, or Three, or . . .

Unlike commercial services, there are no authorities editing or censoring Usenet. Like all anarchies, you'll find the best and the worst humanity has to offer here.

Subscribing to a newsgroup means you have a general interest in its subject. You can unsubscribe at any time. Reading articles is a simple process, once you've subscribed to a group. Usually, all you have to do is press (ENTER).

In most cases, to subscribe you use the *rn* or *trn* newsreader (described shortly in the Reading the News section). If you have a lot of time, and are interested in many newsgroups, there is a way to decide if you want to subscribe to each, one by one. First type the command

```
newsetup
```

This subscribes you to *every* newsgroup. Now, the first time you read the news with *rn* or *trn,* a long, long list of every group is given to you. For instance, a message resembling this appears:

```
***** 144 unread articles in alt.fan.madonna--read now?
```

You should go through the list, one at a time, pressing Ⓤ to unsubscribe from anything that doesn't fascinate you. This will take a little while—there may be thousands of groups to unsubscribe from—but you end up with a list of groups custom-tailored to your curiosity.

Any time there are new newsgroups—and there will be almost every day—you are asked if you want to subscribe.

```
Newsgroup alt.fan.madonna not in .newsrc--subscribe? [ynYN]
```

You press Ⓨ for yes if you're interested in Madonna (the scantily-clad pop singer, in this case, not the religious foremother), Ⓝ for no if you couldn't care less. In some cases—the

EXPERT TIP

If you know how to use a Unix editor you can manually subscribe or unsubscribe to newsgroup names from the *.newsrc* file. Newsgroup names ending in a colon (:) indicate that you are subscribed; you are unsubscribed from those ending with an exclamation mark (!). You may also see numbers after each group. This indicates which messages you have read. A typical entry looks like

```
soc.politics: 1-9334
```

first time you use a newsreader or if you haven't used one in a while—there may be hundreds of new groups. If you'd like to subscribe to them all, you can press (SHIFT)+(Y); to disregard them all, press (SHIFT)+(N).

When subscribing, you may be asked where in the *newsrc* file the new group should be placed. Put your favorite groups first. Press (H) for help to see your options.

Now assume you're interested in reading through the Internet personal ads, but you're not subscribed to an appropriate newsgroup. You can easily resubscribe by typing

```
rn personals
```

or

```
trn personals
```

The newsreader searches for groups containing the word "personals".

```
***** 234 unread articles in alt.personals.ads -- read now [y/n/q]?
```

Some systems may not allow you to subscribe to groups, in which case you'll have to manually request articles from specific newsgroups. In many cases, though, the newsgroups are presented in a well-organized, easy-to-use menu. Browse around until you find an area that interests you—with Usenet's vast selection, it shouldn't take long.

What Do These Weird Groupnames Mean?

There are so many Usenet newsgroups they must be organized diligently and precisely. A typical newsgroup consists of several words separated by periods. For example one popular group is *alt.personals*. The prefix tells you, in general, what the newsgroup is about. (In this case, an alternative subject.) The remaining categories get more and more detailed. There are many different *alt.personals* groups in all, such as: *ads, poly, d, bi, spanking, bondage*. As you can see, Usenet can serve all your, er, needs.

If you are not sure what an acronym in a newsgroup name stands for, subscribe to it. Does *sf* mean science fiction or sexy feet or sinful feelings? You might be pleasantly surprised. You can always unsubscribe later. Table 7-8 should help you sort out the basics.

The italicized groups in Table 7-8 are considered mainstream, and are likely to be found on almost all Internet systems. The others are alternative, and must usually be requested

alt.	Specific topics of an alternative nature. Many, many topics.
bit.	Bitnet mailing lists.
comp.	Computers, computers, and more computers.
info.	Topics from various mailing lists.
misc.	Miscellaneous topics.
news.	Information about Usenet itself.
rec.	Recreation! Hobbies and sports.
soc.	Social subjects and topics, including dating and sensuality.
talk.	Debate and discussion for discussion's sake.
sci.	Sciences.
bio.	Biology and the environment.
biz.	Business, including online commercials!
k12.	Education: kindergarten through 12th grade.
clari.	Real world, local, and special interest news.

TABLE 7-8 A quick list of the most popular Usenet taxonomy

or specially searched for. It is easier to meet people among some of the weirder alternative groups since these groups appeal only to a few people who share the same "craziness."

One last note. Newsgroups that end in *.d* are a discussion of some prior topic. For example, *rec.humor* contains only jokes, but *rec.humor.d* is where these jokes are applauded or (usually) groaned at. Newsgroups that end in *.digest* are online magazines, not discussions. Newsgroups that contain the word *.binaries* are not even text; they are software.

Reading the News

There are many different ways to read Usenet articles, depending on the system you are on. If you have already subscribed to a list of newsgroups, use one of the following newsreader commands:

    rn

or

    trn

Each time you use your newsreader program, it notifies you of all the new articles in your top-five list of subscribed newsgroups. For instance:

```
Unread news in soc.singles 373 articles
Unread news in alt.personals 383 articles
Unread news in rec.arts.poetry 288 articles
Unread news in rec.sports.flyfishing 2999 articles
Unread news in alt.fan.madonna 144 articles
```

You are then asked, for each group:

***** 373 unread articles in soc.singles--read now?

Usually, pressing Ⓨ allows you to start reading the articles. If you press Ⓝ you get a query about your next favorite newsgroup. If you find yourself stricken with a sudden repulsion for Madonna, unsubscribe from the group by pressing Ⓤ. You can press Ⓠ to quit the newsreader. Depending on which newsreader you use, these commands and options vary. Typically, you can press Ⓗ for a list of all available commands.

You can now read through the current newsgroup's articles. If two or more people try reading an article at once there may be a slight delay. You might even be told to try again later. Luckily, there is no lack of interesting articles to read, so if one group is busy, explore another. Table 7-9 summarizes the most important *rn* and *trn* reading commands.

Use the (SPACEBAR) or Ⓝ to view the next article. If the article is longer than a page, you usually have to press (SPACEBAR) or (ENTER) to continue reading it. Press Ⓟ to re-read the previous article. Press Ⓠ to quit the current newsgroup.

One very handy command is the equal sign ⊜. This lists all the remaining articles in the newsgroup, along with each one's subject, as shown in Figure 7-4. You can read what sounds interesting by typing its number and pressing (ENTER).

COMMAND	FUNCTION
(SPACEBAR)	Reads the next article.
Ⓟ	Reads the previous article.
Ⓠ	Quits the current newsgroup.
⊜	Browses through a listing of the newsgroup's new articles.
Ⓡ	Responds privately to the article you just read.
Ⓕ	Allows you to follow up, writing public feedback to the article you just read.
(SHIFT)+Ⓡ	Responds privately, quoting the original article.
(SHIFT)+Ⓕ	Responds publicly, quoting the original article.

TABLE 7-9 Typical commands used for reading Usenet articles

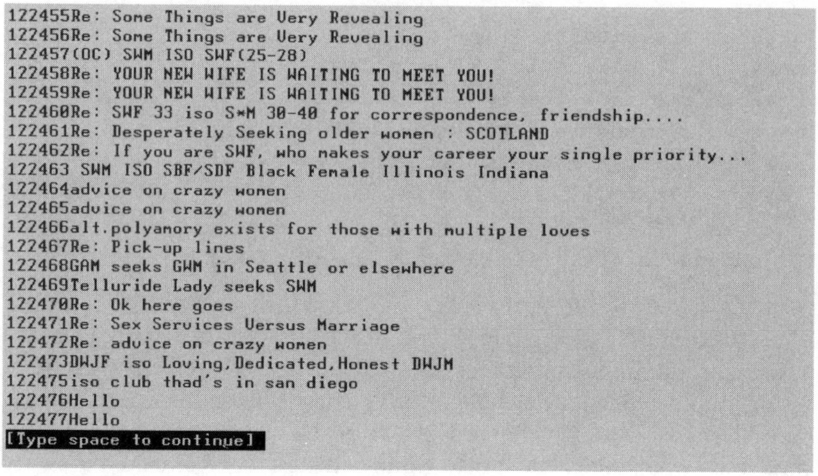

```
122455Re: Some Things are Very Revealing
122456Re: Some Things are Very Revealing
122457(OC) SWM ISO SWF(25-28)
122458Re: YOUR NEW WIFE IS WAITING TO MEET YOU!
122459Re: YOUR NEW WIFE IS WAITING TO MEET YOU!
122460Re: SWF 33 iso S*M 30-40 for correspondence, friendship....
122461Re: Desperately Seeking older women : SCOTLAND
122462Re: If you are SWF, who makes your career your single priority...
122463 SWM ISO SBF/SDF Black Female Illinois Indiana
122464advice on crazy women
122465advice on crazy women
122466alt.polyamory exists for those with multiple loves
122467Re: Pick-up lines
122468GWM seeks GWM in Seattle or elsewhere
122469Telluride Lady seeks SWM
122470Re: Ok here goes
122471Re: Sex Services Versus Marriage
122472Re: advice on crazy women
122473DWJF iso Loving,Dedicated,Honest DWJM
122475iso club thad's in san diego
122476Hello
122477Hello
[Type space to continue]
```

FIGURE 7-4 Browsing through Usenet articles

Here's a sample Usenet article:

```
Path: ucsbcs1!banana.com!lenny
From: lenny@banana.com (Lenny Lovelooker)
Newsgroups: alt.personals, alt.personals.ads
Subject: Re: New movies?
Summary: Duck Soup a quackingly good time.
Keywords: ducks, soup, bananas, movies, me
Message-ID: <1994January1.133423.12632@banana.com>
Date: 1 January 94 13:34:23 GMT
References: <1993December31.092343.23132@reform.gov>
Distribution: world
Lines: 19


In article <<1993December31.092343.23132@moviewatchers.au>
kmarx@reform.gov (Karl Marx) writes:


> Lenny: Do you know where I can find Groucho Marx movies?


I'd like to extend a special invitation to all you idiots to
see Duck Soup. It's about ducking and souping and all that so
see it, you nincompoop. Free cigars to the first 100 who show
up. In particular, I'm looking for a girl to hang onto my arm.
Yeah, yeah, a date. I'm looking for someone well-mannered, tall,
great smile: Anybody who can stand to be seen with me will be
fine. Just remember: I'd never join a club that would have me
for a member.
```

Each article has a header. Most of this is boring technical information. All you have to look at is *From,* which tells you the Internet address and name of the person who wrote the article; *Subject,* which is a brief description of the article; and *Summary,* a one-line synopsis.

Many articles are responses to previous ones. The subject of such articles usually has *Re:* in it. If text in the article is preceded by a greater-than sign (>) then it has been quoted from a previous message.

Certain newsreaders, such as *trn,* can automatically follow an original letter plus its string of responses. This is called a *thread* (the "*t*" in *trn*), and makes a Usenet conversation easy to follow. With most other readers, you read articles chronologically.

Messages can end with a special signature, or *sig.* This is a few lines of pre-designed text which automatically appears at the end of every article you write. Signatures give articles some character, and you can tell who is a regular on a Usenet newsgroup by seeing which signatures appear most often.

Reading Without a Reader

If for some reason you do not have *rn* or *trn* you may have to use an alternative reader. Many systems have their own software, which should run similarly to the *rn* and *trn* readers—ask the system manager if you need help.

Also, try one of the following commands:

```
nn
tin
xrn
xvnews
gnus
gnews
```

These are all popular newsreaders, and may be available. In most cases you can press Ⓐ, Ⓗ, or type

```
help
```

for a list of reader commands.

Perhaps the easiest way to access a great number of Usenet groups is through the Gopher (see the section above). Use Veronica to search for your topic of interest; search for the

EXPERT TIP

You can custom design your own signature with a Unix text editor by creating a *.signature* file. Since this is added to the end of every article you post, it's best to keep your John Hancock under five lines.

newsgroup name itself if you know it. Also, the following Gopher locations have excellent facilities for reading Usenet news, although they may be busy and restrict access during peak hours:

▓ *gopher gopher.msu.edu*, select News&Weather, Usenet News.

▓ *gopher sunsite.unc.edu*, select News, USENET News.

▓ *gopher gopher.tc.umn.edu*, select News, USENET News.

Using Gopher menus, you can now select the newsgroup's category and then browse through all the articles. Although you won't be able to respond directly to articles, you can post Usenet articles through e-mail, as described later in Writing Without a Writer.

Following Up on an Article

When you read something that interests you, you may want to respond. You have to decide if your response should be directed to just the article's author or if you want your message to be readable from any computer worldwide. It is a little tricky to post an article of your own—familiarity with a text editor is important. On the other hand, the only way to make yourself known is to write, write, and write.

Pressing Ⓡ after reading an article allows you to respond privately, through e-mail. If you'd like to follow up publicly, press Ⓕ. You can now type in your Usenet article.

When responding, you may be asked

```
Are you starting an unrelated topic? [yn]
```

Press Ⓝ if your article is a response to the one you just read. Otherwise, type Ⓨ to begin a message with a subject of your own choosing.

Posting Usenet Articles

When you write a Usenet article, at first, it can only be seen by the people at your system. Within a few hours, your message is copied off to several neighboring systems. This process increases exponentially until your wit and wisdom is propagated all over the globe, from the White House to Greenland.

EXPERT TIP

When you follow up on a letter, the Re: is automatically inserted in the subject line. If you'd like the article you are following up on to be quoted automatically in your text, press (SHIFT)+Ⓕ instead of the lower case. You can do the same thing with private responses. Press (SHIFT)+Ⓡ. This can get messy, though, so only quote a message if it is short. If you're comfortable using your text editor, you can quote longer articles and then delete superfluous lines.

Articles typically live about a week before they are deleted to make room for new ones. When your article expires, it is often stored in one of the many Usenet archives, so don't be surprised if you get a response to an article you wrote several months ago.

Some newsgroups are moderated—you may see the term (*moderated*) next to the newsgroup's name. This means there is an editor, a judge, who reads your article and then decides if it is worthy to be posted. The articles on moderated newsgroups are generally of a higher caliber—but sometimes less controversial—than those on do-it-yourself newsgroups. Some moderators take a month's worth of the best articles and combine them into one long magazine called a *digest*, or *e-zine*.

If you are not reading the news and want to begin a message of your own, type

Pnews <groupname>

with a capital P. The <groupname> you use must be valid and exact, so type it carefully. If that doesn't work, try

nnpost

You may now be asked for header information, such as:

Distribution:

To which you can enter

world

Naturally, if you're posting a personal ad in search of nearby dates, you could enter *local;* your message appears only on your local system. You can also usually enter your city name, state, postal code, or country.

You may be asked which newsgroup you want to post to. Enter its exact name. If your article pertains to more than one newsgroup, you can enter several names, separated by commas.

You may now be given a rather ominous warning along the lines of:

This program posts news to thousands of machines throughout the entire civilized world. Your message will cost the net hundreds if not thousands of dollars to send everywhere. Please be sure you know what you are doing.

Are you absolutely sure that you want to do this? [ny]

If you are, press Ⓨ. You are now asked

Prepared file to include [none]:

Press ⒺⓃⓉⒺⓇ, unless you have previously typed up an article using a Unix text editor, in which case you should type in its name.

You now enter a text editor; you may be asked to choose your favorite. Try *vi*. Since *vi* needs to know that you want to add text, press Ⓐ before you begin typing. Type in your

message, line by line, pressing (ENTER) at the end of each line. Finish your message by pressing (CTRL)+(D), or, in some cases, (CTRL)+(Z). If you are using Unix's *vi* text editor, end your message by pressing (ESC), and then the colon (:) and typing

```
wq
```

Once your message is complete, you are then generally given the option to:

```
Send, abort, edit, or list?
```

You can (L) your message, make sure it says what you want it to say, (E) it if need be, and then (S) it away. You are now famous.

Writing Without a Writer

If, for whatever reason, you cannot write a Usenet article through conventional means, you have another option: e-mail (see the Mail section of this chapter for details). Simply send your article to *<newsgroup>@cs.utexas.edu* or *<newsgroup>@pws.bull.com*.

To post your own personal ad, for example, simply enter the command:

```
mail alt.personals@cs.utexas.edu
```

or

```
mail alt.personals@pws.bull.com
```

and then type your message, the way you would ordinary mail.

Newsgroups Related to Dating

The following groups all share one thing in common: people searching for other people.

alt.personals. Thousands of personal ads and related discussion. Subjects range from: "GWM will be in Denver" to "SWF iso Intelligent Life?:)" to "Erotic Female Wrestling" to "Mature woman wanted by young man." You can find everything from cruising teenagers to studly senior citizens; people from every race, nationality, sexual orientation, and intention. Some ad-posters seek online penpals, others are looking for real-life dates who live in their area. Supposedly this newsgroup generates a very good response, especially for females, though it might take some nerve to respond or post your own ad.

alt.personals.ads. Even more personal ads; no discussion. Same vein as above.

alt.personals.bondage. Personal ads by and for people interested in bondage and discipline. Faint of heart should avoid this newsgroup.

alt.personals.d. Discussion about personal ads and dating.

alt.personals.misc. Personal ads where anything goes.

alt.personals.poly. Those who seek multiple loves should check this out. This is for couples interested in meeting other couples and any combination thereof.

alt.personals.spanking. Bad boys and girls can find their proper discipline here.

alt.polyamory. Discussion of multiple love relationships. "Some people involved with this group are interested in three or more people living together and raising a family. Some are more casual. Some are married. Most believe that honesty and openness between all involved is of paramount importance."

alt.romance. Amore online; all love talk not having to do with sex. Romance advice and all its many nuances are discussed in intimate detail here. People seeking romance appear here, as well.

alt.sex. General discussion about all aspects of sex. Beware, much of it is risqué. Much of it is also adolescent. Try *alt.sex.bondage, alt.sex.stories,* and other steamy newsgroups for variations on the theme.

alt.sex.wanted. Straight-to-the-point requests for sex, which don't say much for subtlety. Some subjects include: "Relax, take it one day at a time," "Females: Dolphins are good lovers," "Seeking Beth from North Dakota," and "Anything!"

soc.bi. A place for bisexuals to socialize and to discuss issues.

soc.college. College students can talk here about their social lives, or lack thereof.

soc.college.grad. This is the place for grad students to discourse.

soc.couples. Couples talk about couples here. Discussion of relationships and lifestyles.

soc.men. Card-carrying males can discuss everything from relationships to equal rights, from swimsuits to paternity suits.

soc.misc. A place for miscellaneous social talk, and socially oriented issues.

soc.motss. Members of the same sex. This is where homosexuals can socialize and discuss relevant issues.

soc.penpals. People from various countries and cultures interested in electronic (or even the old paper, stamp, and envelope) penpals invite you to write them here.

soc.personals.ads.fsf. Still more personal ads, organized differently. Females seeking females.

- *soc.personals.ads.fsm.* Females seeking males.

- *soc.personals.ads.msf.* Males seeking females.

- *soc.personals.ads.msm.* Males seeking males.

- *soc.singles.* The best place to meet singles on the Internet. All aspects of the singles scene are discussed here, from frustration about dating to suggestions on where to go to meet people. Some subjects are: "First date: A comedy of errors," "Women don't do it!" "Living well is the best revenge," and "Dental hygienist."

- *soc.singles.nice.* Same as above, but with an emphasis on more mature discussion.

- *soc.women.* Those of the female persuasion can sound off about the issues.

Mailing Lists

Wish you got more e-mail? Now you can! Though most people try to avoid getting their names on mailing lists in real life, over the Internet you'll probably find them a real blessing. Mailing lists are the equivalent of having an entire bulletin board or Usenet discussion group mailed right to you. There is something intimate about e-mail; the people on mailing lists are often closer knit than those on Usenet since articles are sent only to a limited group. Mailing lists are also useful if you do not have access to Usenet.

Once you subscribe to a list, every article it carries appears in your mailbox, where you can read it along with your regular mail. Each list sends dozens of messages a day. It is not a good idea to belong to too many lists; you may find yourself with hundreds of letters to pore through. Pick one or two lists, try them, and then unsubscribe if you'd prefer something else.

Most mailing lists work using a computer program that acts like its own e-mail address, called a *listserver*. To send a command to a listserver, you have to send it mail.

For a wide range of mailing list topics, try *Bitnet* (the Because It's Time Network). Any Usenet newsgroup beginning with *bit.listserv.* is also a Bitnet mailing list. Bitnet is separate from Internet, though there are gateways linking the two together. Bitnet addresses are similar to Internet ones, except they end in *.bitnet.*

Some Internet systems cannot access a Bitnet gateway. Ask your system manager for details.

EXPERT TIP

One popular Bitnet gateway is *vm1.nodak.edu.* If sending mail to an address which ends with the word *.bitnet* fails, you can try sending mail through the gateway. This takes the form

```
vm1.nodak.edu!<systemname>.bitnet!<username>
```

List of Lists

There are many, many, many lists. The easiest way to see what's available is to mail yourself a list of lists. To do this, you must access a listserver. Here are five of the best systems where listservers can be found:

- cornellc.cit.cornell.edu
- mitvma.mit.edu
- vm1.nodak.edu
- ncsuvm.cc.ncsu.edu
- bitnic.bitnet

You should access these listservers every time you want to subscribe, unsubscribe, suspend messages, or get information. Here are the three simple steps you need to use a listserver:

1. Address mail to *listserv@<systemname>*
2. Leave the subject blank.
3. As your message, type the appropriate mailing list command, depending upon what you want to do.

   The command to send yourself a list of lists, for instance, is

   `list global`

   You can also specify a keyword, if you are interested only in lists dealing with a particular subject.

   So, for example, type

   `mail listserv@vm1.nodak.edu`

and press (ENTER) when it asks for the

   `Subject:`

and then type

   `list global`

and end the message by pressing (CTRL)+(D). If you want a list of socially-oriented mailing lists, instead type

   `list global/social`

You should then get two messages back. The first one is technical and tells you that the listserver computer has processed your command. Read it before you delete it; if there is a problem, it may tell you what you did wrong.

The second message may be long. It is an alphabetized catalog containing the name and description of every mailing list the listserver has to offer you.

For instance, when you ask *listserv@vm1.nodak.edu* for a socially oriented mailing list, it returns a list with about 25 items. There are groups about social science, social persuasion, social rehabilitation, nonlinear dynamical social systems (whatever that is), social responsibility, social insect biology research, and a social function Greek list (for college fraternities).

A comprehensive list of Internet mailing lists can also be found in the Usenet newsgroup. The WAIS database also contains a list of almost every known mailing list.

Subscribing

Once you find a mailing list that interests you, write another listerver message. Substitute a slightly different command: *subscribe <mailing-list name> <your real name>*.

For example, if I wanted to subscribe to the *writers* group, I would type

```
mail listserv@vm1.nodak.edu
Subject:
subscribe writers David Fox
```

I would get a technical message back, almost immediately, telling me if I was successful. Pretty soon, my mailbox should begin filling up with articles about all facets of writing.

Unsubscribing

You can probably guess what to do. The command is: *unsubscribe <mailing-list-name>*.

For instance, if I get sick of reading about writing, I would type

```
mail listserv@vm1.nodak.edu
Subject:
unsubscribe writers
```

EXPERT TIP

At times you may come across instructions for subscribing to mailing lists which do not have the *listserv* element in their names. This typically means you must ask a *person*—not a computer—to add you to the list. Send a polite letter with your full name and Internet address, telling the list's moderator that you are interested in joining.

Going on Vacation

If you are away from the Internet for a few days, messages from mailing lists will accumulate. You'll come back and find hundreds upon hundreds of messages in your box. This takes up disk space (which you may have to pay for), and is more information than any human could possibly read.

If you like, however, you can remain subscribed to a list but request that they send you no mail. The command is: *set <mailing-list-name> no mail.*

Again, follow the same general procedure:

```
mail listserv@vm1.nodak.edu
Subject:
set society no mail
```

When you return, you can receive mail by sending the listserver the command: *set <mailing-list-name> mail.*

Mailing Lists Related to Dating

As of now, there are no major mailing lists specifically related to dating. However, the following may be of interest:

The Rainbow Connection. This is for victims of the fated LDR, or long distance relationship. The rainbow connection acts as both a support group and romantic advice network. If you meet your love online, but he or she lives several thousand miles away, this group may be helpful. The group is not for "picking people up." Send a letter asking for info to:

```
rainbow-request@rmit.edu.au
```

Alternates. Advocates of alternate sexual lifestyles—whatever that is, exactly—can meet and discuss here. As you might expect, this is not for the faint of heart or narrow of mind.

```
alternates-request@ns1.rutgers.edu
```

Feminists. A friendly atmosphere to discuss women's issues. Send a letter to the address below containing your full name, e-mail address, and gender. Yes, males are invited to join.

```
femail@hpldlh.hpl.hp.com
```

Men. Here's a list for discussing men's problems and experiences, too. Send mail to:

```
mail-men-request@usl.com
```

Sappho. A "women's only" list for lesbians and bisexuals. Write a letter of introduction to:

```
sappho-request@silver.lcs.mit.edu
```

Mail

Once you are connected to the Internet, you can send e-mail to any one of the millions with Internet access. If you read something by someone interesting, e-mail is the best way to get that person's attention and maintain long-lasting ties.

Most systems tell you if you have any new mail as soon as you log on. If you want to read or write mail, either choose that option from your menu, or type

```
mail
```

If there are letters in your mailbox, you see a list telling you who the letters are from and what their subject is.

Depending on your Internet service provider, you may have to ask to see a list. Try the commands:

```
from
```

or

```
directory
```

Since each Internet site works differently, there is no one way mail is handled. Some systems have easy mouse-driven mail programs (look for programs called POP, Eudora, or Pegasus). Programs such as Elm are not GUIs, but still allow you to use menus and easy commands. Others use a command line interface: a blank screen where you are expected to type in what you want to do. Mailing is a snap once you are familiar with a few basic concepts.

Writing a Letter

This allows you to send someone a message. Typically, you type

```
mail <address>
```

In place of address, you'd type the address (or addresses) of the person you want to reach. To send a letter to Lenny, you'd type *lenny@banana.com* in place of *<address>*.

If the *mail* command doesn't work, try typing

send

by itself and then typing the address when the system asks for it.

Once you address your letter, you see:

Subject:

You can now type a short summary of your message. Try to keep it under fifty characters. If your note is urgent, give it an urgent subject such as *THE FATE OF THE FREE WORLD DEPENDS ON THIS MESSAGE* and it will be more likely to be read first. You may now see a line that looks like this:

cc:

This allows you to send a copy to another user. Just press the (ENTER) key if your message is only meant for one pair of eyes. If you have a party invitation you want to send to four people, *lenny@banana.com; clovelooker@banana.com; hlovelooker@banana.com;* and *klovelooker@reform.gov,* you would go through the following steps:

```
mail lenny@banana.com
Subject: A great party!
cc: clovelooker@banana.com hlovelooker@banana.com
klovelooker@reform.gov
```

Now enter your message, line by line. When you finish typing, press (CTRL)+(D) and your message zooms its way to the proper mailbox. Some text editors require you to press (CTRL)+(Z) or some similar command when your message is done.

If you change your mind while typing a message and decide not to send the letter, you simply press (CTRL)+(C) twice. So, for example, your party invitation could be:

```
Hey fellah, how are you? I was just wondering if you'd be
interested in coming to a party in my neck of the woods this
Sunday. They'll be plenty of horn-tooting and political
philosophizing all around. Bring whatever you can bring, each
man according to his ability. Hope to see you there!
(CTRL)+(D)
```

The letters *EOT* may now appear on your screen. This stands for End of Transmission, and tells you that everything worked the way it should.

Some systems may have fancy text editors, acting like word processors. You can type a message and move around the screen with the arrow keys, editing and inserting text. These usually have their own sets of commands. Often, the commands you need to know (such as saving the letter or aborting it) are printed along the top of your screen. Ask someone at your particular system for more details.

Reading Your Mail

If you have mail waiting for you, upon entering the *mail* command, you should see a list that looks kind of like:

```
*Mail version 2.18 5/19/83. Type ? for help.
"/usr/spool/mail/dsf4185": 4 messages 4 unread
> U 1 lenny@banana.com Fri Apr 13 12:01 4/133 "A Party?"
  U 2 hlovelooker@banana.com Fri Apr 13 16:34 2/237 "Honk"
  U 3 klovelooker@reform.gov Sat Apr 14 11:23 134/
23635 "Let us Unite"
  U 4 clovelooker@banana.com Sat Apr 14 11:24 10/
123 "Whatsa da matta?"
```

This tells you there are four messages waiting, numbered 1, 2, 3, and 4; from lenny, hlovelooker, klovelooker, and clovelooker; the time and date each message arrived; the size of the letter (lines/characters); and the subject. The little arrow (>) points to the next message left unread.

If your mailbox is empty, you see

no mail for <your username>

If you are using a Unix system, you now see an

&

replacing the

%

prompt. This signifies that you are in the mail program. Reading through your mail is simple. To read the next unread message, simply press (ENTER). To read a particular message, type its number. To re-read the previous message, press the minus sign (-). To quit the mail reader, type

quit

Some systems want you to type the word *read* if you are interested in one particular message. For example, to read hlovelooker's message, type

read 2

The easiest way to read mail is to repeatedly press the (ENTER) key. Each message is shown, as in Figure 7-5. If a message is more than one screenful long, you typically have to press either the (SPACEBAR) or (ENTER) to continue.

Mail Headers (The Junk at the Beginning of Letters)

Figure 7-5 shows a typical letter. You may notice that, before you get to the letter itself, there are several lines of what looks like gibberish. This is known as the *header,* and contains

```
& 3
Message 3

Return-path: <lenny@banana.com>
Received: from mail.banana.com by mail.university.edu    (PMDF U4.3-6)
 id <01HBOAFEI7DH55@mail.university.edu); Sat, 15 Apr 1994 01:26:30EDT
Received: from mailserv.banana.com by banana.com for
 redhead@university.edu Sun, 16 Apr 94 00:26:41 CDT
Date: Sun, 16 Apr 1994 00:26:32 -0500 (CDT)
From: lenny lovelooker <lenny@banana.com>
Subject: Pleased to make your acquaintance!
To: redhead@university.edu
Cc:
Message-id: <CMM.1.90.4.763454534.lenny@banana.com>
Content-transfer-encoding: 7BIT

I can't believe you've actually seen some of my movies. So what do you
think of them? I sure have a talent huh? (Just let me know when you
find it!) No, really-- it was nice to "meet" you in IRC the other
night. I never knew anybody could be as snide as I! So tell me some
more about you, I mean, all I know is that you have red hair (and I
don't even know *that*, if truth be told, though I'll give you the
benefit of the doubt.)
→
```

FIGURE 7-5 Reading Internet e-mail

technical information listing the networks the letter came from and got routed through, and what times this all took place. Only two things should interest you:

- *From* tells you who sent the message. Sometimes the person's real name is in parentheses, but the address will always be prominent—remember, the address is always in the form *<username>@<systemname>*. Remember the address, write it down, print it out! If you ever want to mail this person back you'll need to know where to write.

- *Subject* is a summary of what the letter is about. This is a good way to separate junk mail (from mailing lists) and important mail (from your future wife or husband).

Also note that when the Internet talks about *time,* it refers to 24-hour military Greenwich Mean Time.

Cleaning Up

Every letter you get is stored on a computer somewhere, taking up space. Some networks may charge you for how much space you use, or give you a limited amount of room. In any case, computers may crash and your mail may be lost. It always pays to print out your mail, or download it, and then be rid of it.

To delete a message, once you've read it, type

```
delete
```

This deletes the current message. You can delete a group of messages by specifying the range. For example to delete messages 2 through 4, you can type

```
delete 2-4
```

To delete only message number 2, type

```
delete 2
```

Oh No!

If you accidentally delete a message before you read it, you can undelete it with the

```
undelete
```

command. This works in the same way as the *delete* command; you can specify a particular message number or a range of numbers. You must use *undelete* immediately after making your mistake. If you *quit* the mail program all your deleted mail is gone with the cyberwind.

Replying to a Letter

Suppose Lenny sent you a letter. You press (ENTER) and see

```
From lenny@banana.com Fri Apr 13 12:01:02 1994
Received: from server.nyu.edu by mail.nyu.edu
id HD236726 to dsf4185; Fri Apr 13 11:34:33 1994
Date: Fri, 13 Apr 94 12:01:02 PST
From: lenny@banana.com (Lenny Lovelooker)
MessageOId: <2773646525.HD236726@banana>
To: dsf4185@acfcluster.nyu.edu
Subject: A party?
Status: R

I wouldn't come to your party if wild horses dragged me. Heck, I
wouldn't come even on a pony ride.

--Lenny
```

Replying to a letter couldn't be simpler. All you have to do is type, immediately after reading the letter:

```
reply
```

EXPERT TIP

If you understand how Unix files work, you can save the letter, or a group of letters, to your personal directory by typing

```
save
```

to store the current letter. Store letters 1 through 4 by typing

```
save 1-4
```

Now you can begin typing your message. It is automatically sent to the person whose letter you just read. The letters Re: are automatically added to the subject. The letter to Lenny, for instance, would have a subject header: *Re: A Party?*

Again, you type your message and then press (CTRL)+(D) to zip your reply away. Don't be hot tempered. It's the same as regular mail; once you send a letter there is nothing you can do but wait for a response.

```
Who wanted you anyway, you big grouch?
```
(CTRL)+(D)
```
EOT
```

Text Editor Help

There are many more mail commands, allowing you to forward mail, send blind copies of mail to certain people (recipients will not know who received a carbon copy), save mail, and so on. Explore your mail system and its text editor to see what's available. If you get stuck, try typing

```
help
```

or the question mark: (?)

Return to Sender

Elvis isn't the only one who has postal problems. If a letter you send comes back with some strange message about *Unknown Domain,* your mail has been bounced. This means the address you sent to couldn't be found.

You might have sent your mail to the wrong address. It's easy to make typos with such strange addresses. Double check.

Another possibility is that some mail is sent only locally. If your "Internet provider" isn't fully on the Internet, you might need to tell the "mailman" to specifically carry the letter over an Internet gateway. To do this, you surround the address in quotes and precede it with the tag: *in%.* For example, if you want to send a letter to *lenny@banana.com,* try typing

```
mail in%"lenny@banana.com"
```

Chat

It is during live interactive telecommunication—also known as chatting—when the Internet shows its human side. Whether you're interested in going one-on-one with your long-distance sweetheart or being in a roomful of people from South America, the Internet chat resources are definitely worth talking about.

Net-Talk

This is something like talking without a voice. Talking to any person on the Internet is surprisingly easy. If your system has the *talk* command, you can page anyone instantly and then converse in a split-screen format. A horizontal line is drawn across the middle of the screen. Everything you type, as you type it, appears on the top half of your screen; everything your date types instantly appears on the bottom.

Though conversations with net-talk are slower than over a telephone, you can be more poetic and you never miss a single word. Also, it's much cheaper—especially if you have an all-night-long date with a guy from Shanghai.

You must know a person's address to start a conversation. To page your pal Lenny, for instance, you'd type

```
talk lenny@banana.com
```

If Lenny is currently working on the Internet his computer beeps and he gets the message:

```
Message from talk_Daemon@banana.com at 23:12 . . .
talk: connection requested by redhead@university.edu,
talk: respond with: talk redhead@university.edu
```

If Lenny is logged on to the Internet but away from his computer, his system automatically beeps him every ten seconds or so. For each beep, you see the message:

```
[Ringing your party again]
```

If you beep him for a while and still get no response, type (CTRL)+(C) to give up.

If Lenny is not logged on to the Internet, or if *lenny* does not exist at *banana.com,* you see the straightforward message:

```
[Your party is not logged on.]
```

If *banana.com* itself does not exist, or does not have the capability to talk, you see:

```
banana.com is an unknown host
```

Always double-check your spelling if there is a problem.

If Lenny is busy and cannot talk, he might have asked his system to ignore any talk requests. If so, you would see:

```
[your party is refusing messages.]
```

You can refuse messages of your own with the *mesg* command. If you want no messages, type

    mesg n

To re-allow messages, type

    mesg y

If Lenny is busy or not available, it's a good idea to send him some e-mail telling him to beep you when he gets a chance, or to set up a mutually convenient date and time to chat. E-mail, unlike chatting, is not bound by the dimension of time.

When Lenny finally rings you back, you see the message:

    Message from talk_Daemon@university.edu at 23:59 . . .
    talk: connection requested by lenny@banana.com,
    talk: respond with: talk lenny@banana.com

Simply follow the instructions and type

    talk lenny@banana.com

You and Lenny will be exchanging insults in no time.

Talking

If all goes well, you see the message:

    [Connection established]

and may now begin typing. Talk works like a simple line-by-line text editor. You can use CTRL+W to erase a word or CTRL+U to delete an entire line. If somebody else tries paging you, or you get new mail, or something happens to mess up the screen (somebody picked up your telephone), you can type CTRL+L to refresh the display. A typical talk session may look like Figure 7-6.

Treat the talk session like real conversation. If you insult your date and then change your mind and backspace over the remark it makes no difference. Your date has already read your insult as it was typed and is in tears.

Don't worry about spelling. It's too slow to correct each typo. You'll be amazed how well people can decipher each other's misprints. See Chapter 3, The Meet Market, for a list of common abbreviations and smiley-signs to help you communicate even faster.

Many talk programs automatically start a word on a new line if you are at the end of the screen, so just type as fast your fingers can carry you. Remember, you're not writing the Constitution (or even a book about online dating)—you're *talking*.

```
Hey, Lenny, glad I finally got a hold of you.
Heh heh, always joking around, aren't you, Lenny? Anyway, we need to talk.
Now, now, Lenny, you mentioned something about voiding out our contract.
It is? Why?
The _what_?
Oh, come on, Lenny, you can't fool me. Everybody knows that there is no such
thing as Sanity Clause.



TALK 3.3(10)    --------------[Connection Established]-----------------------
I'm so thrilled I could light my eyebrows on fire.
Maybe you need to talk. You can use a face lift while you're at it.
Oh the contract, eh? Yeah, it's null and void now.
Well since you're a little crazy, as anybody can see, the conract is voided
due to the sanity clause.
The sanity clause.
```

FIGURE 7-6 "Talking" up a storm

When you are finished with your gab session, it's considered good manners to tell your date:

I have to go now. BYE?

If he or she agrees, one of you needs to type (CTRL)+(C). This is the cyberspace equivalent of hanging up the phone; if you are talking to someone special, it is just as difficult.

When one of you gets the courage to disconnect you see the message:

[Connection closed. Exiting.]

New Talk

Most Internet computers are as friendly as the people sitting behind them. But sometimes there are communication problems. A Unix system, for instance, talks in a slightly different dialect than an IBM or Macintosh. If you try talking to someone, but all you see is this message stuck on the screen for several minutes:

[Checking for invitation on caller's machine]

it means your talk programs are not compatible. There is a command, however, that makes almost all systems friendly. This is *ntalk,* which works just like the *talk* command. In fact, on many systems, when you use the *talk* program you are actually using *ntalk.* So, to talk to Lenny, you'd type

ntalk lenny@banana.com

and he would respond with:

ntalk <your address here>

If talking still doesn't work, don't despair. You and your date can always talk on a MUD or a MOO (see the next main section). Or, better yet, you can create a private channel on the Internet Relay Chat and gab to your heart's content.

Internet Relay Chat (IRC)

Imagine a social club or pub with hundreds of tables. Around each table people are chatting, telling each other jokes, and flirting and making dates. Each table attracts a particular type of person. There are tables just for Spanish speakers, tables for people who want to discuss computer games, nuclear physics, tables for those who want only erotic talk.

This is IRC, the Internet Relay Chat, a public chat system. Once you enter the world of IRC, you can wander from table to table, eavesdropping. You can just listen, talk publicly, or whisper a message to one particular person. Each table, or channel, has one or more people waiting by it. Some tables are private, encased in soundproof domes. The last time I used IRC, sometime in the middle of the night, there were 681 channels with 1,417 users. It was a slow night.

On IRC you can shed your messy Internet address. You can choose whatever nickname you like—up to nine letters long. To start IRC, find it on your menu or type *irc <nickname>*. For instance, if you'd like to be known as "Lenny," type

`irc Lenny`

You are now in the chat system, as shown in Figure 7-7. Every IRC command begins with a slash (/). For example, to see a list of all commands, type

`/help`

You are shown more commands than you'd ever care to know. The first time you use IRC, type

`/help intro`

EXPERT TIP

If you do not have IRC on your system, you can telnet to it. Try:

`telnet bradenville.andrew.cmu.edu`

or

`telnet ara.kaist.ac.kr`

Log on as

`irc`

```
(TrjnHorse) you?
(dudette) narkoes:s so are you a ned or law student?    or are you undergrad?
(Sher) Alison: where are you??
(TrjnHorse) heya anias
(Orion) Well, last I saw one I did
*** Change: san (~sanja@Mercury.ncs.com) has joined channel #chat
> Hello!
(_pjotr) Alison: What's the population of your city then? Mine (called 'Sneek')
has about 15000 people living here...
(_Icenan_) Th:just chilling.
(san) hi all
*** Change: san has left Channel #chat
(narkoes) dudette: ned, ... i'n gonna operate on you soneday
(Alison) -pjotr : i don't really know
(dudette) narkoes: what a scary thought!
(Orion) Jesus, yours worse than our 40000. pjotr
*** Change: ice (plaw@ganymede.cs.mun.ca) has joined channel #chat
(ice) hey icenan
(narkoes) dudette: don't you trust me?????
(Sher) Alison: Where are you?
(_Icenan_) yo.
(_pjotr) Orion: And they say our town is a big one in Holland :)
*** Change: ice has left Channel #chat
```

FIGURE 7-7 Swimming through the IRC

and

    /help newuser

for helpful hints.

Following is an explanation of the basic commands you need to get around IRC, summarized in Table 7-10. Be aware that some systems require you to type all commands in UPPER CASE. Don't forget to precede each command with a slash.

You now want to tune in to a channel which interests you. Each channel has a short name, and some have longer descriptions. There are channels in all languages.

COMMAND	FUNCTION
/help	Shows the help screen.
/list	Lists all the active channels you can join.
/who <channel>	Tells you who is on channel <channel>.
/join <channel>	Joins channel <channel>.
/me <action>	Performs the action <action>.
/leave <channel>	Leaves channel <channel>.
/nick <nickname>	Changes your nickname to <nickname>.
/msg <person> <message>	Sends a brief message <message> to the person <person>.
/query <person>	Enables a private chat with person <person>.
/mode * +pi	Makes the current channel private.

TABLE 7-10 All the basic IRC commands you need to know to have a great chat

Public channels usually begin with the pound sign (#). You can join a channel already in existence or create your own and wait for people to approach and mingle. To see what channels are available, you can type

```
/list
```

to list the channel topics, the number of people on each channel, and a brief description. This list is very, very long and scrolls by faster than you can see. A better idea is to list only the channels that have at least, say, five people. To do so, you type

```
/list -min 5
```

Popular channels to join are: *#talk*, *#hottub*, *#pub*, *#sex*, *#30plus*, and *#ms0*. If a channel does not begin with # then it is private and you have to be invited into it.

To see who is in a channel you can type */who <channelname>*. For instance:

```
/who #talk
```

Be careful not to enter */who* by itself, or you may have to wait minutes upon minutes while a listing of every IRC chatter scrolls by.

To join a channel that interests you, simply type */join <channelname>*. For instance:

```
/join #talk
```

Remember, you can also specify a channel name of your own and it is automatically created.

If your channel already has people on it, their conversation appears on your screen, much like a script:

```
*** Lenny (lenny@banana.com) has joined channel #talk
> Hello everyone.
<KittyKat> Hi Lenny.
* Redhead curtseys.
<George> Hello, Len my man.
<KittyKat> I am so unbelievably happy.
<George>Oh yeah? I have that effect on people.
<Readhead> Yeah right.
<KittyKat> No really. I just won a hundred bucks in the lottery.
<George> Ooo. A hundred bucks. Rich woman. You know my birthday
<George> is coming up soon . . .
<KittyKat> What should I spend it on?
<Redhead> Internet access, of course!
> If you send it to me, I'd be glad to invest it. *smirk*
```

To say something, just type it. Everything you say is preceded by a >. Other people see:

```
<Lenny> If you send it to me, I'd be glad to invest it. *smirk*
```

If you would like to perform an action, you use the */me <action>* command. For instance:

```
/me dribbles his eyebrows.
```

EXPERT TIP

It's a good idea to use the same nickname each time. This way, people you've met before will know who you are and recognize you on "sight."
You can automatically register your nickname with IRC's nickname service. To read about how to use the nickname server, type

```
/msg nickserv@service.de intro
```

Everyone in your channel sees

```
* Lenny dribbles his eyebrows.
```

Sometimes, due to the tremendous number of people using IRC, there are time lags, and responses may come turtle-slow. If this happens, people may get a topic or two ahead of themselves. Be patient. It takes a little while to get used to IRC, since there are often many conversations going at once. Give it time. It's like walking into the center of a crowded party and trying to listen to just one person talk.

When you are ready to leave a channel, simply type *leave <channelname>*:

```
/leave #talk
```

You can change your nickname at any time. To do so, type *nick <new-nickname>*. If you suddenly feel studly, and want to be known as Studs, you type

```
/nick Studs
```

All the people tuned to your channel (including you) see:

```
*** Lenny is now known as Studs
```

The *msg* message command comes in handy if you want to whisper to just one person. For instance, if you've met Redhead once before, you could type

```
/msg redhead Hey remember me from last time?
```

You see:

```
-> Hey remember me from last time?
```

Redhead sees:

```
*Lenny* Hey remember me from last time?
```

Redhead could be on any channel, even a private one. She still gets the message. If she wants to respond to you, she would type

```
/msg , Sure I do. How are you doing?
```

The comma indicates that Redhead's statement is sent to the last person who sent her a private message—that is, you!

You can create a private channel built-for-two, if you so desire. You must come up with a unique channel name and then send a /msg to your date, asking him or her to join you on your new channel. Supposed you decided on the name *Lennyism*. Type

```
/join #Lennyism
```

#Lennyism is now created. Once your date arrives, you can make the channel private by issuing the command:

```
/mode * +pi
```

You two are now alone together and safe. Very romantic, eh?

If you want to talk only to Redhead, you can tell IRC this by typing

```
/query redhead
```

You are still a part of your channel, and can still see all conversation, but anything you type is seen only by Redhead. You can also query multiple names, for three-way conversations:

```
/query redhead,george
```

When you want to talk publicly again, you simply type

```
/query
```

by itself. Now everyone in your channel sees what you type.

Internet Extras

As if thousands of newsgroups, vast e-mail, and tons of chat channels weren't enough, the Internet has several additional perks that can make cyberspace highly addictive. These include MUDs, MOOs, and BBSs.

Playing in the MUDs

Yes, my significant other and I met through the Internet (although we were only 2 hours apart so it wasn't as difficult as some I've known). We both played on a MUD game based in his city, and since we were both high level wizards, we spoke frequently. We started going out, and 6 months later, I moved in with him. We've now been living together for a year and plan all the love things of the future . . . buying a car (after upgrading our computer again . . . ;)), getting married, buying a house . . . and perhaps even having kids. My mom said I spent too much time on the computer, and she's probably right. I wouldn't trade in my SO for more time off the computer, though . . . .

The fancy name is Multiple User Dimension (or Dungeon). MUDs are an example of text-based virtual reality. All these fancy words amount to one thing: pure, unbridled, addictive, people-meeting fun.

MUDs are role-playing games with real-life characters. Much like listening to an old radio drama, all the action occurs in the mind. MUDs are a strange new world where you can dress up as who or whatever you like. You move from room to room and have the room described in detail for you. You can talk to any of the people or creatures in the room, and they talk back. You can even fight with them. You can do nearly anything your imagination can come up with. The people you meet along the way are not computer programs—they are other Internet users.

It's like Halloween at a singles bar. Beware here. Many men masquerade as women, and vice versa. In fact, many MUDs have genders that extend beyond that, such as elves, demons, or aliens. People are sometimes crass, but always funny. The most introverted of people can live out fantasies here.

The one disadvantage is that MUDs are not usually the best places to find long-term relationships. You can ask people for their addresses, but many will be hesitant to tell you. Actors become so caught up in the illusion, they often forget about the outside world. You may have read a fantasy novel—but until you have MUDed, you haven't been inside one.

To enter a MUD, you need to telnet there. See the Listing of Virtual Realities section later in this chapter. Usually the first thing you do upon entering a MUD is to type

```
register <character name> <password>
```

For instance, if you want to be known as Lenny, with the password "banana," type

```
register Lenny banana
```

On some systems, you may have to register through e-mail. You usually get a password mailed to you within seconds. The next time you call up the MUD, all you have to do to assume your old character is:

```
connect Lenny banana
```

or some equivalent command.

Alternatively, most MUDs allow you guest access, allowing you to take a tour to see if you want to register as a permanent member. Read each MUD's opening screen for details.

Every MUD has its own set of commands. The goal of some MUDs is to win a race or collect a treasure. The goal of some other more violent MUDs is simply to survive. Some MUDs even allow you to program in your own description and to create worlds of your own. All you really need to know to explore a MUD, though, is the following:

Type

```
l
```

or

```
look
```

to get the description of your current room. (Everything, even a forest, is referred to as a room.) For example, you may see:

```
The Church
There is an altar set up here, with two lone candles flickering.
There is a large bible to the side, atop an intricately carved
pulpit. To the right there is a long rope. There's a closed door
to the east. Ahead you can see a stairwell, which you imagine
leads to the crypt. Behind the chorale, to the west, there is a
long, sun-lighted hallway.
Obvious exits are to the north and west.
Redhead, Lenny, Lizard of Oz, and Moosehead are here.
```

You can now visualize the screen. Based on what you are told, you can move *n* (*north*), *s* (*south*), *e* (*east*), *w* (*west*), *u* (*up*), or *d* (*down*). On some MUDs typing

```
nw
```

moves northwest, allowing for even more movement options.

Typing

```
help <topic>
```

usually tells you exactly what you are allowed to do. For example, typing

```
help commands
```

provides an index of available commands. You can then read further help by typing *help <name of command>*. Each MUD has its own set of commands, so don't be afraid to experiment and explore.

Typing *e* or *examine,* for example, usually examines an object in detail. You can examine rooms, articles, or even people. For instance:

```
examine Redhead
```

would describe the Redhead character for you (if one existed in the room you were currently in), telling you her sex, what objects she is carrying, and what she looks like. You can also *r* (*read*) things, *t* (*take*) things, *d* (*drop*) them, *g* (*give*) them, or *u* (*use*) them.

Most important, though, are the communication commands. To say something that everybody in the current room can hear, type *say* or the quotation mark ("). For instance, typing

```
"I am the black knight and can't wait until mourning.
```

causes the following message to be printed on every MUDer's screen:

```
Lenny says, "I am the black knight and can't wait until mourning."
```

You can also emote, or express some sort of action, using the *emote* or colon (:) command. For example:

```
:runs around in circles and collapses.
```

causes the following message to be printed on every MUDer's screen:

> `Lenny runs around in circles and collapses.`

You can *whisper* something private to someone, if you desire. The typical format for this is *whisper "<message>" to <person's name>*. For example:

> `whisper "Meet me in the emerald forest." to Redhead`

Only Redhead would see this message. If Redhead whispers back to you, you see: ·

> `Redhead whispers in your ear, "You want to trap me alone in the`
> `forest, huh? What do you have in mind? *wink*"`

Last, you can *page* someone, even if you're not in the same room. The typical format for this is *page <person's name> <message>*. For example:

> `page redhead "Hey, let's find someplace to chat privately!"`

Only Redhead sees this message. If Redhead pages you back, you see something like

> `Redhead pages you: "How about my place?"`

Milking the MOOs

MOOs—MUDs Object-Oriented—are the next generation of MUDs. MOOs not only have rooms, characters, and props, they have detailed layers of each. You can get complex in a MOO. You can create your own custom nouns, verbs, or adjectives. Many people build their own houses—complete with rooms, decorations, and furnishings—with special locks to make them private.

Since most MOOers have their own cyber-singles-pads, if you're in a crowded hot tub and talking to somebody you find interesting, you may want to invite that person to speak in a more intimate setting. It puts a whole new spin on the "Your place or mine?" line.

Commands in MOOs are constantly growing and changing. You can use the basic MUD commands, listed above, to move around and communicate. But a MOO room may have strange exits. For instance, *go elevator* or *go trapdoor*. Or you may have to *smash button* to activate a secret trap door. MOOs may also have very specific verbs, such as *undress* or *tickle*.

Many universal MOO commands begin with the at sign (@). These allow you to do things like follow people, teleport to any room, search for someone, or program in your own objects.

With a MOO, when you read a description, you can examine parts of that description even further. For instance, one popular MOO room contains a large mural of a circus scene. It mentions specifically that there is a painting of a seal balancing a big red ball on its nose. If you type

> `examine red ball`

EXPERT TIP

An easy-to-use service automatically mails you a list of more MUDs, MOOs, MUSHs, and MUSEs than you'd ever know what to do with. Simply send mail (it can be a blank letter) to

`mudlist@aug3.augsburg.edu`

you are told that the ball is actually a button. You also get a list of verbs you can use on the ball. Pushing the button has no effect, but

whomp red ball

causes a panel on the north wall to slide away, revealing an exit.

Most MOOs have a tutorial or sample obstacle course for beginners. Try

help tutorial

also try

news

for basic information.

Another popular variation of a MUD is a MUSE (Multi-User Simulated Environment). You may also see MUSHs, MUCKs, DIKUs and other such systems. They all amount to basically the same thing: highly addictive fantasy life.

LambdaMOO is one of the most noteworthy social MOOs. It's located deep in a research computer at the Xerox corporation. (Figure 7-8 shows a typical screen.) The Lambda

```
The Hot Tub
The hot tub is made of molded fiberglass: on three sides a bench will seat
   five comfortably (and ten who are friendly), and on the fourth side there is
   contoured couch for one luxurious soak.  There are two rubber mounted buttons
   here.  You may push either the right or left button.  The bright sunlight
   glinting off the water makes you squint.  The underwater light is on.
You see TubToy, Sisal's Place, The Hot Tub Pub, Acme(tn) Blatantly Obvious
   Listening Device, Has Anyone Heard Of Robotech, Nude Beach, Woo-woo document,
   David Bowie, The Alter Ego of WolfrunXen, a red ticket numbered #24, and
   shark cage here.
Syren, Trinity (practicing random acts of weirdness), Plaid_Guest, Rocker
   (dozing), Palli, Pink_Guest, Technicolor_Guest, and Infrared_Guest are here.
Infrared_Guest waves.
Splash!
Pink_Guest so
A scientific calculator flies into the room, hits the wall, and smashes into
   itty bitty bits. This procedure is soon followed by Are.
Splash!
Are says, "hello people"
"Howdy"
Csoul teleports in.
Technicolor_Guest ducks and maneuvers around Csoul's shot.
You say, "Howdy"
```

FIGURE 7-8 Boiling in the hot tub at LambdaMOO

city is large and always crowded, with most of the action taking place in the cozy Lambda lodge. There is even a sundeck with a swimming pool and hot tub. Lambda can be as complex or as simple as you want to make it—you can just hang out in the living room chatting, or you can explore vast jungles, mountains, and deserts. Once you get used to the MOO commands, you can build your own rooms, objects, and even verbs. You can find Lambda on the Gopher or telnet there by typing

```
telnet lambda.parc.xerox.com 8888
```

Listing of Virtual Realities

The best way to find a virtual reality is with the Gopher. Use Veronica to search for the word *MUD* or *MOO*. A huge list of choices presents itself.

Also, read the Usenet newsgroup *rec.games.mud.announce*. This discusses the best MUDs and tells you how to connect. A huge, excellent list of MUDs is updated weekly. Table 7-11 has a few MUDs to wallow in. To connect, simply type:

```
telnet <systemname> <port>
```

Bulletin Boards

There is a vast selection of BBSs connected to the Internet. See Chapter 6 for details on what a BBS offers.

Using Gopher's Veronica, search for the term:

```
BBS
```

A huge list appears, including listings of lists. You can explore to your heart's content. Many are explicitly suited for online dating and romance; see Table 7-12. Also, try *telnet*ing to some of the networks in Appendix B—many specialize in much more than mere Internet access.

Once you know a particular network's name, *telnet* there by typing

```
telnet <systemname> <port>
```

With many systems, you do not need to designate a port.

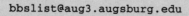

EXPERT TIP

An even easier way to get a huge list of Internet BBSs is to send mail to:

```
bbslist@aug3.augsburg.edu
```

It doesn't matter what your message says. It can even be a blank letter. This is a convenient service that automatically mails you the listing.

NAME	<SYSTEMNAME>	<PORT>
ACTLab	actlab.rtf.utexas.edu	6889
AFserv	pa.itd.com	6889
Amber	amber.ecst.csuchico.edu	6889
Albion Mud	veda.is	4000
AbsolutMUD	b63740.student.cwru.edu	4000
Abyss II	helpmac.its.mcw.edu	8888
Aldara	thrash.isca.uiowa.edu	4000
AlexMUD	marcel.stacken.kth.se	4000
Apocalypse IV	peabrain.humgen.upenn.edu	4000
Arctic	hobbes.linfield.edu	2700
BurningDIKU	next5.cas.muohio.edu	4000
Groan CoolMud	groan.berkeley.edu	8888
Copper Diku	copper.denver.colorado.edu	4000
Crimson	gpx.lis.uiuc.edu	4000
DIRT	alkymene.uio.no	6715
Eclipse MUD	uhs-2.bsd.uchicago.edu	6715
Goonsquad	goonsquad.spies.com	2002
Mirage	agean.nmt.edu	6715
Mustang	mustang.us.dell.com	9173
Northern Light	aber.ludd.luth.se	6715
PaderMUD	padermud.uni-paderborn.de	3000
Sleepless Nights	cs3.brookes.ac.uk	6789
Terradome	cms.brookes.ac.uk	8888
Regenesis	birka.lysator.liu.se	7475

TABLE 7-11 A small fraction of "invisible" virtual realities: MUDs and MOOs

Once connected, you can usually log on as *guest* or *new*. Most BBSs have an opening screen guiding you through the steps. Table 7-12 has 20 amorous and user-packed BBSs to get you started.

NAME	<SYSTEMNAME>	<PORT>	FEATURES
After Five	af.itd.com		adult chat
Bad Boys' Inn	baboy.aue.com		boards, talk
Chess Servers	rafael.metiu.ucsb.edu	5000	online chess
	bentley.daimi.aau.dk	5000	
	ics.uoknor.edu port		
Cleveland Freenet	cwns16.ins.cwru.edu		many conferences
Go Server	shellspark.wharton.upenn.edu		go (Japanese national boardgame)
	flamingo.pasteur.fr		
	bsdserver.ucsf.edu		
Eagles Nest	seabass.st.usm.edu		chat rooms
Endless Forest	orest.unomaha.edu	2001	bohemian hangout
FootHills	marble.bu.edu	2010	chat service
IDS World Net	idsvax.ids.risc.net		games, chatting
Isca	bbs.isca.uiowa.edu		many topics
Leaky House	upsun.up.edu	4000	chat service
M-Net	hermes.merit.edu		party line chat
Olohof's BBS	morra.et.tudelft.nl	2993	chat service
The Picayune	milo.ndsu.nodak.edu		games, messages
Quartz	quartz.rutgers.edu		many discussion boards
The Ragged Edge	wagner.musicnet.ua.edu		diverse topics
Softwords	softwords.bc.ca		online chat
Sparcs BBS	ara.kaist.ac.kr		boards, talk
Tele-Chat	speedway.net	7777	chat service
Virginia Tech	vtcosy.cns.vt.edu		many boards, college chat
Virtual Campus	indigo.lut.ac.uk	5000	chat service

TABLE 7-12 Internet BBSs

Internet Epilogue

The Internet epitomizes what being online is all about. Hundreds of couples have met on the Internet, as have countless numbers of friends and professional contacts. As long as you are connected to the Internet, you'll never be alone; there are round-the-clock messages to read, people to write to, and plenty of lively chatter.

Navigating the Internet is a little complex. This chapter reviewed the basics, but if you find yourself wanting to be more of an Internet aficionado, try The Waite Group's excellent *Internet How-To* reference.

Since networks, software, connections, addresses, and commands are always changing, you (and everyone else) may often feel clumsy as you try to find what you're looking for. You may even feel so bogged down with resources and places to explore that you won't know where to begin. For what it is, however—a continuous free flow of information between millions of people worldwide—the Internet is nothing short of miraculous.

AMERICA ONLINE

800-827-6364
8619 WESTWOOD CENTER DRIVE
VIENNA VA 22182

HERR FIXIT AND I MET ON AMERICA ONLINE

in October 1990. We met in person in November. We continued to talk via phone and online, and in February I moved from Philadelphia to California to be with him. Later that year we moved back to the East Coast. On October 31, 1992 we got married in real life. We decided to have an online wedding the night before our offline one so our friends who couldn't make it could celebrate with us in our time of happiness. The vows that Fixit and I spoke to each other on America Online are the same ones we spoke in our real live wedding. (See the end of this chapter.)

What It Is

America Online (AOL) is a dazzling, colorful service. Completely mouse-driven, AOL is fervently user friendly. Little cartoon-like icons guide you through every nook of the online terrain.

AOL connects your computer to expert technical help, the Internet, business advice, libraries full of software, daily news, stock quotes, encyclopedias, and other typical online conveniences. But, more importantly, America Online is just that: more than 9 million users from all over the United States, all searching for company, interaction, and often romance.

AOL boasts one of the online world's friendliest and busiest chat arenas—the People Connection. No matter where your interests may lie, there's usually an associated *chat room* holding scheduled seminars and discussions as well as spontaneous dialogue. With emphasis on live talking, it's easy to see how close friendships can be kindled on AOL.

America Online is pretty much limited to users calling from the United States. Due to its growing popularity, local numbers are often busy or choppy, especially on late evenings and weekends. Phone connections are often interrupted and, at times, broken.

The biggest problem with America Online is having too much fun, losing track of online time, and running up big bills.

How to Connect

Because of America Online's easy-to-use graphical menus, special software is required. Luckily, everything you need to connect to AOL is offered free of charge; you don't even have to shell out shipping and handling. You can receive software for your MS-DOS IBM computer, for Microsoft Windows, the Macintosh, or the Apple II GS; you may select either 3½-inch or 5¼-inch diskette format.

If you have an IBM, order the Windows version of AOL if you have a 80386 computer or better, at least 4 megabytes of memory, a VGA monitor, a mouse, and a working copy of Windows version 3.1. In any case, you need a mouse to navigate through the AOL departments.

To order the software, simply call 800-827-6364 (703-893-6288 in Alaska and Hawaii), and ask about the free trial offer. You are mailed a compact package complete with your diskette and registration certificate.

The Software

America Online is a cinch to set up and operate. Although there are slight variations in how the AOL software operates from computer to computer, the basic navigation remains the same. The author used the Windows version of the AOL software.

Windows

The Windows version of AOL has the colorful icons and easy control that Windows users have come to expect. The software has a *command ribbon* feature, which graphically displays popular commands across the top of the screen.

To install, insert the disk into the floppy drive. Select Run from the File pull-down menu in the Windows Program Manager and type

```
a:setup
```

and click OK. If your computer has two floppy drives, you may have to substitute

```
b:setup
```

DOS

This version is for IBM PCs and compatibles that use DOS without Windows. Installing is just as easy. America Online makes use of a Windows-like background called GEOS. Insert the floppy disk in the drive and then access the drive containing the AOL disk by typing either

```
A: ENTER
```

or

```
B: ENTER
```

at the DOS prompt. To get everything copied onto your hard disk and set up, simply type

```
install ENTER
```

Macintosh

Insert the disk into the drive. You may have to double-click on the AOL disk icon. Double-click on the *Install* icon when the AOL folder pops up. That's all!

Apple II

Insert the disk in the drive and type

```
aol ENTER
```

Charges

The first month you use America Online, you're allowed five to ten hours of free use, depending on AOL's current membership offer. Once you become a regular member, you have access to all of AOL's services for $9.95 a month, entitling you to five hours of use.

After those hours pass, it's an additional $3.50 an hour. Use the keyword *time* to check out how long you've been online. Your up-to-the-minute bill can be viewed by using the *billing* keyword. (Keywords are explained later, in the Getting Around section.)

Unlike many other services, America Online doesn't charge you extra for certain departments. There are no surcharges (unless you call from outside the continental United States), and you can call up any time of day at the same hourly price.

You must have a major credit card (VISA, MasterCard, Discover, or American Express) or a checking account number to sign on.

Logging On

The first time you run the America Online software, it automatically sets up an account for you. Simply follow the instructions, using the mouse to click on the appropriate buttons. The software is configured to fit your system's abilities. Be sure your modem is on, because AOL automatically dials up an 800 number to locate your two closest public data networks (see Chapter 5, Buckling Up).

You should then see a screen with a touch-tone keypad, a detached cable, and a golden key. The keypad glows as your modem dials, the cable glows as you connect to the service, and the key lights up as your password information is checked. It may seem like a lot is happening; just sit back and enjoy the ride.

If your local access number is busy, or if there was some problem connecting, click on Sign On to try again. Click on Setup to fiddle around with the particulars, such as inserting special dialing commands. For instance, some business phones require the number 9 be dialed first, to secure an outside line. You can also use the Setup area to automatically disable call waiting.

Your America Online startup kit should include a registration certificate. You are asked for your registration code. Type it in the space provided, exactly as it appears on your certificate. Press ⟨TAB⟩ to move into the next blank area, known as a *field*. Alternatively, you can access a new field simply by clicking inside it. Once you are within a field, type your temporary password, which is also printed on the registration certificate.

EXPERT TIP

If you ever move to a new area code or upgrade from a 2400- to a 9600-baud modem, you have to have the AOL software learn your new local access number. Click on the "AOL On the Road/Access Number List" selection in the Member's Online Support area (keyword *help*). From here select the "Search Access Numbers" option. If you're in Alaska, Hawaii, or Canada, click the Help menu for local access numbers. Note the hefty surcharges!

Since America Online is an ever-changing service, new departments and graphics are added all the time. The version of software you have may not be the most recent. If not, you have to wait a few minutes while AOL automatically sends you the appropriate files and installs them.

To proceed, you have to enter your billing information. Select the credit card you'll be using and enter its number.

Everyone on America Online is known by a three to ten-character *screen name*. You may now choose yours. If your name is not unique, AOL adds a number onto the end of it. You can either try to think up a less common name, or you can approve your first choice.

You now have to enter a password of your choice (four to eight characters) in both the spaces provided. Type the word, press (TAB), and type the word again.

The next time you call America Online, signing on is simple. If you are using the Windows version of AOL, type your password in the space provided; other AOL users are asked to type in their password a little later. Now click on the Sign On button. That's all! The software dials your local access number and warps you online.

Logging Off

To log off, simply select the Exit option from the File menu. Depending on which version of AOL you're using, the system may ask if you'd like to Download the files in your File Manager (files you've previously marked for retrieval). You are then asked if you want to sign off temporarily—in case another member of your family wants to sign on—or exit the entire application. Click on the appropriate option.

Getting Around

If you are familiar at all with the Macintosh or Windows environments, you already know how to use America Online. See the Wise GUIs section in Chapter 4, The Datemobile. Table 8-1 lists the various icons you may come across. When a list of options appears, these icons usually precede each item. This way, you know exactly where you're heading, quickly and easily.

You always get more than one doorway into a particular America Online section. Buttons are strategically placed, so that you can navigate the service by whimsical interest. For instance, the main Discover AOL window has a button with a picture of two hearts entwined: America Online Highlights. Click on it, and you get a ever-changing list of AOL's latest features. Click on one of these features, and you go to it. Click on a picture of a microphone, and you can talk live with other users. Click on a disk and you can download software relevant to the area you are currently in. Click on a notepad and you can write messages.

One of the easiest ways to get where you're going is to search the Directory of Services, under the Go To pull-down menu. Simply click on Search The Directory of Services and then type in the word or words best fitting the topic you're interested in. A list of potential areas appears. For example, if you wanted to find areas relevant to dating, you would type

`dating`

and one item appears: The Romance Connection. Double-click on an item to read more about it. Click on Go to take an express train there.

As you browse through AOL, you may come across long lists of choices—hundreds of digitized photographs to download, for example, or dozens of personal ads to skim. If a list of selections or options is lengthy, the More button appears. Simply click on it to continue browsing down the list using its scroll bar.

Since all versions of AOL work in a GUI environment (see the Wise GUIs section in Chapter 4, The Datemobile), you can easily close and resize all windows. To return to a previous window simply click the tiny box in the upper left corner of the current window.

📋	Chat auditorium.
🗁	A folder containing a bundle of information and options.
📇	Software downloading.
📄	An article you can read.
🔳	Chat area.
🗂	Bulletin board.
◇	Takes you to another section of America Online.

TABLE 8-1 America Online's cute little icons

EXPERT TIP

You can customize the Go To menu with your favorite keywords. Simply select the Edit Go To Menu item from the Go To pull-down menu. You may give custom names to up to six menu entries, so long as you specify a proper keyword. Each of your favorite keywords now has its own shortcut: Simply press (CTRL)+(1) to automatically move to the first keyword, (CTRL)+(2) to access the second, etc.

Keywords

Keywords are special shortcut commands that let you zoom in on a particular department, from any location on AOL. To type in a keyword, simply press (CTRL)+(K). Enter the keyword and click on the OK button or press (ENTER).

Alternatively, you can click on the Go To pull-down menu and then select the Keyword option. Windows users can click on the Keyword icon (an arrow pointing to an AOL screen) in the command ribbon.

Welcome!

Figure 8-1 depicts a sample welcome screen. This is the first screen you see each time you connect—or sign on—to America Online. The four buttons on the right change constantly and contain the "hottest" areas, online meetings with famous people, or brand-new features. The bottom-most button contains the hour's top news story.

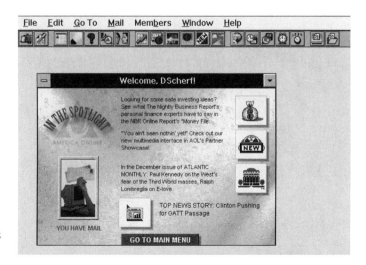

FIGURE 8-1 America Online's welcome screen

On the left side of the screen, there are three important buttons. If your mailbox has something waiting in it, your computer beeps (or even talks, if you have the appropriate hardware). Click on the New Mail button to read your goodies (see the section on Electronic Mail, a bit further on). If you have no mail, the button is dimmed and reads No Mail.

To begin wandering among the main AOL departments, click where it says Browse the Service or Departments. Depending on which version of the AOL software you're using, the Departments window may be called Main Menu.

If you're an AOL beginner, take a guided tour by clicking Discover AOL and then trying a taste of America Online Highlights.

Departing to Departments

There are many ways to access the Departments window, shown in Figure 8-2. The easiest is to press (CTRL)+(D). You can also click on the Go To pull-down menu at the top of the screen and then select Departments.

In addition, some versions of AOL have a ribbon bar at the top of the screen with an icon button for each department. The DOS version of AOL makes use of a general Browse the Service window, with eight department icons along its top border. To move to a different department, just click on its icon (as shown in Figure 8-2) at any time. The layout of the AOL departments varies slightly depending on whether you are using the Windows, DOS, or Macintosh version of the software. For example, the Windows version of AOL has an additional Newsstand department, where you can easily access any online magazines and newspapers.

The eight main America Online departments are:

News & Finance (keyword *news*). All of today's news is here. There are special areas for sports buffs, stock market gurus, and people who own small businesses. This is also the place for discussing current events.

FIGURE 8-2 The Main Menu

The travel and shopping department is an ideal place for lonesome wanderers to pick up travel partners.

- *People Connection* (keyword *pc*). The social hub of America Online. See the Chat section later in this chapter.

- *Lifestyles & Interests* (keyword *lifestyles*). Click here for a listing of America Online clubs. Some special areas include the latest whatnot about such topics as aviation, wining and dining, and writing, to name just a few. Each club, or forum, has its own sprawl of software libraries, chat rooms, and message areas.

- *Games & Entertainment* (keyword *games*). America Online has dozens of role-playing and strategy games you can play against the computer or other users. There is a casino, Broderbund's MasterWord game (a hybrid between hangman and Scrabble), a place for you to coach your own sports teams, and a stock market simulation game. The play-by-mail area hooks you up with other strategy gamers who battle you via e-mail. For role-playing fans, Advanced Dungeons and Dragons has a fantastical Neverwinter Nights game where you can create your own characters, trek through fantasy landscapes, and meet wizards, monsters, and other AOL characters along the way (keyword: *neverwinter*). Check out LaPub here (keyword *lapub*), if you're interested in lounging at an online bar—bring your own drinks. This is also the place for messages/chat about sports, science-fiction, trivia, and the wide and oft-glamorous entertainment world.

- *Travel & Shopping* (keyword *travel*). Here's the fastest way to spend your money. Load up on cars, computer or office equipment, software, music, and even flowers (in case you meet someone extra special online). A computerized travel agent is here, and the EAASY SABRE service automatically makes reservations for you on airlines, hotels, and car rentals, as well as automatically sending you all your tickets and vouchers. Discuss your travel plans with other AOL users, too, and find the best tapas bar in Madrid or how to avoid diarrhea in Malaysia.

- *Computing & Software* (keyword *computing*). Click here for technical talk, product reviews, access to over 45,000 software files, online promotions from various soft/hardware companies, computer magazines, and the latest computing news and reference sources.

- *Learning & Reference* (keyword *learning*). This section is handy for students and teachers of all ages. Click here for *Compton's Encyclopedia*, a dictionary of computer terms, course listings and registration from colleges and major universities across the country, online homework help and tutoring, student and teacher discussion forums, a book catalog from the Library of Congress, and a CNN current events discussion. A variety of online magazines, including *Disney's Adventures* and the Kid's Only Online center (KOOL)

are ideal places for junior cyberdaters. There are areas that contain tips on choosing and getting into the right college. There is also a section with reams of valuable career counseling and job listings. Spend time here and you may just get a crush on one of the online teachers.

Members' Online Support (keyword *support*). If you click on this area, you are told about AOL's latest features. There's even online customer support available. Click on Customer Service Live for immediate questions (keyword *cslive*). Billing information is also available here. You can explore this department as long as you want; it does not count toward your hourly online fee.

Downloading

Transferring files from AOL's computers to your own is one of the simplest ways of getting free software in the online world. Though most programs aren't applicable to online dating, you

FIGURE 8-3 Roberta and Paul both worked for America Online for a while; he as a technical service member in Virginia, she as a Brooklyn-based online algebra teacher. Over AOL, their friendship rapidly blossomed. In 1988, they finally met at a Boston computer conference. Two years later, they were married. The pews at the church, they say, were divided into the Mac side and the DOS side. Of the sixty people at their wedding reception, only about ten were *not* from the online world. Their future plans? To live happily ever after.

EXPERT TIP

You can highlight all the software you want and then download it later, automatically disconnecting from AOL when you're through. To do so, double-click on each file and then click on the Download Later button. Whenever later comes around, download everything at once by clicking on the File pull-down menu at the top of the screen and selecting Download Manager. You can view the descriptions of the files you have previously selected, delete the ones that no longer interest you, or change the destination of the download. Then click on Start Download. There is a little box in the download window next to the words Sign Off After Download. Click on the box if you do want to sign off automatically once you've got everything.

can find many pictures of fellow America Online users, lists of BBSs, and other information that may lead to a more productive online love life.

To access a download library, click on the picture of the diskettes: The Software Center icon. You can search America Online's entire collection by clicking the "Search Over 45,000 Files" option. (Windows users can select the File Search icon from the ribbon; it's the picture of the magnifying glass and a diskette.) You can select from top downloads, applications, games, graphics, utilities, and more.

You can also enter the keyword *quickfind* at any time, which allows you to search AOL's entire library for any particular file of interest. To reduce the search time, click on the relevant categories. You can even search for descriptive words, such as "love" or "romance." All relevant files are listed. Figure 8-4, for example, shows the results of the search for "dating." Double-click on whichever file interests you. You get a description of the file, including its requirements and how long it'll take to download.

If you want the file, click on the Download Now button. A percentage bar tracks the progress of your download. Unless otherwise specified, your file ends up in the

```
C:\WAOL\DOWNLOAD
```

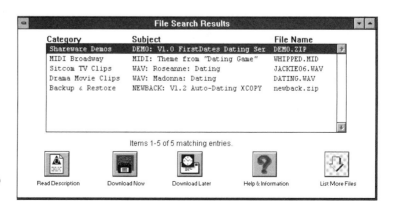

FIGURE 8-4 A list of America Online files having something to do with dating

directory (or the Online Downloads folder on the Macintosh). If the file is compressed, it ends in a .ZIP or .ARC suffix. America Online conveniently decompresses all files for you once you log off.

America's Most Wanted

America Online features an easy way to pinpoint those who share your interests, and makes it easy for them to find you. The *member profile* area is a well-stocked catalog of people you'll want to meet.

It's a good idea to fill in your profile sheet the first time you log on. Click on the Members pull-down menu and select Edit Your Online Profile. Along with the standard information, you can enter your marital status, hobbies, and occupation, as well as a favorite personal quote.

Pressing (CTRL)+(F) at any time finds out if your friend is online. Simply type in his or her screen name. If your pal is in a chat area, you find out exactly where. Pressing (CTRL)+(G) gets member profile information. Just type in the screen name of the person you're interested in, and if he or she has a profile you can read it. Figure 8-5 illustrates a sample profile.

The Search Member Directory command, within the Members pull-down menu, allows you to hunt for whatever attributes fit your style. Click Search Member Directory and then type in broad, descriptive words, such as "film" or "rock and roll" or "dating." A list of people who share your interests appears. Click on someone's name and then click Search. That person's profile pops up for you to browse.

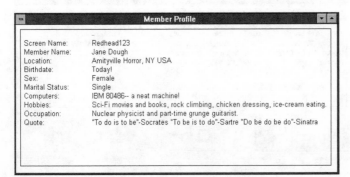

Screen Name:	Redhead123
Member Name:	Jane Dough
Location:	Amityville Horror, NY USA
Birthdate:	Today!
Sex:	Female
Marital Status:	Single
Computers:	IBM 80486-- a neat machine!
Hobbies:	Sci-Fi movies and books, rock climbing, chicken dressing, ice-cream eating.
Occupation:	Nuclear physicist and part-time grunge guitarist.
Quote:	"To do is to be"-Socrates "To be is to do"-Sartre "Do be do be do"-Sinatra

FIGURE 8-5 Using AOL's user profiles, you can find out juicy tidbits about Redhead123 before ever chatting with her

Messages

There is no one place to go for messages; they're scattered everywhere. Most every online magazine, forum, department, and topic has its own message area. Whenever you see the Pushpin icon, you are at a message base. Luckily, all the bases work in the same general way. Messages are grouped by category, topic, subject, and then by chronological time entered.

For example, suppose you're heading away on an intensive hike around the wilds of upstate New York. It sure would be nice if you could find a partner! You press (CTRL)+(D) and click on the Lifestyles & Interests department. A list of areas appears, including "Backpacker Magazine Online." You double-click on it. You can now read all about backpacking, chat in the "Back Talk" section, or click on the Trailhead Register. A list of three message forums appears, one of which is "Find a Hiking Companion." You click on it, and may now read about fellow New York hikers or post a message of your own.

That's all it takes to enter any of the AOL bulletin boards. Click on a message base to enter it (you may have to double-click, if the base is part of a longer list). You typically see a summary screen, which tells you the total number of categories or topics (depending on the intricacy of the particular board), number of messages posted, and on which date the latest message was posted. Click on List Topics or List Categories to view all the available areas. You can also click on Find New, which only displays messages posted since the last time you've read the forum. Click on Find Since to display only the more recent contributions; you may be asked to type in the number of past days whose messages you wish to view.

Figure 8-6 depicts a typical screenful of topic folders. If you've chosen to only look at new or more recent topics, the screen appears slightly different. You have the option to Read 1st New message, List New messages, or to List All.

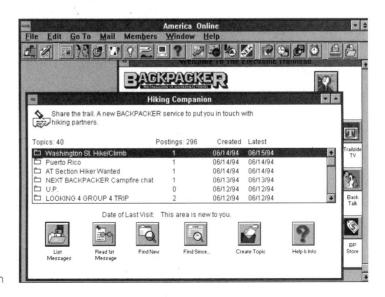

FIGURE 8-6 Skimming through some of the topics at the Backpacker Magazine Online's "Find a Hiking Companion" forum

Each line of the topic list describes the topic, tells you how many individual messages have been written about that topic, specifies the date the folder was originally created, and cites the publication date of the most recent article.

Reading

If this is the first time you've seen the topic, click on Read 1st Message to begin reading all the relevant articles. To read only the latest messages, click on Find New or Find Since.

You can also browse through a listing of article subjects by clicking on List Messages, which displays a screen similar to Figure 8-7. Browsing is a good idea if there are more messages in the topic than you have time to pore through; just double-click on the ones you like.

When you're done reading a particular message, you can either reply to it, click the upper left corner of the window to return to the subject listing, or click on the Previous Message or Next Message arrows—if available—to display adjacent articles.

Posting

Very simply, click on the Post Message button while in the appropriate topic folder. Enter a descriptive subject in the space provided, press (TAB), and then enter your message. Figure 8-8 depicts a typical article drafting session. When you're finished, click on Post.

You can also respond to something you've just read. Click on Add Message. The subject of your message is set automatically, preceded by "Re:".

If you're a trend setter and want to start a whole new rap session (within the general subject of the current message area), click on the Create Topic button in the topic-listings window. Each forum allows a maximum of 50, but unused topic folders are automatically deleted after about a week to make room for new ones. If there are already 50 topics, you see the message

`This category is full. Topic cannot be created.`

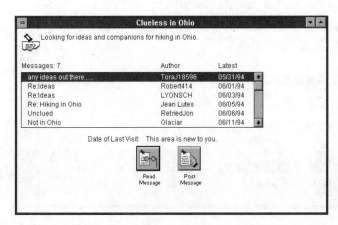

FIGURE 8-7 A lotta, lotta messages for your reading pleasure

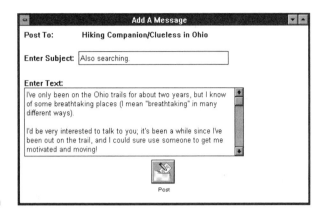

FIGURE 8-8 Composing a resplendent article of your own

Try creating your topic at some future date, or in some similar message area.

If there is space, however, you get your new topic folder. Type in its title. Give a brief description when the system asks for it. For instance, if you're in the "Wine and Dine" message area and want to invite a date to join you at a local wine tasting exhibition, create a topic called

```
Looking for a Sweet, Full-Bodied Grape
```

When asked for a description, type something along the lines of

```
I heard through the grapevine that lots of people on here love
wine tasting exhibitions. This is the place where fellow tasters
can hook up and have a grape time.
```

EXPERT TIP

A great way to save time and money is to read and write long messages offline. To save any message you're currently reading, click on its text and then click on the Save option under the Files pull-down menu. Enter a descriptive name, and the message is stored on your hard disk, in the DOCUMENTS directory or folder, for you to read at your leisure.

You can compose your articles offline, as well. Before you Sign On to America Online, click on the New option under the Files menu. Type in your Pulitzer Prize winning masterpiece and save it. Later, once online, go about posting a message as usual. When it's time to write your article, Open your saved file (under the Files menu), highlight the text using the mouse, and then select Copy from the Edit pull-down menu. Click on an area in the Enter Text: box and then choose Paste (also under the Edit menu).

Note: Windows and Macintosh users may paste their text directly from the clipboard, allowing them to type messages using their favorite word processor.

It's considered good form to now click on the Add Message button and enter an introductory article, to get the ball rolling. Simply type a subject and your text in the boxes provided, and click on Post.

Dating Messages

I was online one afternoon in the infamous Romance Connection listening to the chatter. When checking the profiles I came across one that "flashed" at me. It was the strangest thing, it seemed as if the screen seemed to glow. Now really, I am a quite stable professional male with a level head, intelligent, and in full grasp of what is real in the world but I was somehow drawn to this woman without ever having met or even typed a word to her. Being the gentleman that I am, I sent a private message to her that said something like "You misbehavin' over there?" It was to become one of the defining moments of my life! We struck up a conversation and talked for a very few minutes and then signed off . . . I was starstruck! I came to call her "Blue Eyes" and we began what would become a great love story. The sheer excitement in the beginning was so intense that I didn't know if I could take it! I was running home from work to send her a note and read what she had sent. We had no idea what we were really in for . . . it was a Coast to Coast affair . . . I felt like a teenager again! It could seem strange to you but until you experience it, you will not understand! Learning to love someone from the "inside out" instead of the other way around is very powerful.

America Online has a special area particularly suited for cyberdaters. Use the keyword *romance* to enter the "infamous" Romance Connection—a well-thought-out personal ads section. People are organized by age and by region. You act as your own matchmaker, browsing through the messages. Don't be afraid to post one of your own, even if you're just looking for a pen pal. Select one of two topics:

- *Make Your Match: Find By Age Group* contains the categories: Teens, 20s, Over 30s, Over 40s, Single Again, and All Ages.

- *Make Your Match: Find By Region* contains seven categories: Northeast, Southeast, South, Northwest, Midwest, West Coast, and Southwest.

You might enjoy reading the "Happy Endings" boards, where AOL users who found love online rave and kvetch about it. You can find everything here from *West Side Story* to *Fatal Attraction*. If you happen to find an online soulmate-for-life, this is the place to post your wedding invitation.

The Gay and Lesbian Community Forum (keyword *glcf*) also includes a special "Heart to Heart" matchmaking area.

Dating goes on in other forums, as well. For example, you can visit the Afterwards Coffeehouse (keyword *afterwards*) and hang out with the AOL bohemians, smoking clove cigarettes, adjusting your beret, and discussing art, music, and literature.

Mail

> Me and another married woman had a brief affair. Guilt and stress forced us apart. We both were on AOL, though, and used e-mail to help cheer each other up. We now send e-mail to each other every day. Actually in a way it is more exciting than the beginning was. We already know each other as physically as possible, and now we are finding out more and deeper things.

America Online's mail services, while simple to use, are packed with a variety of useful options.

Reading New Mail

If anyone has e-mailed you, you are notified as soon as you log on. Click on New Mail. If you get new mail while you're online, the tiny Mailbox icon appears (or lights up) in the upper left corner of your screen. Some versions of AOL even talk to you, saying, "You have new mail!" in a sweet lil' voice. Click on the mailbox icon or press (CTRL)+(R) to start reading it.

You see a list of the subjects of all your "unopened" letters and the screen name of the people who sent them. Double-click on what you want to read. A screen similar to Figure 8-9 appears. That's all there is to it!

Mail is stored for one week after you've read it, and then automatically deleted. To browse through your old letters, select Check Mail You've Read from the Mail pull-down menu.

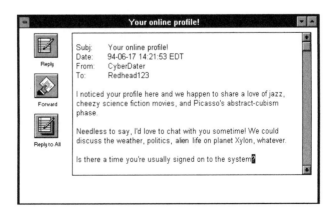

FIGURE 8-9 A typical (or perhaps not so) piece of e-mail

If someone sent you a software file along with a letter, you can download it by clicking the Download File button. You can click Download File Later if you want to retrieve the file at the end of your AOL session using the File Manager.

Replying to Mail

You can automatically respond to a letter by clicking the Reply button. This is just like sending mail, only you don't have to enter the mailing address or subject. Just type in your reply, click Send, and you're done.

If the letter you're replying to was sent to several people, you can reply to the whole lot of them by clicking the Reply to All button.

Forwarding Mail

If you want to share some good e-mail news with another AOL user, simply click on the Forward button. Type who the mail should be forwarded To:, along with an initial Comment:, if you'd like.

Sending Mail

Press (CTRL)+(M) to compose new mail. The compose screen, shown in Figure 8-10, appears. Type the screen name of the person you want to send mail to in the To: box. You can send a letter to as many people as you like; simply separate screen names by commas. Press the (TAB) key to enter the CC: field, which sends additional "carbon" copies. If you don't want the recipients of your letters to know who else was on your mailing list, surround their screen names with parentheses.

Press (TAB) again and enter a tantalizing subject in the Subj: field. One more (TAB) gets you to the File: field, where you can type your letter. Click on the winged Send button when your note is signed and ready to fly.

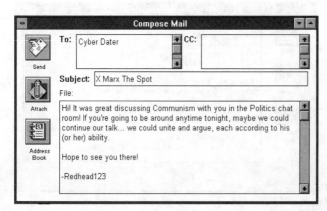

FIGURE 8-10 Composing a letter to that special someone

You can save countless online hours if you compose your mail offline. Before you log on, select the Compose Mail option under the Mail pull-down menu. Enter your mailing address, subject, and text as usual. Switch to the Sign On window, sign on, and switch to the Compose Mail window. Click on Send to send the mail.

Windows and Mac users can use the Cut and Paste options from the Edit menu to highlight text from any file, cut it, and then paste it into the body of their letters.

DOS users can also use AOL's notepad (select New from the File pull-down menu) to write a letter offline. Once you've written the text, select the Save item from the File menu to save your letter to disk. You can now sign on. Click on the File pull-down menu and select Open to view your letter; it should be in the DOCUMENTS directory or folder. Click on the Mail pull-down menu and select Address Memo. The Compose Mail window appears, with your text already filled in. Type in the relevant information, and then click Send. Voilà.

To remind yourself what you wrote yesterday, select Check Mail You've Sent from the Mail pull-down menu. Click the Show Status button to see if a piece of mail was received, when, and by whom. The actual text of your old mail is also stored for a week—just double-click on the letter you want.

The Attach File button allows you to mail any piece of software along with your letter. This is like uploading a program directly to your friend's mailbox. If you have a digitized picture of yourself, for example, it might be nice to send it to a prospective date along with a nice little *carté de amour*. If you decide against sending up a file, you can simply click the Detach File button.

Address Book

Assume you have ten very close friends on America Online. Further, assume you know some of them by their real names (John Q. Private, Jane Dough, Lenny Lovelooker), and others by screen names (Cyberdater, Redhead123, Freddie987, Lenny). You can organize all this information by using the address book.

Click on the Edit Address Book selection of the Mail pull-down menu. Depending on which version of AOL you are using, you may need to click on a Create button. You can now click on the Group Name field and type the name of the person or group whose screen name you want to store. Then (TAB) to the Screen Names field and enter either one screen name, or—for a group—a listing of several names separated by commas. Click OK when done.

From now on, when sending or forwarding a letter, click on the Address Book icon to automatically access the list of your favorite people. Just click on the appropriate group (or person), and AOL puts the proper screen names in the To: box.

Chat

Chatting is the paramount feature of America Online. Almost every discussion area, lifestyle, and interest group has its own chat room. In most cases, chatting is as simple as finding an area you like. Once you're in a chat room, the talk scrolls down the screen in a scriptlike format. Whenever you want to "say" something, type it and press (ENTER) or click Send. It's even easier, perhaps, than real-life conversation!

Instant Messages

No matter where you are on America Online, you can send any other user a quick, private message by pressing (CTRL)+(I). Type the screen name of the person you want. Click the Available? button to see if your pal is currently online. If so, enter your message in the provided field and then click on the Send button.

If someone sends an instant message to you, click the Respond button to get back to them. Depending on the version of AOL you're using, your instant message session appears one message at a time or as a complete sideline conversation as in Figure 8-11. In either case, once you type in your comment, click on Send.

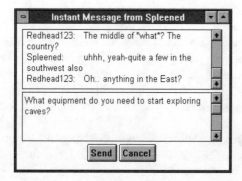

FIGURE 8-11 Sending an AOL instant message

EXPERT TIP

If your computer has a sound card (as many Macintosh, Apple II, and Windows-based systems do), you may have noticed that AOL speaks to you, saying things such as "Welcome!" or "You have new mail!" You can also transmit your own sounds during chatting. Chat Room Sounds must be enabled in the Preferences section of the Members pull-down menu. Any time you type:

```
{S <soundfile>}
```

anyone in the chat room who has the capacity for sound hears the sound file you just played, as long as they have the <*soundfile*> file in their AOL directory or folder.

The People Connection

The People Connection comprises the hundreds of chat rooms sprinkled everywhere around AOL. The fastest, easiest way to enter the People Connection is to press (CTRL)+(L). You have many other alternatives: You may select Lobby from the Go To menu, click on the People Connection icon in the Departments window, or use the keywords *pc, peopleconnection,* or *chat.* Chances are, no matter what you do, you'll soon wind up in the thick of the People Connection.

The Lobby

So you've meandered into the lobby . . . . There is usually a host here who shakes your hand, makes you feel welcome, and answers any questions you may have. Tell the host what mood you're in and the host (whose name will begin with the word GUIDE) points you in the right direction. See Figure 8-12 for a sample chat screen.

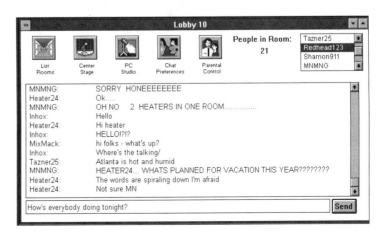

FIGURE 8-12 Getting oriented in AOL's Lobby

EXPERT TIP

Highlight is a neat feature that lets you color or underline everything one specific user "says." This makes it easy to keep track of who is who, and gives each chatter a voice of his or her own. An *H* precedes the names of people who you've slated to be highlighted.

Click on Rooms to see the many places where people are conversing. Click on Available Rooms to see which public rooms are currently empty; click on one to activate it, should you be interested. From this window, you can also enter the customized Member Rooms. Both Public and Member rooms are described later in this chapter.

If you are using the DOS version of AOL, you can click on People to see who is in the current room. Other AOL users have a list automatically displayed on the upper right of their screens. Double click on someone's name and then click Get Info to view a chatter's user profile. Clicking on Message allows you to whisper an instant message to whoever's name is currently highlighted.

Clicking on Ignore gives the cold shoulder to whichever screen name is currently highlighted. If you're not interested in reading what someone has to say, you can mute his or her on-screen yammering. Click Ignore again to give someone a second chance.

Public Rooms

America Online has dozens of public rooms, as depicted in Figure 8-13. Check out the listing—you are told the name of each room and how many people are inside it. The list of room names scrolls for a long time; click on More to continue the listing once you get to the end of the current batch.

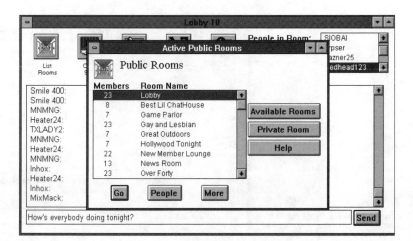

FIGURE 8-13 Just a tiny sliver of AOL's available public rooms

Clicking on People gives you a sneak-peek of who's inside a room. You can check out their profiles and see if there are any interesting souls. Where else can you learn the biographies of everybody in a room before you boldly strut in?

To enter one of the rooms, highlight the room name on the list box and select Go.

Rooms Where Datin' Is the Rage

Although online dating occurs in all of AOL's rooms, some places are better than others for meeting new people, finding companionship, or old-fashioned flirting. Rooms such as Teen Chat, Gay & Lesbian, and Over Forty cater to more specific groups of people, while the rooms below cater to anyone with a pulse:

- *The Romance Connection.* A place custom designed for 24-hour cyberdaters. There may be several of these rooms, numbered 1, 2, 3, and so on, since they usually fill up pretty fast. Most people begin by typing their age/sex/state. Folks usually end by pairing up in private rooms.

- *The Flirt's Nook.* Very similar to the romance connection, only with a more sensual sort of slant to it. This is the area for cyberteases.

- *Best Lil' Chathouse.* Folks 'round these parts chat it up about everything from hard rock to rock collecting.

- *The Meeting Place.* The place to meet, greet, and even, at times, turn up the heat.

Member Rooms

There may be hundreds of these at any one time. Member rooms are usually more profane and, though AOL discourages it, most have to do with sexual topics. Some usuals are: Over 50, Pierced and Tattooed, Jewish Singles, Married and Restless, Ebony, and Psychic Chat. Click on Create to invent a room reflecting your own interests. Just type in the new name, such as "Gregorian Chanting Fanatics," and either wait for people to join you or invite them through e-mail or instant messages.

PC Studio

This is AOL's remote control and TV guide all in one. Search the Event Rooms Guide for listings of upcoming meetings; the Event Rooms Schedule has more detailed information, telling you what to expect and what mood to bring. Use the keyword *pcstudio* to get here.

From the studio, you can also access AOL's cartoon and comic strip gallery; a gallery of AOL members' photos; an advice and tips section containing lawyers, psychics, home-makers, doctors, and advice-columnists; a gRaFfItI area; a gossip area; clubs for teens and trivia masters; and the game parlour.

Conference Centers

The symbol of a microphone indicates a conference center. Magazines and software support areas may have an online customer service representative, ready to answer any questions you may have. Other conferences are where people who share special interests or lifestyles can chat it up.

Some interesting forum areas include:

- *LaPub.* Whether you're the type who downs a straight-up Scotch or sips Coca Cola, LaPub welcomes you. LaPub is one of the more close-knit discussion rooms, with a resident bartender who helps kick off the conversation. Use keyword *lapub*, and then select Enter LaPub. LaPub has its own dart games, occasional online weddings, holiday and birthday parties, and more. Check out the Events and Contests listing to see what's up and coming.

- *The Bull Moose Tavern.* No bouncer, no fake IDs, no brawls. What more could you want out of a collegiate-type bar? Keyword is *bull moose*.

- *The Lambda Lounge.* An online gay bar. Use keyword *glcf*.

Setting the Stage

At various places around AOL, you may come across a symbol of a coliseum, or a man speaking at a podium. These are large forums for staging game shows, celebrity speeches, seminars, and other public shows and events.

You generally receive directions on how to go about interacting before you enter a forum. In most cases, there is a moderator, who chooses the best remarks and questions from the audience—yours, with luck—and asks them on your behalf.

EXPERT TIP

Sometimes AOL features door prizes to the first fifty or so audience members. These include free online time, T-shirts, and books.

Click on the Interact button during celebrity interviews, game shows, elections, or auctions. You can then Ask a Question or just Make a Comment. When appropriate, you can also cast your Vote or Bid.

Chat Rows typically hold eight people each. Any comments you make are only heard by people in your row, kind of like "whispering" to your date during an opera. You can move from row to row, so long as the row has room. For events that you imagine will be popular, get there early. People in the front rows get first dibs in asking questions.

Clicking on the People button shows you who is in your current chat row. You can also click on the Who's Onstage? button to get information about the speaker, as well as highlighting his or her words.

Usually, the onstage guest of honor cannot "hear" your questions as you type them; however, the conference moderator may occasionally turn on the microphones in your chat row, allowing you to make a direct comment.

Some chat coliseums include:

- *Games Parlor* (keyword *gaming*). A variety of strategy, number, and trivia games. Check the Online Gaming Forum for schedules and game rules.

- *It's Time* (keyword *time*). *TIME Magazine* has a special odeon featuring live interviews and speeches by "faces" direct from the pages of *TIME*.

- *Center Stage* (keyword *centerstage*). This is AOL's main event stadium, featuring a different guest of honor most every night.

- *The Omni Odeon* (keyword *omni*). UFOlogists, ghost hunters, near-death experiencers, and maybe even an occasional ET or two discuss topics of interest to readers of *Omni Magazine*.

- *Computing's Rotunda* (keyword *rotunda*). Software designers, hardware manufacturers, and all sorts of computer know-howers meet here to discuss the cutting edge of the industry.

- *Classrooms* (keywords *ies* or *classes*). The Interactive Education Services of the *Learning and Reference* department contains customized classrooms where you can get tutoring in everything from S.A.T.s to computer software. There are even college and career workshops and business investment seminars.

America the Beautiful?

Since America Online's software makes moving around so simple, it is ideal for novices who want a taste of the cyberspace life. In no time, you are downloading, writing messages, sending e-mail, and chatting, chatting, chatting the night away. And with AOL's colorful icons, each screen is as easy to look at as it is to use.

Due to AOL's friendliness and laid-back atmosphere, it is often crowded. This can be a good thing—in the dead middle of the night, when you're looking for somebody to talk to, for example. However, AOL tends to run slowly during prime time.

Most of the people who call America Online, it seems, are looking for companionship. As such, it's almost impossible *not* to make new friends each time you call. America Online's popularity also makes it a hunting ground for a large number of individuals who treat it like cheap phone sex. Female cyberdaters should expect inappropriate instant messages, cumbersome chat come-ons, and similar cybersleaze. Once you learn to turn off instant messages and ignore people (as explained earlier in the Chat section), your online environment will be much more comfortable.

My fellow Americans, get online!

Wedding Vows of TallTassle and Herr Fixit:

[Justice of the Peace] Boblooo: As I look out into the audience here tonight I'm struck by the diversity of those here to share in this event. Some of you I've known for a long time and we are old friends. And I mean OLD . . . LOL!!! Some of you I've known for a long time, even though you might be half my age . . . . This is the glory of the Electronic Community . . . . We can all come together and be known for our ideas . . . our humor . . . our caring . . . our sharing . . . . Something that is so very hard in the "other world." I won't say the "real world" because this, too, is the real world. And the friendships that are made here are many times stronger than those we make at work or in our local communities because of all of the roadblocks that are put up for the real development of friendships. Here we have two folks who met, shared some e-mail and some IMs [Instant Messages], things that many people around us would say "Huh???? What are you talking about?" But it's real, and their friendship has grown to love . . . and blossomed to the point where they are now here coming before us, their friends, to share the greatest gift that can be given to another . . . their love for each other. It gives me great pride and joy to be here tonight sharing in this moment. And I thank our bride and groom for not only asking me to join them but for doing this online so we can all share in it. And with that it's time now that we get on with what this is really all about . . . the sharing of the Vows.

TallTassle: Walt . . . from the first time we met in person two years ago I knew you were something special. I am so very glad that you kept IM-ing me and sending me e-mail. I am also glad that you wouldn't take no for an answer. Today we start a new life together, a life no longer you and me . . . but us. A life built on trust, sharing, and love. I may not do things in a straightforward manner but I will try. I promise to be open and honest, caring and sensitive to you, and what you want as we share our life together. This ring that I give you is a symbol of all those things. A never ending unbroken circle of love, sharing, trust, and communication. A symbol for the things that brought us together. I love you now and forever.

Herr Fixit: Kate, The past two years with you have been some of the happiest I've known. I know our life together will be full of love. I love you and am so glad you answered your mail that night two years ago. I promise to be honest, open, caring, and sensitive to your needs, hopes, and dreams as we go through life together. I know we'll have a wonderful life as long as we're honest, loving . . . and remember that communication is key. I may not seem the most romantic of men, and I tend to forget little things like birthdays and anniversaries, but I promise to be here when you need me and to make our life together a treat. I love you!

Boblooo: Though this is but a rehearsal of what will take place tomorrow, I think we have witnessed the reality of this marriage ceremony. The exchange of their concern and love for each other. And with that I present to you our couple!! And invite you all to LaPub to share in this Celebration of Love!

Herr Fixit:::Kissing the bride::

Boblooo:::listening to exit music::

TallTassle:::Kissing the groom::

Boblooo: Get your rice ready, folks . . . hehehe . . . .

COMPUSERVE

800-848-8990
P.O. BOX 20212
COLUMBUS OH 43220

COMPUSERVE IS A GOOD PLACE TO DATE,

or, yes, fall in love. Just ask my wife, who says she wants to leave me for a man she met online. And I'm the one who kept trying to convince her that CompuServe was a great way to meet new people. Oh well. I suppose our marriage was doomed anyway.

What It Is

The granddaddy of online services, CompuServe Information Service (CIS) is where the pros hang out. Though CompuServe has a tidy, businesslike environment, there are hidden water-coolers where folks loosen their ties, let down their hair, and flirt.

CIS has the best of the most. The most online stores to shop from. The most forums geared towards software and hardware support. The most perks and features. And although CompuServe may not have the most cyberdaters, there are plenty of meeting spots, if you know where to look. CIS's e-mail is among the most versatile and full-featured in the online world. And armed with CompuServe's powerful CB simulator, you can hold a dozen private conversations at the same time.

If you like data, expert advice, and lots of it, then CompuServe is your best bet. Although CIS is not targeted toward the novice user, its new graphically-oriented software makes it a snap (or mouse click) to navigate. Pricewise, CompuServe has a

low monthly rate, which gives you access to a basic stable of options. These options, however, won't gallop too far when it comes to online dating. If you want to ride off into the sunset of love, you'll probably find yourself paying an hourly fee.

How to Connect

Although you do not need special software to access CompuServe, it is highly, highly recommended. First of all, CompuServe is just too large and information-rich to try to navigate using monotonous text menus. Second, the CompuServe software has time-efficient features which save you quite a bit when it comes to online fees. Last, depending on how much you pay for the CompuServe software, you are given a $10 to $25 usage credit; the price of the software is nominal.

The software is called the CompuServe Information Manager (CIM), and its retail price is $49.95; usually it's on special for less. Call 800-524-3388 with your credit card ready and CompuServe will gladly send you a copy of CIM. Your membership kit also includes two booklets, a monthly subscription to *CompuServe Magazine,* and, most important, your registration number and temporary password. If you're the cautious type, you'll be glad to know there's also a 30-day money-back guarantee. The opening screen of the WinCIM software is shown in Figure 9-1.

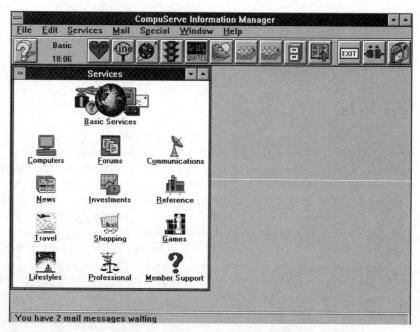

FIGURE 9-1 WinCIM at a glance

If your modem or computer came with a CompuServe membership kit but no CIM software, or if you feel comfortable with your communications software, you can download CIM yourself, for free. Downloading costs $10, but you're given a $10 time credit. Before you download, you have to be a CompuServe member. Call CompuServe to get a free membership booklet, which includes your registration number and temporary password. Become a member, as detailed later in the Signing On Without WinCIM section.

Now type

```
go wincim
```

Alternatively, type *go maccim* or *go doscim*, depending on which version of the software you want. Select the menu number corresponding to the Download CIM option. You may need to download two separate disks. After agreeing to the licensing information, select your protocol; you can use Xmodem, Ymodem, Kermit, or CompuServe's own B protocol. The entire program takes about an hour and a half to download at 2400 baud.

WinCIM users now have two files, called DISK1.EXE and DISK2.EXE. Log off CompuServe and go to the DOS prompt. Put an empty high-density floppy disk in the drive and type

```
DISK1 A: (ENTER)
```

Now put a second blank, high-density floppy disk into the drive and type

```
DISK2 A: (ENTER)
```

You now have a copy of CIM! You can go about installing it as detailed in the next section.

The Software

The CompuServe Information Manager is one of the most powerful online software packages available. Whether you get WinCIM (for Windows), DOS-CIM (for DOS), or MacCIM (for Macintosh), the features include:

- *Mouse/Pull-Down Menus.* Navigate and access CompuServe features by pointing the mouse to a menu item and clicking.

- *Automatic Log On.* You don't need to memorize your CompuServe user ID or password. Each time you use CompuServe, CIM signs you on automatically.

- *Time-Saving Shortcuts.* By keeping track of your favorite places, favorite people, and favorite forums, the software frees up your memory for more important things than cryptic CompuServe ID numbers and forum names.

Filing Cabinet. By composing and storing text offline, you can save hours of online time. These are also a big help when it comes to managing your mail.

Without the CIM software, you're only seeing the tip of the CompuServe iceberg. If you are already a CompuServe member but do not have the CIM software, you can either download it (see the Expert Tip in the above section) or order a copy online by typing *Go order.*

This chapter deals primarily with WinCIM. Although the screen layout of MacCIM may differ, the commands are essentially the same. DOS-CIM contains no icons (pictures), but its menu layout is generally the same as WinCIM's.

WinCIM

WinCim combines the power of the Windows environment and the features of CompuServe. Some of its features include quick and easy icons, context-sensitive help, cutting and pasting from any Windows document, multitasking, and multiple windows. In other words, if you don't WinCIM, you lose some.

To install, insert the disk into the floppy drive. Select Run from the File pull-down menu and type

`a:setup`

and click OK. If you are using your second drive, substitute

`b:setup`

You are asked if you want to install the Sign On software. Click YES. Once WinCIM is installed, double-click on the Membership Service Sign On icon to get started.

DOS-CIM

DOS-CIM may not be as colorful or snazzy as the other CIM programs, but it gets the job done. To install, type

`A:` `(ENTER)`

or

`B:` `(ENTER)`

at the DOS prompt. To copy the program onto your hard disk, type

`install` `(ENTER)`

MacCIM

MacCIMize your online time. This version of the CompuServe software is nearly as feature-rich as the Windows version, allowing you to use CompuServe while using typical Macintosh multitasking functions. Insert the disk into the drive. Double-click on the

CompuServe disk icon. When the CompuServe folder pops up, double-click on Install. The software transfers onto your hard disk.

Other CompuServe Software

CompuServe, in association with other software companies, has developed alternate front-end programs. To find out more about each of the following software packages, read the information online.

▧ *CompuServe Navigator* allows you to plot out your CompuServe session in advance. Once you decide which forums you want to visit, what messages you want to read and write, and what letters you want to read and write, the Navigator quickly logs you on, performs all the necessary tasks, and then logs you off so you can view all your new messages offline. *Go order* to find out how to order the Macintosh or Windows version of this program. *Go winnav* to download the Windows version.

▧ *Autopilot*, for Amiga computers, provides an easy way to navigate around the CompuServe world. *Go amigavendor* for details.

▧ *Golden CommPass* works with the OS/2 operating system. *Go CommPass* for details.

You can always *Go cissoft* to find out about the latest CompuServe software releases.

Charges

In the bad old days of online telecommunications, CompuServe used to be known among cyberpeople as Compu$erve. It had extravagant hourly fees and lots of steep surcharges. Lately, though, CompuServe has trimmed its prices and is more on-par with the other American online services.

CompuServe has so many different pricing schemes, it's easy to get dazed trying to figure out how much you're supposed to shell out. With the "standard" plan, you pay $8.95 per calendar month (though your first month is free), for all the bone-basic options, such as e-mail, movie reviews, shopping, and the encyclopedia. Options like message forums and the CB chat simulator, though, cost an extra $4.80 per hour at 300 to 2400 baud, and $9.60 per hour at 9600 baud or higher.

EXPERT TIP

There is no need to use CompuServe at 9600 baud or higher in forums or chat areas since reading messages and chatting takes about the same time at all bauds; it depends on the speed of your reading and typing, not the modem. If you are downloading, however, it usually pays to log on at as fast a baud rate as possible.

In addition, there are certain premium services—indicated, when you run across them, by a dollar sign ($)—that can cost up to an additional $35.00 per hour. You are warned, online, if you attempt to access one of these services. Read instructions closely for exact fees.

In some cases, the "alternate pricing plan" may pay off for users of extended services, while the "executive service option" may be best for business-oriented users. *Go rates* to get the latest information. Always consult your CompuServe manual, or call up customer service, for exact prices.

You can *Go charges* at any time to get an explanation of your bill, your current account balance, billing history, or current activity. *Go bill* to change your billing address or method of payment.

CompuServe has its own telephone network, covering about 80 percent of the continental United States. If you are using this network, there are no hourly phone surcharges no matter when you call. The CompuServe network is available in most international countries as well, though there is a $7.70 per hour surcharge if you call during prime time (from 8 A.M. to 7 P.M., Monday through Friday).

If you must use an 800 number, Tymnet, SprintNet, DataPac, or some other international network, the price begins to rise. This runs from $1.70 to $35 an hour, depending on when you call, your location, and your modem speed. Call CompuServe or *Go networks* online to get exact prices.

Logging On

Signing on to CompuServe for the first time is a relatively painless process. Be sure to read all the online instructions, questions, and warnings, since they often change.

Signing On Without CIM

If you feel comfortable with your communications software, you don't need CIM to access CompuServe. After calling CompuServe and getting your free membership kit mailed to you, you can become a CompuServe member by signing on manually.

Set your terminal's settings to 7 data bits, even parity, full duplex, and 1 stop bit. See Chapter 4, The Datemobile, for details on how to use your communications software. The introductory membership booklet supplied by CompuServe lists many network access numbers. If the number for your area is not listed, follow these steps:

1. Dial 800-346-3247 with your modem.

2. When you see the *CONNECT* message, press (ENTER).

3. When asked for a *HOST NAME,* type

   `phones`

4. Type in your area code and baud rate, when prompted to do so.

A list of numbers appears. Alternatively, you can voice call 800-635-6225 and press ① to obtain a list of local numbers.

Once you have a local access number, use your communications software to dial it. Press (ENTER) a few times, until you're asked for the *HOST NAME.* Type

`CIS`

and press (ENTER).

Type in your temporary User ID number, as printed on your membership materials, and press (ENTER). You no longer need this ID number once you type it in. A permanent User ID number is issued to you at the end of the sign-up procedure.

Now type in your temporary password. A second temporary password is issued at the end of the sign-up procedure. Your *permanent* password will arrive in the mail in about a week, whereupon your temporary password will expire.

You now have to enter your personal and billing information. You may conduct the sign-on in English or German, by pressing ① or ②, respectively.

When prompted, type in your Agreement Number, exactly as it is printed on your CompuServe Membership package. Likewise, type in your Serial Number.

You are now asked personal information, such as your name, address, phone number, social security number, and payment method (Visa, MasterCard, American Express, Discover, or electronic transfer from your checking account). When asked if you want your name listed in the CompuServe directory, it's a good idea to select Yes, since this makes it easier for potential dates to locate you.

You are now issued your permanent User ID and temporary password, which you need from now on every time you log on to CompuServe. Write them down. You are now an official CompuServer!

LOVE BYTES

EXPERT TIP

If you ever move to a new area code or upgrade to a high-speed modem, you have to have the CIM software learn your new local access number. To do this, *Go phones* while online and enter your area code, when asked. Write down the number that applies to your baud rate. Now, select Session Settings from the Special pull-down menu and enter your new number in the Phone box. If the local access number does not belong to the CompuServe network, there is a surcharge. *Go logon* for pricing information.

CIMple Sign-On

If you are using CIM, click the Membership Sign On icon. The software hunts your closest local access number. Type your temporary User ID number, password, Agreement Number, Serial Number, personal information, and billing information in the appropriate boxes.

To automate CIM so that it connects you to CompuServe, without having to type in your ID or password, select the Session Settings option from the Special pull-down menu. If you signed on to CompuServe using the CIM software, then CIM already knows a lot about you. If it's not already there, enter your local access phone number in the Phone box. Also fill in the appropriate Baud Rate, Connector COM Port, and Dial Type (Tone or Pulse).

Now enter your *Name, User ID,* and *Password* in the appropriate boxes. Your password appears as a string of asterisks, for your security. You'll have to return to this Session Settings menu in about a week to update your password, when your permanent one arrives in the mail. Click on the Password box, backspace over the asterisks, and carefully type in your new password.

From now on, to log on to CompuServe, simply run CIM and select any command. You automatically connect and that command is performed. For example, if you want to receive mail, first thing, select the Get New Mail option from the Mail pull-down menu. If you want to browse forums, click the Forums icon in the Browse window.

Logging Off

To log off CompuServe while keeping CIM running (in order to check your file cabinet or read mail offline), click on the Disconnect icon (the picture of the two separating cables)

EXPERT TIP

If you want to change your password (once you receive your permanent one), *Go password.* You are asked to enter your old password and then type in the new one, twice. You should get in the habit of changing your password from time to time.

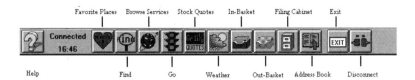

FIGURE 9-2
WinCIM's default
button bar

or select Disconnect from the File pull-down menu. If you want to exit the entire CIM program, click the EXIT icon or select Exit from the File menu.

If you are not using CIM, you need to type

```
off
```

at any exclamation point (!) prompt.

Getting Around

CIM makes it simple to navigate CompuServe. To access a command, simply select it from the appropriate pull-down menu or click on its icon in the *button bar,* a special ribbon of buttons, found in WinCIM and MacCIM, that allows you to perform typical commands with a single mouse-click. See Figure 9-2.

As you browse through CompuServe, most of your options appear as part of a list or menu. For instance, the Human Sexuality menu is shown in Figure 9-3. If you have a mouse, you can double-click on any item to access it. Otherwise, you can use your keyboard arrow keys to highlight the topic you're interested in, and then press (ENTER) to go there.

Favorite Places

This is part of the Services pull-down menu. The favorite places list displays the CompuServe areas you access the most. Instead of remembering the right *Go* word for routine CompuServe services, you just click the Favorite Places icon, see a list of your usual CompuServe destinations, and double-click on whichever item you like.

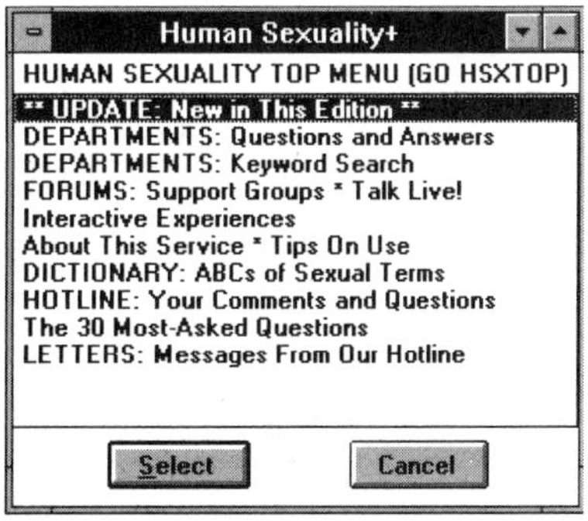

FIGURE 9-3 The Human Sexuality menu; a diverse (and popular) topic

Click Add to put a new favorite place on your list. Type in a description—such as the full name of the forum or service—in the Description box. Type that service's unique name—the name you would normally *Go* to—in the Service Name box. See the Find command, below, for information on how to add topics you often search for into your favorite places list.

Find

Find is part of the Services pull-down menu. Click the Find icon and type in any word or words. A list of places around CompuServe where that word is found is shown. For example, if you type

```
dating
```

a screen similar to Figure 9-4 appears, listing the two Human Sexuality forums.

To add one of the topics to your favorite places list, just highlight it and click the Add button. Double-click on a topic to go there directly.

Go

Also part of the Services pull-down menu, Go is the command that really takes you places. Every CompuServe service, forum, and area has its own unique name, usually indicated at the bottom of its menu. Clicking on Go and then typing the unique service name in the Service: box brings up the corresponding menu.

For example, Go is one way to access the CB Simulator menu. Click on Go, type in

```
CB
```

and press (ENTER).

If you don't know a CompuServe service's exact name, you can either guess it (Go transports you to the closest match), or you can search for it with the *Find* command.

Go tour takes you on a quick tour of CompuServe's basic features.

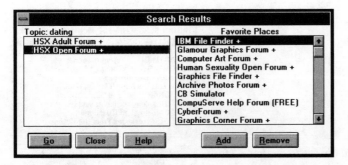

FIGURE 9-4 Looking for "dating" over CompuServe

Don't Waste the Baskets

The In and Out Baskets, found under the Mail pull-down menu, are tremendous money-savers. They work just like an office's in and out baskets would.

Any mail or forum messages you compose offline are placed in the Out Basket. Later, once online, you can have CompuServe empty your Out Basket by clicking on it, automatically sending all letters to the appropriate recipients and posting all messages to the specified forums.

The In Basket is similar. Any time you Get New Mail, all your new letters are dumped into the In Basket. If a minus sign (-) precedes the entry, you haven't read it yet. Once offline, click on the In Basket icon to read all your new mail, delete it, and even reply to it if you want.

If your In or Out Basket is empty, its icon appears dimmed.

File Cabinet

The File Cabinet—which provides permanent storage for any text you read or write online—is found under the Mail pull-down menu.

Whenever you read a letter or forum message online, you have the option to File it. See the Messages and Mail sections of this chapter for detailed instructions on how to slip something into your customized cabinet. Items are stored in their original formats; in other words, you can still reply to a letter or forum message as usual. You can read anything in the File Cabinet both online and off; simply double-click on the folder, and then the item that interests you. When you no longer need an item, Delete it.

Within the File Cabinet, you can create as many folders as you like with the New button. Just type a descriptive name for each folder, such as "LETTERS FROM POTENTIAL DATES." Every letter or forum message you type is conveniently stored in the Auto-File folder for later reference. There is also a General file for miscellaneous and temporary text.

Browsing the Services

By default, the Browse screen first appears every time you run the CIM program. You can access the browse screen at any other time by selecting Browse from the Services pull-down menu or by clicking on the Browse globe icon.

Browse organizes all the CompuServe services into a baker's dozen of categories. There is plenty of overlap; for instance, the CB Forum can be found under the Forums category, the Lifestyles category, and the Communications category. Simply click on a category's icon to access its menu. Double-clicking on a menu entry accesses yet another menu. Continue like this until you've found a service that interests you. The categories include:

- *Basic Services.* Choose from CompuServe's many basic services. These are free under the "standard" pricing plan.

- *Computers.* The online world's most extensive professional support teams await you here. Discuss everything about computing, from building to buying to business.

- *Forums.* All of CompuServe's forums are organized within this category. If you want to write and read messages, but aren't sure where to check out, browse this category.

- *Communications.* Information on e-mail, FAXing, postal mail, international connections, and other CompuServe communications is available here. Naturally, you can also access the CB simulator from this area.

- *News.* All the latest news and weather is yours at a keypress. You can also debate current events or view news photos here.

- *Investments.* Funds, markets, mortgage, and other money matters.

- *Reference.* An encyclopedia, *Consumer Reports* articles, health information, a dictionary, drug references, and college profiles are available for you to search through. This is also the place to find IQuest, a service that searches hundreds of databases and finds almost anything you could possibly be looking for (at around $9 a search). Many other costly—but information-rich—databases are also available.

- *Travel.* Transportation and accommodation information from across the nation (and internationally, too).

- *Shopping.* A huge online mall awaits you. Classifieds are also available here, but there are no personal ads. Browsing through the CompuServe mall is free.

- *Games.* Many silly little time-killers, such as trivia, quizzes, and text adventure games, are here. However, there are also interactive play-by-e-mail games and multi-player online games available. *Go* to the *PBMGames, MTMChallenge, Gamers,* or *MPGames* forums for more details. The Epic Megagames option allows you to download the month's hottest new shareware game for only $3 (plus you're given $3 credit on your CompuServe account, so the game is virtually free). The Entertainment Center (*Go ECN*) allows you download quality graphics games—such as backgammon, checkers, chess, or StarSprint—and play them with other CompuServe members. Members of the CB Club (explained in the Chat section) can access the Entertainment Center at reduced hourly rates. Finally, *Go Sniper* to download and play graphical wargames with other CompuServe warlords.

- *Lifestyles.* Forums and information for those interested in such things as food/wine, hobbies, arts/music/literature, and other special interests can be found here.

- *Professional.* Doctors, lawyers, programmers, business people, engineers, scientists, journalists, and other pros can use the databases and forums in this area to network.

- *Member Support.* Billing information, account status, and other CompuServe help is available here.

Downloading

Along with messages, every category in every forum also has a download library. You can find all sorts of relevant articles, graphics, and software—including digitized photographs of other CompuServe members. For example, the Gallery & Profiles library in the CB Forum contains biographies and GIF photographs of many CompuServe cyberdaters. See the Messages section of this chapter for information on how to access a forum.

Once you've joined a forum, select Browse from the Library pull-down menu or click on the Browse Library icon. A list of the forum's categories appears. Double-click on the library you want to browse. All the files in that library appear, the most recently posted files first. You can see each file's title, size, and date, plus the number of people who have already downloaded it.

Double-click on a file to read its description. You can mark a file for later downloading by clicking an *x* in its adjacent box or by clicking the Mark button. To download all your marked files, select Retrieve from the Library pull-down menu. To download the file immediately, click Retrieve. Once you opt to mark or retrieve a file, you can save it under any name you want, though it's usually best to click OK and save it by its default filename.

A gauge appears, graphically displaying the percentage of the file already downloaded and the total estimated time.

To search lists of all CompuServe files, *Go*

- *GRAPHFF.* To find a particular graphics file.
- *IBMFF.* IBM files.
- *MACFF.* Macintosh files.
- *AMIGAFF.* Amiga files.
- *ATARIFF.* Atari files.

You are able to search by file name, date, or several descriptive key words. Click on a category to search for it. To display a list of found files, double-click on Display the List of Files.

Viewing a File Online

If the file you're interested in is a text file or a GIF graphics file, you can use CIM to view it online. Simply click on the View button, if available.

Once you view a file, you can save it, if you wish, by accessing Save from the File pull-down menu.

Graphical (GIF) files can be found in the Computer Art, Photography, Fine Art, Glamour Graphics, Archive Photos, or Graphics Corner forums, to name a few. Use the Find command to search for the word *GIF*.

Finding CompuServers

To search CompuServe's entire membership list, select Member Directory from the Mail pull-down menu at the top of the screen. You can search by first and last name, city, state, or country. Enter as much information as you know.

A list of matching members names appears. Click Address to add the currently highlighted person's name and ID number to your address book. Double-click a name to find out more detailed information about it.

Messages

CompuServe specializes in unique and eclectic forums. Whether you want a hobbyist's paradise, a database of facts, a club for those who lead similar lifestyles, support for a particular piece of software or hardware, a professional guild, or a place to catch the latest news, you'll be hooked on forums in no time.

Each of CompuServe's services has its own forums, and each forum generally has its own message topics, its own libraries of topical text and software available for download, and its own conference rooms.

To find a forum that fits your interest, you have several options:

- Search for it by clicking on the magnifying glass Find icon or by using the Find option under the Services pull-down menu. Type in anything at all, and there's probably a forum that covers it. For example, you can Find all "dating" areas, and see a list of the Human Sexuality forums, as shown in Figure 9-4.

- Explore any of CompuServe's dozen or so main services, browsing through menus until a forum catches your eye. Most CIS forums are tagged with the plus sign (+),

If you meet someone in a forum or in the CB Simulator, and only know the person's nickname or handle, you can also search by CompuServe ID number to find out your mystery date's real name.

meaning that they have an hourly charge. Or check out the Forums service, which organizes all the available forums into categories, making it easy to find exactly what you need.

Search offline using the CompuServe directory. The directory has detailed information about nearly 500 different forums. Select CompuServe Directory from the Help menu or balloon.

The first time you enter a forum, you are welcomed. The opening screen describes the forum and invites you to join it. It also tells you who the forum's sysop is. You can just *Visit* a forum if you'd like, browsing around and getting a feel for the topics and the people. You might as well just *Join* the forum, though, since there is no additional cost, and members get full access to all the chat rooms, libraries, and message areas.

When you join, be sure to fill in the Interests box. Whenever you're in a forum, its members can browse your profile, read your interests, and learn what makes you tick (or ticks you off).

WinCIM provides an easy *toolbox* panel to the right of your screen, which allows you to navigate around the entire forum. The toolbox and its associated commands are shown in Figure 9-5. All toolbox commands are also available from applicable pull-down menus.

To leave a forum and return to basic services, click on the Leave icon (the picture of the open door on the command bar), or select Leave from the File pull-down menu.

Your Messages

If anyone has responded to a message you posted, you find out as soon as you enter the forum. Check the bottom of your screen for a message like "You have 10 messages waiting."

Click the Get Waiting Messages icon or select Get Waiting from the Messages pull-down menu. A list of all the subjects that contain messages directed to you is shown. Double-click on a subject to read what's there.

Figure 9-5 Your forum control panel: the toolbox

In this way, each forum acts as a sort of voyeuristic mini-mailbox. When you reply to people's messages, they'll know immediately, without having to browse, and will usually reply back to you. In this way, you can exchange messages. Anyone else who is flipping through the forum can also read your exchange, and join in.

Browsing the Messages

Forum messages are divided into sections. Some sections require special permission to access; you need to send mail to your *forum leader* (FL), another word for the sysop.

To browse through a forum's messages, simply click on the Browse the Messages icon (the picture of the finger shuffling through the sheets of paper). A list of all the sections, similar to Figure 9-6, appears. You are told how many different sections and total messages there are.

If you want to browse just one section, double-click on it. To browse all the sections, click on—you guessed it—All. You can also *x* the box next to some of the sections you're interested in and then click on Select. A listing of subjects appears, as in Figure 9-7.

Again, mark the subject(s) that interest you and then click on Get.

You can also search for individual messages. Click on the Search Messages icon or select Search Messages from the Messages pull-down menu. You can click an *x* on the categories you're interested in searching. If you'd like, you can specify a particular topic, sender, or recipient, by typing its name in the corresponding box. You can also Mark the items you find so you can download them later.

Reading

Each message you selected is shown, one by one. If the message is too long to fit on one screen, click on the scroll bar to flip to the next page of text.

Messages are organized in *threads*. This means that a new message is treated as a forefather (or mother), and all its replies are treated as children. If someone replies to a reply,

Since 4/20/94 3:02 PM		
Title	**Topics**	**Msgs**
Dear Dennis N.	10	54
Family Crisis	0	0
Counselor's Corner	5	9
Gay Alliance	6	6
Singles Club	15	58
Matters of Morals	2	7
Software Exchange	0	0
Shyness Workshop	6	33
Pen Pals	5	10
HSX Contest	3	36
More Than Skin Deep	1	9
Naturist Lifestyles	7	13
Living With AIDS	13	60
Sex and the Law	2	3

[Select] [Mark] [All] [Close]

FIGURE 9-6 A listing of some of the sections in the CompuServe Human Sexuality forum

FIGURE 9-7 Getting into the nitty gritty: browsing the list of current subjects

there may be grandchildren and great-grandchildren and so on. To see the thread's "family tree" click on Map. The arrow buttons allow you navigate through a message thread. Clicking the right arrow is the logical choice, displaying the next message in the thread. You can continue clicking on the right arrow until all the replies have been shown. You can also see the previous message by clicking the left arrow. The up arrow shows you the current message's parent.

Replying

Click on Reply to respond to a message and to create a new child in the message thread. If you want to send a private reply over CompuServe e-mail, click an *x* into the little Via Mail box. Otherwise, go ahead and write your message, as detailed in the next section.

Writing a Message

Click on the Compose Forum Message icon (the graphic of a hand writing on some paper) or select the Create Message option from the Messages pull-down menu. Enter an eye-catching summary of your message in the Subject box. If your message is for everyone, you can either leave the To box blank, or address it to Sysop or to All. If your message is directed toward one particular person, enter his or her name in the first box and

EXPERT TIP

You can download entire sections of messages, saving you vast amounts of online time. Select each topic you're interested in and click Mark. Select Retrieve Marked from the Messages pull-down menu. Then click on Get All. You can even *x* the Disconnect When Done box to automatically log off when your download is complete. If one doesn't already exist, a corresponding forum folder is created in your filing cabinet.

CompuServe ID number in the adjoining box. Or, click on the To button to select a name from your address book.

If the forum you wish to post to is not already printed in the Forum box, click on the box and select from the list of all your forums. Click on the Section box, as well, if you want to change the default. The section list (shown in Figure 9-6) appears. Select the section where your message best fits.

Click on the Via Mail box, putting an *x* in it, to send your message privately over e-mail (in which case you could've just sent e-mail to begin with). You can also *x* the Private box so that only the appointed reader can see your message. Not all forums allow the use of private messages.

Finally, you can type in your message in the space provided. Click on Send to post your message immediately, click on Out Basket to hold the message until later.

Exploring Human Sexuality

Not surprisingly, given its self image as a serious, professional service, CompuServe doesn't have many message areas suitable for the flagrant flirt. One exception may be the Human Sexuality Forum. *Go HSX* to access the Human Sexuality main menu, shown in Figure 9-2. Over the *Hotline* you can ask confidential questions about any love, sex, dating, or relationship problems you may have. You can also search the hotline by double-clicking the Search The Hotline option. Type in a keyword, such as "*dating*," and a list of relevant questions and answers appears for you to browse. Answers are provided by such famous therapists as Dr. Ruth Westheimer and Dr. Joyce Brothers, as well as local CompuServe experts.

The Human Sexuality area has two support group forums, the Open Forum and the Adult Forum.

≋ Open Forum (*Go HSX100*). This is for tame discussion of sex and related subjects. Some of the categories include The Singles Club, Gay Alliance, Shyness Workshop, Pen Pals, More Than Skin Deep, Naturist Lifestyles, Living with AIDS, A Matter of Morals, and several confidential discussion hotlines.

≋ Adult Forum (*Go HSX200*). This area is strictly for uncensored questions about any aspect of human sexuality, from hang-ups to hang-downs (whatever that means).

CB Forum

If talking on the CB isn't enough for you, you can write messages about it, too. *Go CBFORUM.* Some of the many categories include Teen Talk, CHATTers Lounge, CB Games Info, and more.

Sneak a peek at Cupcake's CB Gossip Column (*Go Cupcake*), where the antics of your favorite CB pals are tracked with a keen eye. Who snubbed whom? Who is dating whom? Who cares? Read exclusive profiles of some of your favorite CB personalities. You can even have Cupcake publish *your* articles, gossip, or stories.

Participate

The Participate forum is a customized area where CompuServe users create their own messages areas and subjects. As of now, it is not available through the standard CIM interface, and is a little confusing to use. *Go participate* for more information.

Mail

CompuServe charges for mail, but the "standard" pricing plan includes the equivalent of 60 three-page letters per month, which should be enough. *Go mailrates* for detailed information. If you send e-mail from a forum, or respond to a classified ad, that letter does not count as part of your allowance.

Special mail, such as FAXes, Internet messages, CupidGrams (available around Valentine's Day, and perfect for compu-couples), SantaGrams, CongressGrams, and forum mail each have nominal costs. See Chapter 13, Shouting Over the Wall, for details on sending mail from CompuServe to other parts of cyberspace.

Reading New Mail

When you first connect, the Mailbox icon, shown in the upper-right corner of Figure 9-8, appears if you have any new mail. You can also click on the Get New Mail option of the Mail menu. If you're not already connected to CompuServe, CIM logs you on and gets you a listing of all your new, unopened mail. Double-click on a message to read it, then and there. You can also click on Get All to stuff all the new messages in your In Basket for later perusal.

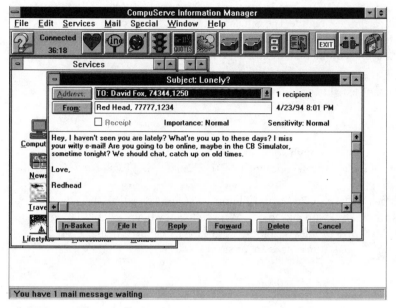

FIGURE 9-8 Reading a letter using CIM is even easier than reading one in real life. No paper cuts!

Later, on or offline, access your In Basket and double-click on whatever mail you wish to read. A window like the one in Figure 9-8 appears. Use the scroll bar at the side of the text to read extra-long letters. Click on Next, if available, to read the next letter in your list.

You can also select Print from the File pull-down menu to print your message, or Save As from the File menu to save your message as a text file. You can also click the File It button to save the letter in your file cabinet.

Replying to a Letter

To immediately respond to a letter, click the Reply button. A new message window appears, with the Address and Subject boxes already filled in appropriately. Click an x into the Copy Original box to reply to all the recipients of the original message.

See the Writing a Letter section for details on how to compose your electronic *billet-doux*.

Forwarding a Letter

To send the letter you just read to somebody else, click on the Forward button. The recipient list and new message windows appear, just as if you'd opted to write an original letter. You can then edit the letter, take extracts, or add comments. See the next section for instructions on writing a letter.

Writing a Letter

You can compose a letter either offline or on. Select the Create Mail option from the Mail menu or *Go mail*.

First, the Recipient List window pops up. Type in the addressee's name (or nickname) in the Name: box, and the CompuServe ID number (which looks something like 70000,0000) in the Address: box. Then click Add.

You can also send a letter to a name already in your address book. Just click on the Address Book listing and select as many people as you like. To add the name to your recipient list, click on the Copy>> button. Likewise, you can add people from your recipient list into your permanent address book by clicking on their names and then clicking <<Copy. The address book is discussed later in this chapter.

By default, any names after the first one you enter are designated as CC (carbon copy) recipients. You can also click the BC circle and then select (or type) a name to blind copy someone, if you don't want the other addressees to know that the current person was on your recipient list. Alternatively, you can click on the Show Recipients box to remove the x. This way, *nobody* you send the letter to receives a copy of your recipient list.

In this way, you can send mail to as many as 50 people at a time if you need to. Click OK when done.

The Create Mail window now appears, as in Figure 9-9. Enter a descriptive summary of your letter in the Subject box. You can now click on the big message box and type in your letter.

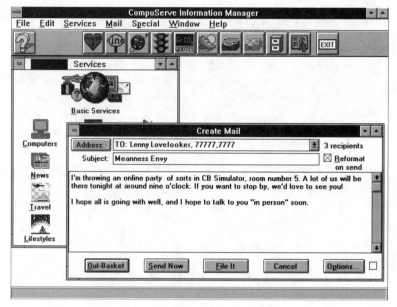

FIGURE 9-9 Wait a minute, Mr. Postman! Composing a letter on CompuServe

When you're done entering (or importing) your letter, you have a few options. To send it, click the Send Now button at the bottom of the message box. Your message is delivered within a few minutes. If you are composing your mail offline and want to send the message later, click Out Basket. The File It button is ideal if you want to save a copy of your current message in an area other than the Auto-Filed folder in the filing cabinet, where it is automatically stored.

As with the United States Postal Service, you can designate several nifty delivery options. Click on Options. You can have a receipt automatically sent to you when your letter is read, akin to certified mail. There is a $.15 charge for this service. You can also change the message to Low or High priority, or Private, Personal, or Confidential sensitivity. You can even designate the mail as Cash On Delivery, which means your poor recipient is charged for the letter, not you.

If, for some reason, you want to type a message now and have CompuServe not send it until a later date, you can specify a date in the Release Date box. You can also change the number of days the mail will be held in the recipient's mailbox before being deleted (1 to 90 days).

Sending Files

If you mail someone a scanned photograph of yourself, a word processing document, a graphical Valentine's day card—anything other than text—it is referred to as a *binary file*.

To send a binary file, select Send File from the Mail pull-down menu. Set up a recipient list, as usual (detailed in the previous section). Now enter a brief summary of the file in the Subject box. Click on the File button to browse your hard disk for the appropriate file, or just type its full name in the box.

Click on the circle next to Binary, Text, or GIF depending on the type of file. You can include some comments in the Additional Information box, such as brief instructions on how to use the file. You may now place the binary file in your Out Basket or send it immediately, by clicking on the Send Now button.

Downloading a Mailed File

If somebody sends you a file over e-mail, simply read the "letter" as you normally would. Instead of text appearing, a gauge indicating how long the download will take appears. The gauge looks just like the one for a file you're pulling out of a forum library, as described earlier in the Downloading Files section.

Address Book

CIM's address book is one of its keenest features. You can easily transfer the names of anyone you ever meet, read, or receive mail from on CompuServe into your address book. You can then send e-mail and write forum messages to these people without having to memorize their IDs.

Click on the command bar's Address Book icon or select Address Book from the Mail pull-down menu. The book, shown in Figure 9-10, appears.

To put a new name in the book, click Add. Enter any name or nickname in the Name: box, and enter that person's CompuServe ID number in the Address: box. Click OK. You

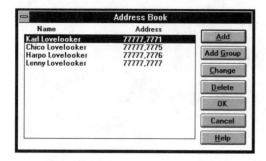

FIGURE 9-10 The Address Book: an easily accessible list of CompuServe friends

can also enter a FAX or Telex number, Internet, or MCI Mail address, or even a postal address. See Chapter 13, Shouting Over the Wall, for details on sending mail out of CompuServe.

You can also enter a few comments about each person, helping you keep track of who is who.

If you need to, you can always edit the address book: Click on the Address Book icon. Highlight a name and click on Delete to erase it. Click on Change to review or edit a name. You can also click on Add Group to place several names and addresses under one address book heading.

Chat

There are two powerful ways to telecommunicate live over CompuServe: You can discuss one particular subject in its forum conference area, or you can go truckin' through cyberspace, shootin' the breeze with hundreds of people via CompuServe's CB Simulator.

Ten Four, Over and Out, Good Buddy

CompuServe's CB Simulator is just that—a radio-style running bull session without the static, without the greasy food, and without the voice. Simply *Go cb* to access the main menu.

If you haven't already done so, you should fill in your CB profile. This is a little auto-biography that other CBers can read at any time. Double-click CB Profiles and fill in your nickname, location, occupation, and interests.

EXPERT TIP

If you're a CB junkie, it pays to join the CB Club. For $25 a month your CB time is billed at $3 an hour (for $50 monthly, CB time is only a buck an hour). Also, you can reserve your own handle, guaranteed to be yours and only yours. Double-click Special Pricing–The CB Club from the CB Simulator main menu. You must re-apply to the CB Club at the beginning of each month.

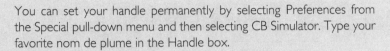

EXPERT TIP

You can set your handle permanently by selecting Preferences from the Special pull-down menu and then selecting CB Simulator. Type your favorite nom de plume in the Handle box.

Once you're ready, you can access one of the three CB bands:

- *General Band.* You can find anything and everything discussed in the General CB band—so long as it's rated PG or below. There are channels for most European languages, age groups, and even for a few hobbies. There's a poetry reading channel, a college corner, a teens-only room, and a holodeck, to name just a few. Channel 9, Heart to Heart, might be of special interest to those who want to happen onto other lonely hearts.

- *Adult I Band.* Most of the 36 chat channels in the Adult Band are not labeled. However, there are dedicated *Adult, Gay Lifestyles,* and *Lesbian Talk* channels. As you become a CompuServe veteran, you may find that different cliques of people meet in the different channels each night. Listen in for a while to decide if a channel is too hot or cold for your tastes.

- *Adult II Band.* The second Adult Band was created because the first band often fills up completely, becoming slow and choppy. If you're looking for a less crowded atmosphere, check it out.

When you first enter a CB band, you are asked to choose a handle—a creative nickname you want to be known by, such as Redhead, HotLegs, Cyber Dater, or Lenny. Your handle can be up to 19 letters long. The CB toolbar now appears to the right of your screen, shown in Figure 9-11.

You are now asked to select a channel. First, click on Status, and a window similar to Figure 9-12 appears. This tells you how many people are gabbing in each channel. You wouldn't want to tune in to an empty channel, unless you'd like to wait for some friendly soul to join you.

Change Channel

Who's Here?

Change Your Handle

See List of Friends

Invite

Ignore

FIGURE 9-11 Your CB control dial keeps you truckin'

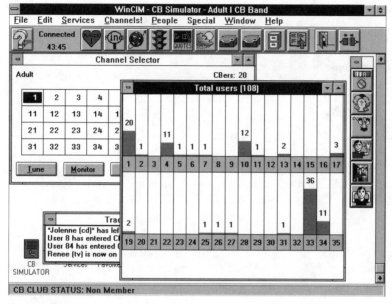

FIGURE 9-12 The status window shows you where the action is

Next, click on a channel that looks interesting and then click on Who. Click on the little Chan circle to display a list of the people currently in the channel. You can double-click on a name to read the person's profile. If the people sound interesting, the next step is to eavesdrop on their conversation. To do so, click Monitor. If the talk is moving too fast, you can click on Freeze to slow down the action. Click Freeze again when you're ready to continue.

Finally, when you've found your dream channel, select Tune. You are now in the middle of all the excitement. To talk, just type whatever you like and press (ENTER). Figure 9-13 displays a typical CB session.

While you're talking, you can change your handle at any time by clicking the Change Handle icon (the Groucho glasses).

EXPERT TIP

The Friends list is similar to an address book, keeping track of all your CBer pals. Every time you meet someone special, interesting, or funny, select Friends from the People pull-down menu. The Friends List box appears, letting you record nicknames and ID numbers for later reference.

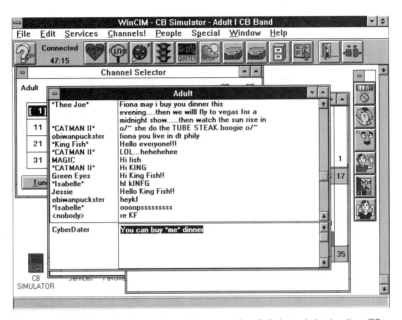

FIGURE 9-13 You don't need an eighteen wheelin' rig to join the live CB action, just a home computer, a modem, and a subscription to CompuServe

To list a roster of the people currently on your channel, click on the Who's Here icon (the picture of heads and the question mark). A window similar to Figure 9-14 opens. You can opt to view All the people in the CB Simulator (a hefty list), the people in the current Chan, or a designated Group of people. Simply click the little circle next to whichever option you want. You can also click the Only Friends box to list only those people whom you've previously designated as friends.

FIGURE 9-14 Hey, who's here?

Every time a person leaves or enters the channel, the Who's Here list alters itself. To freeze the list for a moment so that you can take a look at it, click on Freeze. Double-click on a nickname to get that person's profile. Click on Talk to hold a private conversation (see the next section) with the currently highlighted person.

Selecting Ignore from the pull-down menu, or clicking on the Ignore icon (the rather resolute man with his fingers in his ears) allows you to tag people you don't want to hear from. Then if they type something, try talking to you, try inviting you to a private party, or try anything short of e-mail, they are snubbed.

To exit, click the Leave icon or select Leave from the Files pull-down menu.

A Private Party

You can invite a bunch of people to a private channel by clicking on the Invite icon (the beckoning, smiling man leaning out the open door). Click on whoever you're interested in, placing an *x* in his or her associated box. Then click on Invite. The group gets a formal invitation to join you. A special group conversation window opens, like a scrambled CB channel of your very own.

Indeed, the time may come when the following message appears across your screen:

Would you like to join in a group discussion with Redhead?

Click on Yes and you step into Redhead's private room, closing the door behind you.

Talking One-to-One

If you want to hold a sideline conversation with someone in the Who's Here window (shown in Figure 9-14), highlight that person's nickname and click on *Talk*. A small peripheral window opens and you can hold a private chat session with your date while still taking part in the general banter of your current chat channel. Whenever you want to say something, click on whichever window you want to talk in.

If somebody Talks to you, a window suddenly appears on your screen. If you're too busy to chat, say so. Remember, if the same people keep bothering you with requests to talk, you can click the Ignore icon and squelch them to oblivion.

Be careful. If you talk to too many people at once, your screen fills with a collage of windows, each a different conversation. Remember, to close a window, just double-click on its upper-left corner.

Forum Conference Rooms

Most every forum has its own group of conference rooms. These are ideal places to meet experts in particular fields, address specific issues, or gab with people who share your interests.

Click on the Enter Conference Room icon from your toolbox (See Figure 9-5, back in the Messages section) or select Enter Room from the Conference pull-down menu. Figure 9-15 shows a typical conference room list. You are told the name and number of each room. To enter a room, double-click on it.

FIGURE 9-15 The list of conference rooms in the Adult Human Sexuality forum

As in the CB Simulator, you can pull down the Conference menu (or click the proper icon) to Set A Nickname, Invite, or Ignore. You can also select Who's Here from the Conference menu (or click its icon) to list the people currently in the forum. If you want to see who is in a particular chat room, click Room and type in that room's number.

Select Descriptions from the Conference pull-down menu to get an overview of each room, including a schedule of the daily goings-on. The Notice, also under the Conference pull-down menu, tells you if a celebrity guest is slated to appear in one of the conference rooms, and may contain additional information.

To speak up in a conference, all you have to do is type.

You have now mastered the third dimension of the CompuServe forum; you've left your letters and messages, downloaded your files, and now you know how to have your computer serve up endless hours of talk.

Final CompuServe Comments

CompuServe is one of the most feature-rich online networks available; it lives up to its own billing as "The service you won't outgrow." No other provider has as much support and service for U.S. and international callers alike.

Although CompuServe's shirt is a little stiff when it comes to online dating, people are people and you can find your share of flirts, fun-lovers, and ordinary folk just looking for some feedback. Even right-wing giant Rush Limbaugh met and married his match using CompuServe e-mail. Although the service is indeed targeted toward computer experts, the CIM software has opened up the CompuServe world to users of all experience levels.

Due to CompuServe's reputation, high-end extended price, and experienced user base, it can be thought of as the country club of telecommunications services. If you've mastered the techniques in this chapter, however, you deserve full membership privileges, virtual golf clubs and all.

PRODIGY

800-PRODIGY (776-3449)
P.O. BOX 191486
DALLAS TX 75219-1486

I MET A GIRL IN JUNE '88 VIA Q*LINK,

an old Commodore online service. She became my fiancée. However, she broke the relationship twelve days before our wedding. I met another girl on PRODIGY (while I was engaged) whom I am still friends with; she "set me up" with her best friend, who was rooming with her in Texas. It was a long-distance relationship for nearly three months before I actually went out to meet them both in person. I've since moved her (the best friend) out here to Virginia and we got married last April.

What It Is

Sears and IBM jointly own and operate PRODIGY, and it shows. From the moment you log on, you feel like you're browsing through an enormous, crowded high-tech mall. You'll be offered airline tickets, flowers, lingerie, computer hardware, clothes, books, and plenty more. However, as any suburban teenager knows, malls are sometimes the coolest places to cruise, picking up dates.

PRODIGY is by far the cutest commercial network. You move around the screen, selecting neatly-labeled buttons. It's easy to explore and hard to get lost. Most screens are aflame with colorful magazine-style layouts and near-photo-quality pictures. There are weather maps, cartoon animals, graphs, charts, and more. PRODIGY blasts you with commercials on the bottom of each screen, which you may find either annoying

or fun. There are many tiny time-wasters to check out, and online game-shows and contests are popular.

Prettiness has its price, though. PRODIGY's dashing good looks come at the expense of speed. Even at 9600 baud, PRODIGY runs a good deal slower than other online services. Depending on how fast your modem and computer are, PRODIGY may spend several minutes drawing each screen.

PRODIGY is America's largest commercial cyberspace station, currently sporting over three million users. There's a good chance of running into your old high-school buddy or, even better, your old high-school sweetheart.

Though there are plenty of places to leave messages, the PRODIGY service has just begun to offer limited real-time chatting with other users. Interaction through bulletin boards is popular on PRODIGY, but using them runs up an hourly toll. Each e-mail letter you send also has a nominal fee.

How To Connect

Because of its fancy graphics and easy layout, PRODIGY requires its own communications software. A startup kit is available at most every computer store for about $14.95. (I've even seen it in supermarkets.) If you don't mind waiting, you can order the software for free (well, $4.95 or so for shipping and handling) directly from PRODIGY at 800-284-5933.

The Software

The PRODIGY menus, graphics, and options all work pretty much the same no matter which computer or operating system you use. There are three versions of the software: Windows, MS-DOS, and Macintosh. For IBM computers, both the 3½ and 5¼ inch diskette sizes are available.

Windows

This is PRODIGY's newest and snazziest software program. It is specially geared toward navigating PRODIGY with a mouse, allowing standard Windows gizmos such as pull-down menus, cutting and pasting, and multitasking. This version also supports digital sound cards, allowing for music, and has the ability to display photo-quality images, such as news and sports photos, or photos of online celebrities, as in Figure 10-1. Windows PRODIGY is also the only version currently offering a chat facility.

EXPERT TIP

Get a current PRODIGY user to request software for you. You get a free sign-up package and your friend gets extra bonus hours.

FIGURE 10-1 PRODIGY transmits photos online. This technology may eventually allow cyberdaters to see each other while they interact

You must own a copy of Microsoft Windows version 3.1 (or higher). It is also recommended that you have at least an IBM 80386 PC running at 16Mhz (consult your owner's manual), 3.5 megabytes of room on your hard drive, 4 megabytes of RAM, a mouse, and a VGA color monitor. Anything less and the software is much too clunky.

Installing the Windows version is easy. Be sure Windows is up and running, and then insert the PRODIGY diskette into the drive. Using the mouse, click the Program Manager's File pull-down menu and then select Run. If the PRODIGY disk is in drive A, type

    a:install (ENTER)

otherwise, type

    b:install (ENTER)

MS-DOS

This version of PRODIGY is for IBM PCs and compatibles that aren't powerful enough to work with Windows. Although it lacks multitasking, chatting, and photo-quality, it looks and functions pretty much the same as the Windows version. You need DOS version 2.0 (or higher), 640K of memory, and a video graphics card (Hercules, CGA, EGA, VGA or better). Installing is just as easy. First, place the PRODIGY diskette into the disk drive. If the disk is in drive A, type

    a: (ENTER)

otherwise, type

    b: (ENTER)

Then type

    install (ENTER)

Macintosh

You need a Mac Plus machine (or better) with at least 1 megabyte of memory, running System 4.1 (or higher). The Mac version of the software, while currently on par with the skimpy DOS version, is slated to support sound and photographic images eventually. Installing PRODIGY requires only a few clicks of your mouse.

Put the PRODIGY diskette in the drive and double-click on the Disk icon when it appears. Then double-click on the PRODIGY Configure icon and select the Setup option. Enter your computer's configuration, modem speed, and other technical details. Next, double-click on the Install icon, which places the software onto the Macintosh's hard drive. Finally, click on Launch The Service to achieve liftoff.

Charges

The first month on PRODIGY is usually free, allowing you to get a taste of the service before you become a full-fledged member. After that, you are subscribed onto the Value plan, for a flat fee of $14.95 a month. Table 10-1 lists some of PRODIGY's main pricing plans. You can switch plans online by Jumping to the Payment menu. PRODIGY also offers money-saving long-term plans.

Once you exhaust your pricing plan's free hours, you have to pay an additional $3.60 an hour. Most of PRODIGY's areas—online games, encyclopedias, shopping, and news—are *core* services, which, under the standard Value pricing plan, have unlimited free usage. Unfortunately, the best places for online dating—namely bulletin boards—fall under the *plus* services category, and may run up your bill. Also, e-mail costs $.25 a message, although you are allowed 30 free "stamps" under the Value plan.

More generously, there are no local surcharges and no fines for speeding; 9600-baud users pay the same as anyone else.

General billing help and information can be found under the Account Menu, which can be accessed from PRODIGY Tools. Here you can look at your monthly statement or check the status of your latest payment.

PRICING PLAN	MONTHLY CHARGE	FREE SERVICES	FREE E-MAIL
Value	$14.95	All *core* services; 2 hours of *plus*	30 messages
Alternate	$7.95	2 hours of *core* or *plus*	None
Alternate 2	$19.95	8 hours of *core* or *plus*	None
Alternate BB	$29.95	25 hours of *core* or *plus*	None

TABLE 10-1 An overview of PRODIGY's pricing plans

Under this menu you can also change your Payment Method, and allow your credit card or bank account to be billed automatically, which may be more convenient than a monthly tab.

Logging On and Off

Once you are a PRODIGY member, simply run the PRODIGY software to connect. Windows and Macintosh users should click on the PRODIGY® Software icon, DOS users need only type

```
prodigy
```

Your PRODIGY startup kit will walk you through your first sign-on. Type the service ID and temporary password from the paperwork that came with the software into the slots provided on the screen, and press (ENTER). Then answer the technical questions that appear—simple stuff like the speed of your modem and whether or not you have call waiting (which PRODIGY automatically disables for you). PRODIGY now calls a special 800 number, retrieving the number of your local public data network. If you have trouble finding a local access number, call PRODIGY customer service.

Next you are asked for your personal stats: name, address, etc. Once everything is entered, you're able to choose your password. Type it in, twice. You can change your password later online by Jumping to the Change Password menu. You are now officially PRODIGY's newest member.

Autologon

To access this feature, Jump to *autologon* when you're online. You may select from the following:

≋ *Full Autologon.* You never have to enter your pesky PRODIGY ID or password again. Simply click on the Autologon icon (for Windows), or run the PRODIGY software as usual. You'll be online in a jiffy. Of course, if any strangers have access to your computer, they can be online in a jiffy too.

≋ *Partial Autologon.* For security, you may not want access to your PRODIGY account to be a simple keypress away. If your computer is located in a public area, you may appreciate the Partial Autologon option. Each time you connect to the PRODIGY service, you have to enter your password.

≋ *Switch Off.* To turn the autologon capability completely off.

Logging Off

To disembark from the PRODIGY service, type Ⓔ and press (ENTER) or click on the Exit button at the bottom of the screen. You get a chance to change your mind, or to sign on another member of your family.

Getting Around

Think of the PRODIGY screen as the dashboard of a cyber-spaceship. Along the bottom, there's a *command bar* containing the main navigation controls and status indicators. On the Macintosh and Windows versions, the navigation controls are represented by single letters and symbols. The DOS version uses full words to represent the various commands. You can catch a glimpse of the standard Windows command bar at the bottom of Figure 10-1.

At any given moment, all applicable commands are displayed in bold text. To access a command, click on it if you have a mouse. If you're mouseless, press the underlined letter; on some versions of PRODIGY you need to hold down (CTRL) while pressing the applicable letter. All the commands can also be found in the Mac and Windows pull-down menus. Last, most commands have their own special hot keys—which differ slightly with each version of the PRODIGY software.

For instance, if you are reading a long letter, pressing Ⓝ displays the next page of text, as does clicking the Next arrow ⊙, as does selecting > from the Page pull-down menu, as does pressing (PGDN). Different people prefer accessing their commands in different ways. Fool around with the software to figure out which keystrokes or mouse-glides suit you best. Table 10-2 summarizes the basic functions of the navigation buttons. Remember, not all navigation buttons appear at all times.

The rightmost corner of the command bar also tells you what type of service you are currently using:

- *Free.* These areas, such as advertisements and member services, never have an hourly charge.
- *Core.* Core areas are free to those who belong to PRODIGY's basic Value membership plan.
- *Plus.* This includes bulletin boards, stock quotes, and company news. There is often an hourly toll for these areas, although Value members are allowed two free hours a month.
- *****.* This is for areas such as mail, where pricing depends on how many letters you send.

DOS	MAC/WIN	HOT KEY	FUNCTION
[~]	[~]	F5	Takes you directly to the PRODIGY Highlights screen.
>	>	PGDN	Displays the next page of information.
<	<	PGUP	Displays the previous page of information.
Menu	M	F9	Brings you back to the last menu screen you were at.
Jump	J	F6	Enters a *jumpword* to access a specific PRODIGY area.
Path	P	F4	Moves to the next item on your path list.
	V	F3	Displays the path list.
A-Z	A-Z	F7	Allows you to select from PRODIGY's alphabetical index of jumpwords.
Xref	X	F8	Allows you to browse other areas of current interest.
Zip	Z	CTRL + Z	Returns you to wherever you were before "Looking" at an ad.
Action	A	F2	Verifies that you want to make an online purchase.
	Pr	CTRL + P	If your printer is set up, prints the current screen (text only).
Tools	T	CTRL + T	Selects from PRODIGY's billing and personal account tools.
	R	CTRL + R	Reviews the PRODIGY areas you've visited most recently.
Exit	E		Logs off the PRODIGY service.
Copy			Allows you to copy the current text to your disk, clipboard, or printer.
?		F1	Guides you through PRODIGY sign-up, navigation, and software.

TABLE 10-2 PRODIGY's navigation commands

A color-coded ribbon winding down the left side of the screen tells you which department you are currently in. Generally, the right side of the screen contains menu buttons, which take you wherever you wish to go.

Above the command line, the screen changes constantly. Sometimes it's a menu, allowing you to select from a list of options. Other times it's text or pictures, like a page in a magazine. No two screens are the same, and layouts are often revised and revamped, which makes PRODIGY fun to bump around in. Ads are always splayed along the bottom of each screen.

Generally, each option is surrounded by a rectangle, giving it a button-like appearance—whether it's a picture, a number, a navigation command, a blank space for you to type in, or a sentence. To select an option, simply move the mouse arrow over it—the arrow changes into a pointing finger—and then click. Otherwise, you can highlight the option's border (which promptly flashes) and then press (ENTER). Generally, PRODIGY highlights the option that makes the most sense, depending on the context. To highlight a different option, simply use the up and down arrow keys. Alternatively, (TAB) highlights the next selection.

At times there may be a numbered list of choices. You can either highlight one of the items, as usual, or simply press its number.

Next/Back

If the message or letter you are reading is longer than a single screen, selecting Next flips the electronic page. Next flips forward, Back flips, yes, back.

Menu

This takes you back to the last menu you were using. This is often useful. For instance, if a menu with several tasty entrees appears, simply choose the first selection you want, read it, and then access the Menu command. You may now choose the second selection, third, and so on.

Jump

Jumpwords are the true secret of being a PRODIGY prodigy. They work like a book's index; you type in the jumpword and you're zipped directly to the appropriate page. Upon selecting the Jump command, you are asked which jumpword you're looking for. If you know the exact jumpword, enter it. Otherwise, just guess. PRODIGY displays a list of valid jumpwords closest to matching your guess. For instance, if you try to jump to

    dating

you get a list of actual areas ranging from Classifieds to Personal Ads to Singles BB.

A-Z Directory

The A-Z command allows you to browse a list of every jumpword known to PRODIGYkind. You can also click on a specific PRODIGY department, such as Communications A-Z, to browse through relevant jumpwords. In addition, the directory has an easy search capability. Simply highlight the black Type to Move List box and type in the first few letters of a topic you're interested in. All nearby jumpwords are displayed.

If you want some information about a particular jumpword, highlight it and press ⑦. To jump somewhere, click on an item or highlight it and press (ENTER).

The Path Less Taken

At times the PRODIGY forest can be thick, dark, and spooky. The Path command allows you to mark up to 20 of your favorite areas to visit, comprising what is known as a *path list*. The first time you access Path, you automatically jump to the first item on the predefined pathlist. Select Path again and you jump to the second item. Et cetera.

PRODIGY's built-in path list is, in fact, the best way to take an unguided tour. Repeatedly select Path. You jump from a weather map to the latest news story to stock quotes to football scores to . . . .

If you'd like to see the current stops along your path, select the ViewPath command. Figure 10-2 illustrates a common path list. By selecting any feature on the list, you can jump to it. In this way, the path keeps track of the PRODIGY jumpwords you use most often.

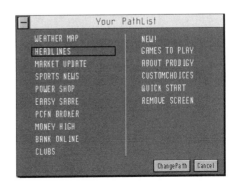

FIGURE 10-2 A peek at PRODIGY's popular paths

To create a path of your own, simply select the ViewPath command and then access the Changepath option. Select Add, and then Other Location. In the Add box, type in a valid jumpword. You are asked in which position (from 1 to 20) you want to place the word. Place your most favorite words first. You can continue typing in new jumpwords, either building your path list from scratch or modifying the current list to better suit your needs.

Alternatively, you can jump to ChangePath at any time.

Cross Referencing

If you're the type who likes to pinball around online services, tasting a little bit from the smorgasbord of options, you'll enjoy the Xref command. Any time you read, see, or do anything which interests you, selecting Xref brings up a list of similar services. To jump to one of them, simply select it.

Action

PRODIGY is chock-full of ways to separate you from your wallet's innards. If you're not careful and click on the wrong series of buttons, it's possible to order yourself a $5,000 computer system. Luckily, the PRODIGY service takes this into account (pun not strongly intended) and provides a safety measure: the Action command.

Selecting Action is the way of telling PRODIGY, "Yes, yes, I *do* want to buy what is currently on the screen." Obviously, only access the Action command if you really want to act. You can usually review your order and enter your mailing and billing address and your payment method. You can also Cancel most orders at the last minute.

Tools

The PRODIGY toolbox is a handy menu containing everything you need to keep your account in tidy order. Through the Tools command, you can change your password, update or specify your method of paying bills, create PRODIGY accounts for other members of your household, set up the autologon feature, and check the status of your account and its finances.

Look/Zip

If an advertisement piques your interest, you can *Look* at it. You can read the stats, order what you like. When you want to return to whatever you were doing prior to Looking, access the *Zip* command, and you automatically zip right back.

If an ad flashes by before you get a chance to Look, you can access Ad Review under the Jump pull-down menu. Using the Next/Back commands you can flip through PRODIGY's current crop of advertisements.

EXPERT TIP

You can custom design your highlights screen so that each time you log on to PRODIGY the cover screen of one of the ten PRODIGY services appears. Jump *change highlights.* If, for example, you spend most of your online time scrounging through bulletin boards and sending mail, try selecting the Communications Highlights screen.

Service Highlights

PRODIGY is organized into ten main services: News and Weather, Business and Finance, Sports, Communications, Entertainment, Reference, Shopping, Computers, Travel, and Home/Family/Kids. In addition, there is the free Member Services area, which contains everything you've ever wanted to know about PRODIGY but didn't know where to ask. To access one of PRODIGY's services you can Jump to it, select it from the Contents pull-down menu, or select the appropriate button from the main Highlights screen.

The PRODIGY Service Highlights screen, shown in Figure 10-3, is like the front page of a very colorful newspaper. You can access the Highlights screen any time you're online by clicking on its icon (a square with a yellow stripe atop it) in the lower left corner of your screen.

Highlights contains the top three or four news stories of the day (usually including an online photograph or two), a daily poll, special shopping bargains, and other noteworthy news such as the arrival of an online celebrity. If you have new mail, the word Mail appears in the top right corner, or a picture of an envelope appears in the bottom right corner.

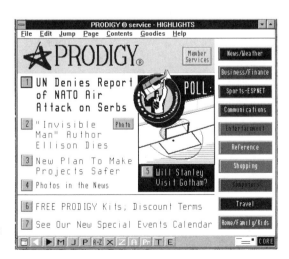

FIGURE 10-3 Spotlighting the PRODIGY Highlights screen

Some versions of PRODIGY even tell you, in a sassy voice, if you have any mail waiting. See the Mail section later in this chapter for more information.

All the PRODIGY services are also listed to the right of the screen, color-coded and ready for you to select. Each service has its own relevant news stories, products, polls, and bulletin boards. Remember, if you get lost, you can return to the opening screen at any time by selecting the Highlights icon at the lower left corner of your screen.

PRODIGY's main services are:

- *News/Weather:* the bare facts. PRODIGY is very much a fully-functional newspaper. From the News/Weather service, you can flip through the latest business, sports, health, entertainment, weather, international, local, and other news. This is also the place for news discussion, selected reviews, and polls.

- *Business/Finance:* the bulls and the bears. The Business/Finance service is stocked with the latest news, economics, market quotes, online trading, online banking, bill paying, office help, tax info, small business advice, money discussion, and other such topics.

- *Sports-ESPNet:* the Chicago Bulls and their buddies. Sports news, scores, stats, player info, and more can be found under the Sports-ESPNet service. Using PRODIGY's fantasy simulations, you can manage your own football or baseball team and play a season or two against other PRODIGY managers. Also, PRODIGY's Network Golf Tour, for an additional monthly fee, allows you to create your own computerized courses, choose from a roster of pros, and tour against other PRODIGY swingers.

- *Communications:* shooting the bull. Figure 10-4 displays the main menu of the Communications service, PRODIGY's cyberdating hub. Mail, Bulletin Boards, and Personals are three choices you may be interested in. There's also an Internet forum here, where you can learn how to send messages over the information superhighway. See Chapter 13,

FIGURE 10-4 The cover screen for PRODIGY Communications services

Shouting Over the Wall, for more details. Select the Greeting Cards option to send personalized, colorful messages to your PRODIGY friends. Many cards are animated and even play little tunes. This feature can take some of the monotony out of regular e-mail, and is a good idea for birthdays, holidays, anniversaries, and especially Valentine's Day. There is a nominal fee for each card sent. You can preview each card before you buy and send it.

Entertainment: where the silver screen meets your computer screen. You'll find the latest Hollywood news and gossip and even the Total TV online TV guide. You can also lay your finger on the pulse of today's culture by finding out what's hot and not in television, videos, music, games, movies, books, dining, and people. Select Games to enter the Game Center, shown in Figure 10-5. You can select Adventures/Role-Playing Games for the graphical adventure game *Mad Maze,* or the geographical *Carmen Sandiego* detective game. Select Strategy/Sports for fantasy sports simulations, strategy games such as *Guess the Next Move Chess,* or *Rebel Space,* an intergalactic exploration and trading game (which has an hourly fee). The Quick Games selection contains a handful of fun little time-fillers, and the Humor, Stories, & Other Amusements selection is the place to go for your online one-liners, stories of all kinds, and a lovely online art gallery. You can also choose to download games of your own. For an additional monthly fee, you can find out how to access Game Point, a separate online service where you can play live action games with other cyberdaters. (Most of PRODIGY's regular games contain no human interaction.)

Reference: your online neighborhood library. If you seek any common info, you'll probably be able to find it in the Reference service. Search your heart out through an online encyclopedia, *Consumer Reports* product reviews, political profiles, White House memorandums, software guides, travel guides, movie guides, or city guides.

FIGURE 10-5 PRODIGY takes games seriously

- *Shopping:* the marketplace in your home. Between PRODIGY's specialty shops, classifieds, bargains, giveaways, perks, mail-order catalogs, and online company support, you should be able to buy nearly anything you'd normally have to trudge through a mall for.

- *Computers:* ready-reference technobabble. The Computers service has all the latest news, reviews, expert support, software guides, and more.

- *Travel:* a do-it-yourself agency. Using PRODIGY's Travel service, you can make bookings with hotels, car rental agencies, or airlines. There are also several city guides to help you and your real-life date decide where to go for a night on the town. You'll also find weather maps, travel tips, culture tips, and special travel deals and discounts here.

- *Home/Family/Kids:* domestic living at its most computerized. Whether you want to bone up on the latest Health/Fitness news, settle down with the Home/Family, dig your teeth into some Food recipes and tips, or discuss your favorite Hobbies, the Home/Family/Kids service of PRODIGY is a nice place to visit. There's also real estate and automotive information, as well as a section just for kids.

- *Member Services:* get hip to all facets of PRODIGY, for free. You can find out about what's new or up-and-coming with PRODIGY, or quick tips on how to use the PRODIGY service. Membership and account stats are also available here, as is a question-and-answer area, where any trouble you're having with PRODIGY is solved.

Downloading

PRODIGY charges for most downloads, depending on the file. Prices range from free (for promotional items) to upwards of $50 for commercial-quality software. There is no additional hourly cost while downloading software. To check out the companies that allow you to download their programs via PRODIGY, select the Download button or Jump to one of the following distributors:

- *Ziffnet.* Some of the highest-quality shareware programs are offered through Ziffnet. Choose the Ziffnet Selections feature to browse through the catalog, searching for software by category or title. You can either pay for each download, or Enroll in Ziffnet for the price of $7.50 for one hour a month of downloading or $14.95 for a three-hour spree.

- *Download Superstore.* The superstore contains top-quality software, not shareware. Browse through the catalog for a detailed description of each file.

- *Royston.* This company only offers one item of software: PRO-Util. This program works hand-in-hand with your PRODIGY for DOS software, turning PRODIGY into a faster, more convenient network. PRO-Util allows you to compose messages offline, see how long you've been online, and more.

When you've highlighted a file you like, select Download Now to see the ordering information. Review the charges and select a billing method (you can usually just tack the price onto your PRODIGY account). Select Download. You are told the file's name, and the directory or folder it will appear in (usually it shows up in your default PRODIGY directory). Now select Download again or Authorize Purchase & Begin Download. You get instructions, online, about how to use your new software. You only pay for the file if the download is successful.

Searching for the Prodigal Son

This is about a different kind of couple meeting on PRODIGY. I found my half-brother that I hadn't seen in 24 years. We were not raised together. We had only seen each other three times in our life. One night on PRODIGY I looked at the member list and typed in his name, checking all the states. He was from Massachusetts, but I found him in Montana. I wrote to him asking if he was related to me and within 24 hours he wrote back. He flew to Nebraska to see me two weeks later. It was a great family reunion for me because I lost my husband last year and have no other family. We had both bought our computers around the same time and had signed onto PRODIGY almost the same week. I now have a brother who has a wife and three kids! My brother was also able to tell me where my other brother and sister were. I was not as lucky with them; they have not been very receptive, but thanks to PRODIGY I have a family again.

Since PRODIGY has so many members, users often run across old teachers, friends, classmates, roommates, lovers, relatives, and more. To search PRODIGY for someone, Jump to *Member List*. You can locate a person by name, city, and state, or by city and state alone. When asked to enter a first and last name, type in the first few letters of each.

You can now either select one state or choose Search all states to perform a nationwide search. A list of possible names appears. Select a name from the list and you are told that person's city, full name, and PRODIGY ID number. If this is the person you were looking for, select Add to add that person's name to your personal address book, for easy future reference. You are asked to type in a name or nickname. See the Address Book section, a bit further on.

If you're not sure that you've found the right John Q. Public, you can ask the person through a polite e-mail message. You can select Write to send the person some mail right away.

If you'd like to be unlisted you can select Delete Your Name From the List at the Member List main menu. To add your name, if for some reason it isn't there, select Add Your Name to the List.

Messages (Notes)

It finally happened when I really wasn't looking. I had only been on PRODIGY three days. I had never signed on to a bulletin board before, I just happened onto it by mistake. What made it special was that I could be myself, and I wasn't trying to impress anyone with my physical attributes. Not that I am bad-looking, but California men have this idea that all women should look like beach bunnies. Kevin and I got to know each other from the inside out and ultimately in a relationship, that is what counts. We are

all going to grow old sooner or later but basically we don't change much on the inside. We realized that not only were we attracted to each other for our personalities, but also the physical attributes as well when we finally met. I never imagined that I could care for someone so fast, I had always been so careful and protective, but knowing that he was in another state I could open up completely to him and tell him my deep down feelings. It's a great way to meet; I would recommend it to anyone who is tired of the singles scene, and believe me, I tried everything in San Diego from disastrous blind dates to personal ads. I just knew that I didn't want to be alone for the rest of my life. I guess this just goes to prove two things: There is someone out there for all of us and it happens when we least expect it to. [Saundra and Kevin were married June '94.]

Bulletin boards, or BBs, are the forums where PRODIGYers can cavort, argue, buy, sell, write, or discuss. You can find more BBs around PRODIGY than in your average air-gun. Apt BBs can be found under each of the eleven PRODIGY services. To see a list of all the BBs, Jump to *Bulletin Boards*.

PRODIGY's notes are divided by board, topic, then subject. Select Boards A-Z to scan a list of almost fifty general categories of bulletin-boarding. You can type in a few letters and press (ENTER) to quickly search for a particular board. You can now select Go To to access that particular board, or select About to read a summary of topics and to find out what is usually discussed there.

You can also directly search the list of PRODIGY's hundred or so discussion topics. Select Topics A-Z. Again, you can type a particular topic to access it directly, for instance:

`dating`

Those topics marked with an asterisk (*) are read-only topics, which means you cannot reply or write your own messages.

Select a topic and you are taken to the appropriate bulletin board's cover screen. Figure 10-6 illustrates the look of the Singles BB.

Once you know which BBs interest you, you can Jump directly to them at any time. For instance, Jumping to Singles BB is much faster than going through the list of boards and topics.

Reading Notes

Each BB is its own club. The cover screen of a BB contains that club's latest announcement by the *Board Leader*—the PRODIGY staff member or members responsible for keeping the board organized. If you have any questions about a BB, you can always e-mail its leader.

EXPERT TIP

PRODIGY's terminology is a little out of synch with the rest of cyberspace. It generally refers to e-mail as "messages" (not letters) and bulletin board articles as "notes" (not messages).

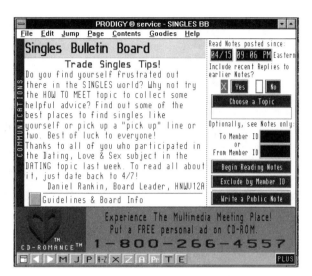

FIGURE 10-6 The cover screen of PRODIGY's Singles BB

Select the Guidelines & Board Info button for a more detailed description of the BB, as well as its applicable rules.

Due to PRODIGY's huge number of members, BBs are constantly inundated with notes. Therefore, you have lots of options as to what exactly you want to read. As a default, you only read notes that have been posted within the last hour or so. If you'd like to read further back, access the date and/or time slots at the top of the screen and type in the new time you want to begin reading from.

PRODIGY's notes are well organized. Each individual note, and all its replies, are bundled together in one easily-readable package. If you only want to read new notes, and not new replies to earlier notes, then select No where you're asked "Include recent replies to earlier notes?"

If you're interested in reading notes exclusively to or from one particular PRODIGY member, you can enter that person's ID number in either the To Member ID or From Member ID box. If there are people whose notes always annoy you, select Exclude by Member ID to ignore their words of nonwisdom.

Once you have your reading criteria down, you may choose a topic. Each BB has anywhere from 5 to 40 different topics. Select the Choose a Topic button. A topic list similar to Figure 10-7 appears.

EXPERT TIP

You can Change Access to prohibit other members of your household from accessing certain BBs. Simply go through the options, selecting what is on and off limits to whom.

FIGURE 10-7 The topics you can browse in the Singles BB area

FIGURE 10-8 A subject list for you to peruse

Scroll through the pages, if the list is long, by accessing the Next command (or by pressing (**PGDN**)). Choose your favorite topic. You may now select Begin Reading Notes.

A subject list, similar to Figure 10-8, appears. If you are searching for a particular subject, you can type it in. For instance, many of the personal areas of the Singles BB sort their subjects by area code. To search for someone looking for love in New York you could type Manhattan's area code:

(212)

and all subjects beginning with (212) appear.

You may now choose a subject to read by selecting it. Alternatively, you may select the Notes - Subject Order button, which shows you a detailed listing of each subject, how many notes were written under the subject, by whom, and how many replies there are to each note. Browse through the listing, placing an x in the box which precedes each note you want to read. When you've x-ed everything you're interested in, select the Read choices button. If you'd like to read all the notes, select the Read all button.

You may now read through your final selections, one by one, as in Figure 10-9. Many notes have quite a few replies. To read through the replies, select the Reply Preview button and click on whichever replies sound interesting. To read the next note in the current subject, if applicable, select Next Note. To begin reading the notes belonging to the next subject, select Next Subject. You can continue like this until you run out of replies, notes, or subjects, whichever comes first.

When you are finished reading, you can access the Options button, where you can either select a new subject, select a new topic, or return to the bulletin board's main cover menu.

The Export Business

To save costly online time, you can browse through a list of subjects, choose what interests you, and then save all the subjects (along with their replies) on your disk. Later, after

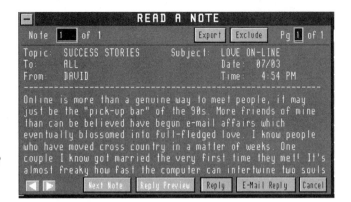

FIGURE 10-9 Anything for love? A sample note in PRODIGY's Singles BB

logging off PRODIGY, you can read the messages at your leisure, as you would any other text file.

To do all this, change the Note Preview area of the subject listing. Originally, this is set to Off. If you'd like to store all of a given subject's notes onto your disk, select On w/ Subject Export. If you'd like to browse through the various notes first, select the On w/ Selective Export button.

Now, click on the subject you want to export. You should see a screen telling you how many notes there are and how many replies each note has. You are also given a preview of the first line of each note. If you choose the Selective Export feature, you may now pick the notes you want, one at a time, putting an *x* in each one's check-box. To save everything, select Export All Notes and Replies on the Subject. Enter a filename and, in a few moments, PRODIGY downloads all the notes to your hard drive.

You may now select Subject to export a different subject, or select Topic to return to the bulletin board's main topic listing.

Replying to a Note

If you read something that deserves a public retort, applause, answer, or further comment, simply select the Reply button.

If your reply is of a more personal nature, you can send the note's author a private e-mail message. Select the E-Mail Reply button. See the section on Mail, a bit further along, for more help.

Writing Your Own Note

There are two ways to post a note of your own:

🔖 If you're reading the note under a particular subject and want to say something that isn't exactly a reply, but still pertains to the topic, select Write a New Note in This Subject from the Options button list.

EXPERT TIP

You can save a great deal of online time by composing your notes offline first. Using your favorite editor or word processor, type up the note. Be sure to save it as a text file. Now, log on to PRODIGY and go about posting a note, as usual. When you get to the note-entry screen, select the Import button. Type in the name of the file where your text is stored. Your words automatically swoop up from disk space into cyberspace.

Otherwise, you have to create a new subject. From the main cover screen of a bulletin board (as in Figure 10-6), select Write a Public Note. You are then asked to select a topic, if you have not already done so. You should now see a list of every subject that has ever been written under the current topic. Browse through the list. If you see something that fits what you want to say, select it. Otherwise, select the Add a New Subject button.

You can now type your note. A screen similar to Figure 10-10 appears. Unless you're addressing the note to one specific person, leave the Note To: box blank. If you haven't already chosen a subject, type one in the appropriate box. Then begin typing your message.

When you fill up a page, you can write some more by accessing the Next command (or pressing (PGDN)). If your train of thought switches tracks and you want to retype your note, simply select the Clear button. You can also Cancel Note entirely. Once you finish typing, select OK and then select Submit My Note. Any one of PRODIGY's three million members may now be reading your handiwork!

Where to Date

PRODIGY has quite a few areas designed especially for those who are lookin' for love, in all its shapes and sizes. Explicit language is prohibited on the family-oriented PRODIGY,

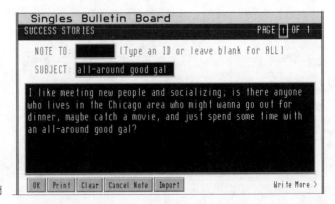

FIGURE 10-10 Writing a note onto a PRODIGY bulletin board

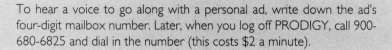

EXPERT TIP

To hear a voice to go along with a personal ad, write down the ad's four-digit mailbox number. Later, when you log off PRODIGY, call 900-680-6825 and dial in the number (this costs $2 a minute).

and you may not find much steam, but there's plenty of fire. Mature individuals who seek the same abound in great multitude.

Online Personals

The Tele-Publishing Corporation offers an easy-to-use personal ad service over PRODIGY. The price you pay depends on how long your ad is and how many months it runs. The cheapest ad can be placed for around $2 a month. Select Browse or Place, and then select Place An Ad. Type in your ad the way you would any other note. After you select a billing method, your personal is posted online. You will receive e-mail about how to record your voice message on Tele-Publishing's 900 "greetings" number.

Browsing the ads is free. Select Browse or Place and then select Browse. You can search any particular area code within one of the following categories:

- Men Seeking Women
- Women Seeking Men
- Men Seeking Men
- Women Seeking Women

See Figure 10-11 for a typical ad. You can send e-mail to anyone you're interested in by selecting the Reply button. See the Mail section of this chapter for more information.

Lifestyles BB

Some of the topics in the Lifestyles bulletin board include:

- *Alternate Lifestyles.* For discussion by those leading gay, lesbian, bisexual, transgender, communal, or any other mode of living that differs from the mainstream.
- *Men's Issues.* A place for men, and women, to discuss those subjects that daunt all men.
- *Pen Pal Requests.* Match up here, finding friends to trade e-mail, phone calls, or regular mail.
- *Relationships.* What's the chemical formula for love? Is cheating always wrong? What's the best way to celebrate an anniversary? What's the best way to break up? If it's on your mind, and it's troubling you, then it's probably because of a relationship. Let's talk, here.

FIGURE 10-11 Meet a star over the PRODIGY Service!

🐚 *Sexuality.* Sex is discussed, advised on, debated, and sought here.

🐚 *Women's Issues.* Fair is fair. This is the place to discuss those subjects that daunt all women.

Teens BB

Being a family-oriented service, PRODIGY has many areas catering to an oft-overlooked gang of cyberdaters: teenagers. Whether you're looking for your first date or needing to talk to somebody your age about whatever's on your mind, the Teens bulletin board will make you feel at home. Topics of interest include:

🐚 *Alternate Lifestyles.* For those teens who are faced with more than the usual "boy meets girl" relationships.

🐚 *Dating Issues.* When is too young to date? When is too old? What role should parents play? What attributes should I look for in a date? Teenagers help teenagers get on the track to a comfortable love life.

Singles BB

I was another one of those people who would look at the PRODIGY Success Stories and say, "This will NEVER happen to me!" I have many friends on PRODIGY, but no one that I felt that I could totally tell everything to. I decided to check the Pen Pal Requests in the singles BB, and found someone who sounded pretty neat. I picked up enough courage to write her, and a couple of hours later, she wrote back, and I found out that we had tons in common. Soon, we were writing several letters a day. I felt an emotion so strong, yet so new, and it was indeed the strongest of them all . . .

LOVE! Soon I'll be flying to see her in person. I can't wait to finally see my one true soulmate, who I care for more than anyone or anything in this whole world. So, to everyone still searching out there, please DON'T YOU DARE GIVE UP, there may be someone out there for you who is closer than you think. And for those who have found someone . . . isn't life grand?

PRODIGY's Singles bulletin board is the source for cyberdaters nationwide:

- *Dating.* You asked for it, you got it. The how, why, when, what, and where of it all is discussed here.

- *How To Meet People.* Browse through here for tips about how to be less shy, where to find your type of people, things to say, how to dress, ways to act, and other dating dos and don'ts.

- *Coping.* Being single is, quite frankly, often a drag. Luckily, as long as you can log on to PRODIGY, you're never completely alone. Folks here help other folks cope with the rough-and-tumble of the amusement park called love.

- *Pen Pal Requests.* Looking for Mr. or Ms. Write? Here's the place where fellow letter-scrawlers can meet.

- *Success Stories.* Those who have met their soulmates can brag to the world here. The love stories detailed here occurred online as well as off.

- *Suddenly Single.* What do you do if, after a decade or more, you are thrown back in that great blue sea of love? Here's the place to discuss how to go fishing again, and how to avoid the sharks.

- *The Meeting Place.* This is a *free* personal ad area. Though not as well-organized as the online personals feature, browsing through here may turn out to be just as fruitful. Subjects are generally grouped by state or by area code.

Advice Columns

PRODIGY has many advice columns, including one specially geared toward answering personal questions. Concerns about dating, mating, love, or anything else are answered weekly. Jump to *advice* and browse through the list of available columns.

Mail

Sending and reading e-mail over PRODIGY is a very straightforward process. As mentioned earlier, PRODIGY likes to refer to its e-mail letters as "messages."

When you first log on to PRODIGY, if you have new mail the words New Mail appear in the upper-right or a picture of a tiny envelope appears in the lower-right corner of the screen (see the opening Highlights screen in Figure 10-3). Select the New Mail button or symbol to read your messages.

You can also access the mailbox at any time by Jumping to *mail.* Figure 10-12 shows the contents of a typical mailbox.

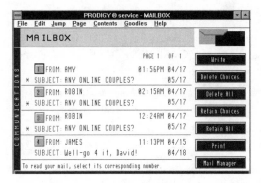

Figure 10-12 Yay, I have mail!

To print out your list of mail, either select the Print command at the bottom of the screen or select the Print button at the side of the screen.

If you've already read a message and no longer need it, highlight its corresponding number and then select Delete Choices. You can also Delete All your mail.

Likewise, if you'd like to store a mail message in order to re-read it later, highlight its number and then select Retain Choices. You may wish to Retain All your mail. Retained mail is automatically deleted in one week. If you'd like to "renew" the scheduled deletion date, you can Retain All at any time.

Reading New Mail Messages

Reading your mail is as simple as selecting the number that appears next to the message you want. Brand-new messages are tagged with an asterisk (*). Messages you've earlier retained are also listed.

When you're reading a mail message, a screen similar to Figure 10-13 appears. Scroll through the message, page by page. When done reading, it's a good idea to either Delete the mail if you're done with it, or Retain the mail for a week if you want to refer to it later. Mail that is not retained may be gone from your mailbox the next time you check it, depending on how fast PRODIGY's housekeeping is.

To read your next mail message, if there is one, select Next Mail.

EXPERT TIP

If you're on a pricing plan where you have to pay for PRODIGY by the hour, it's a good idea to read your mail offline. Storing your mail on disk is also useful if you want to save it someplace safe. To put a mail message onto your hard disk, select the Copy To Disk button. Type in the filename, or just press (ENTER) to save it under the filename MAIL. If you're saving more than one message, you can put them all in the same filename. Just select Append to File when asked.

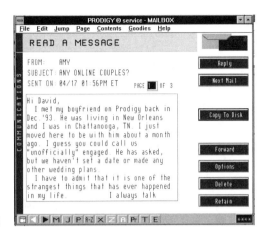

FIGURE 10-13 Reading a piece of mail

If you'd like to print out your mail, you can either select the Print command from the bottom of the screen or choose an alternate Print option which appears once you select the Options button.

The Options button also brings you the Add option, which automatically adds the author of the current message into your address book. Simply type that person's name or nickname. From now on, when you want to send that person mail, you need only type his or her nickname instead of bothering to memorize yet another pesky PRODIGY ID. See the Mailing List section, later, for more information.

Replying to or Forwarding Mail

Simply select Reply after you've read a piece of mail. The mailing address and subject are automatically filled in and you can begin entering your message. See Writing Mail Messages, next.

If you'd like to share a message you've received, select the Forward button. Go about sending mail as usual (see the next section). The message you want to forward is automatically tacked onto the end of whatever you type.

Writing Mail Messages

Select the Write button from the Mailbox screen shown in Figure 10-12. A screen similar to Figure 10-14 appears. If you know the PRODIGY ID number of the person you want to mail to, type it in the To: box.

If your friend's ID number is on your address list (see the next section), you can just type in his or her nickname. To pick a nickname directly from your address book, select Address Book. Likewise, if you've previously set up a mailing list, you can select the Mailing List button to perform a mass mailing.

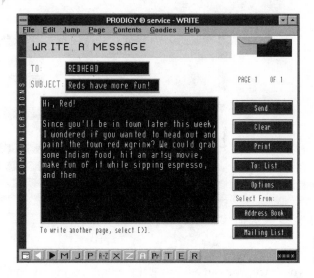

FIGURE 10-14 Writing a mail message to a PRODIGY friend

To search for a particular person's ID number, select the Options button and then select Search. See the Searching for the Prodigal Son section, earlier in this chapter, for information on how to initiate the search and how to add that person's ID number to your mailing list.

To send the same message to several people, select the To: List button. The distribution list appears. To add people to your list, you must either know their PRODIGY ID numbers or have previously added their names to your PRODIGY address book. You can select the Address Book button to select from a list of the people currently in your book. Likewise, selecting the Mailing List button allows you to choose a group of people from a previously-entered mailing list.

You can now Change ID or Remove ID, if you'd like. When your distribution list is complete, select the List Complete button.

Now press (TAB) to enter a brief SUBJECT:. Press (TAB) again and you can type in your message. If you run out of room, access the Next command to begin typing on a new page. When your message is complete, select the Send button.

EXPERT TIP

You can see how many letters you've sent this month so far by selecting Options and then choosing the Count option. Remember, with the Value plan, the first 30 messages are free.

The Address Book/Mailing List

Since PRODIGY IDs are about as warm and human as social security numbers, it's a good idea to build up an address book to keep track of everybody you meet. In this way, if you want to send someone mail, you need only remember the nickname.

You can automatically add a name to your address book while reading your mail or searching the member directory. For details, see the Reading New Mail and Searching for the Prodigal Son sections earlier in this chapter. If you ever want to add a person's ID to your address book (while reading a note on a bulletin board, for instance), Jump to *Address Book*.

Select Add and then type a memorable nickname and an ID number in the appropriate slots. That's all!

The mailing list works in a similar way. Jump to *Mailing List*. Instead of typing a nickname, type a group name in the appropriate slot, such as

    cyberdaters

Then type in the PRODIGY ID numbers of all the cyberdaters you know. Later, you can do a mass mailing.

Chat

PRODIGY only recently added a chat facility, and only onto the Windows version of its software (see Figure 10-15). (Mac and DOS chat systems are in the works.) At the time of this writing, chat is still a little clunky, some features are disabled, and only a few PRODIGY users can actually enter it. However, PRODIGY chat has the potential to be full-functional and easy-to-use someday soon.

If your version of PRODIGY does not support the chat system, your only chatting options are to send e-mail back and forth (which is kind of like passing notes in class, only slower), using the good ol' fashioned telephone, or rendezvousing on another online service.

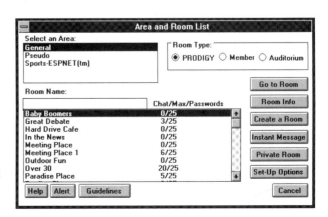

FIGURE 10-15 PRODIGY's latest addition: chat. Pick a room, any room

LOVE BYTES

Try Jumping to *chat.* If your software supports chat, it gives you an intro and some guidelines. Click on the Choose Nickname button and type in an anonymous nickname, 4 to 12 letters long. The first time you use chat, select Set-Up Options and type in the biographical information the system asks for, such as your town and birthdate, and a short personal statement.

You can also customize your chat environment in the Set-Up section. For instance, if you unselect Allow Display of My Member ID, you are truly anonymous. Of course, if somebody wants to send e-mail out of the blue, he or she won't be able to find you without asking you for your ID. You can also specify whether or not you wish to receive instant messages. Be sure Allow Members to Send Me Instant Messages is not selected unless you want people to engage you in private conversations.

You can now click on Enter Chat. PRODIGY has dozens of available chat rooms, as depicted in Figure 10-15. Begin by selecting from the three types of rooms:

- *PRODIGY Rooms.* These are standard rooms with topics such as Meeting Place, Paradise Place, Prodigy Chatters, Singles, Current Events, and so on.
- *Member Rooms.* These are custom rooms created by other PRODIGY members.
- *Auditoriums.* Every so often, PRODIGY invites a famous or renowned celebrity to address the online community. If you type a question, it goes to a moderator who may then decide to pass it on to the featured speaker.

You may now select a broad chat area, such as Clubs, General, or Sports. A listing of all available chat rooms is displayed. For each room, you are told how many people are present and whether or not an *Entry* password is required. Click on Room Info to see who is in the currently highlighted room. To enter a room, double-click on it. If a password is necessary, type it in when the system requests it.

Each person's words appear in the upper box, as shown in Figure 10-16. To talk, type what you wish to say in the empty box at the bottom left of your screen and then click the Send Text button or press (ENTER).

To the right of the screen, a list of all the room's occupants remains in constant flux. To find out more about a person, click on his or her nickname. Select Member Info to see that person's profile, if there's one on file.

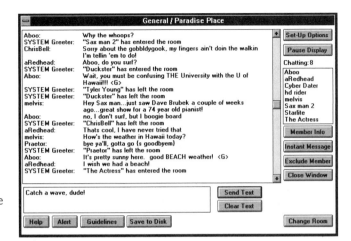

FIGURE 10-16 Shootin' the virtual breeze with other PRODIGY folk

Building Your Own Room

It's easy to create your own room, private or public. Select the Create a Room button. You are asked to type in the room's name and to specify how many members can occupy it (from 2 to 25).

Instant Messages

If you'd like to hold a one-on-one conversation with another PRODIGY member, click on the name of the person you want to talk with and then click on the Instant Message button. You can now type in your message, clicking Send Text when done. You can hold a bunch of instant message conversations simultaneously; a list of all the people you are currently speaking with appears on the left of your Instant Message window. Click on a name to send a message to that person. But beware—if you're conversing with too many folk, things get confusing; be careful not to send the wrong message to the wrong person.

EXPERT TIP

If you want to make your room private, enter a password in the appropriate box. Make sure Room Name Appears on Member Room List is not selected. Only those who know your room name and its associated password will be allowed to enter (by clicking on the Private Room button). You can use instant messages to invite someone to your invisible abode.

EXPERT TIP

If you like, you can type another PRODIGY member's ID in the Send To box. In this way, you can send instant messages to someone who is currently logged on to PRODIGY, but who isn't in the chat area.

Does Prodigy Make the Grade?

For novices, PRODIGY acts as an encouraging introduction to the online world. By using your mouse to press friendly buttons, you can access all that PRODIGY has to offer. Being America's largest online service, tons of people meet over PRODIGY all the time, and PRODIGY is responsible for more than a few relationships and marriages. Those who post personal ads typically receive hundreds of responses.

Unfortunately, PRODIGY doesn't provide full chatting for all its users, leaving some people trapped in the time lag of bulletin boards and e-mail. For the impatient, PRODIGY's slow-drawing screens and slothlike responses may grate on the nerves. PRODIGY is also consumer-oriented, with constant online commercials designed to separate you from your money. But if you're interested in fun-filled hours of shopping—for merchandise or love— you'll appreciate the ambiance of PRODIGY.

GENIE

800-638-9636
GENERAL ELECTRIC INFORMATION SERVICE
401 NORTH WASHINGTON STREET
ROCKVILLE MD 20850

YES, CRAIG AND I MET THROUGH GENIE . . . .

If memory serves me right, I checked online profiles and found out that he worked for the same employer that I did . . . so I thought I'd contact him figuring we'd at least have something in common to talk about . . . . :) We also belonged to a group called Texnuts where Texans could send each other e-mail. We talked for a few months, then lost contact for about six months or so. He hunted me down after I had changed my e-mail address and unlisted it. Funny . . . I was sitting at work wondering how he was doing when I went home and found an unexpected message waiting in my mailbox from him! You could imagine how I felt when I heard from him again after such a long time of silence . . . . Now Craig's and my e-mail address on GEnie is TNT, as in Texas 'n Tennessee, our home states. We always said when we finally got together we'd be DYNA-MITE! :) Even ended up with a little "firecracker" . . . Carly D'Anne *(see Figure 11-1)* . . . . She's really a neat little girl . . . . I wanted to name her Genie but my husband didn't see the humor in it . . . haha . . . . Oh well . . . .

What It Is

General Electric's idea is to offer a sound, well-stocked online service for a low hourly fee. But GEnie has lots of soul, too.

Thanks to a snazzy "The most fun you can have with your computer on" ad campaign, GEnie has established itself as a hip, in-yer-face kind of online service. In part, it has become a smoky Bohemian café, attracting a highly eclectic online crowd and featuring quasi-famous artists, writers, and other cultural icons. GEnie's message areas are among cyberspace's weirdest, always a little off-kilter and discussion-provoking.

If you're one of those who thinks love is just another game, then maybe you'll find your fellow Pac-Mate in GEnie's multi-player games arena. In between blowing your enemies up, outstrategizing 'em, and stealing their gold, there's lots of live chatting. The superb graphics, sound, and depth of GEnie's games make them among the best in cyberspace.

There are just a few caveats: GEnie charges astronomical rates if you use it during business hours; the GEnie tree is only suitable for night owls. Also, though GEnie has a bit of everything the online world has to offer—entertainment, business, reference—it is often difficult to find what you're aiming for. You must often pore through menus; there are no easy icons or mouse-clicks. However, GEnie has just released a version of its front-end software—similar to America Online, PRODIGY, and CompuServe's CIM—which makes navigating much easier. This software is still in its testing stage, though. It is slow and full of errors, lacking many essential features, but at least the GEnie folks are on the right track.

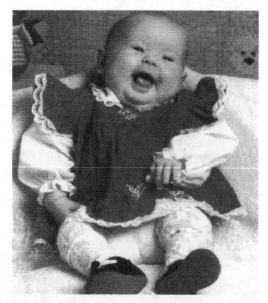

FIGURE 11-1 Carly D'Anne, one of the world's first (and cutest) "cyberbabies"

How to Connect

You must use your own communications software to sign onto GEnie. Your software must be set up for eight data bits, no parity, and one stop bit (8N1). You must also change your settings to half-duplex (local echo), at 300, 1200, or 2400 baud. See Chapter 4, The Datemobile, for information on how to set up your modem and dial.

Dial 800-638-8369 with your modem. In Canada dial 800-387-8330. When you have connected, type

HHH

You should see a prompt that looks like

U#=

type

signup

and press (ENTER).

You get a number of questions about your communications software. In most cases, you can just press (ENTER) to use the default settings. Type in your name when the system asks for it: last name first, then a semicolon, then your first name. For example, Lenny Lovelooker would type

Lovelooker;Lenny

When prompted, enter your city, state, phone number, and other personal information. You must then select a method of payment. You can either type in your credit card information or use your checking account number.

Next you get a local access phone number. Write it down—you will use it to call GEnie from now on. If the number requires long-distance tolls, you may use the more widely-available SprintNet instead—but there's a $2 per hour surcharge.

The GEnie membership agreement then comes up. Read it and then type

agree

if you agree with it. You are now a GEnie member. The system tells you your User ID and password, and your e-mail address—which usually consists of your first initial along with your last name and a number (like L.LOVELOOKER3). Write these items down, as well.

The Software

GEnie recently got on the easy-to-use bandwagon and designed its own front-end software. Try it out. It's not perfect, but it has several distinct advantages over GEnie's standard command-line interface:

- Automatic log on and log off.
- Support for your mouse, so you can navigate the system by double-clicking the menus.
- Colorful icons—a talking cartoon character for a Chat area, a red pushpin for a bulletin board, a stack of diskettes for a file library, and an open book for another menu—to help you identify useful destinations at a glance.

EXPERT TIP

To change your password, once you're online, type

set

and then select the Change Password option from the menu.

SOFTWARE TIP

If you are running the GEnie front-end software, change your password by selecting the Change Password option from the Online pull-down menu.

- A tool bar with more icons for frequent commands like menu-hopping or searching the member directory.
- Offline support for mail and messages, to save you online charges—with a full-screen editor, almost a word processor (also available online).
- Automated address book, so you can keep track of your friends' e-mail addresses and reach them easily.
- Automated "to-do" list, keeping track of files, mail, and messages for a mass download when you log off.
- And a filing cabinet to capture anything interesting, for reading later at your leisure.

If you don't mind waiting, GEnie can send you a copy of the software through the mail; call them up. Since the software is still in its early test stages, it is free of charge; however, that may soon change.

You can also download a copy of the front-end package, free of connect charges. Simply log on to GEnie, as usual. Type

```
m 1465
```

to access the front-end software menu. Select either the Download GEnie for Windows or the Download GEnie for Mac option. Choose a protocol (preferably Zmodem) and then have your communications software download the file. See Chapter 4, The Datemobile, for more detailed downloading instructions.

GEnie for Windows

GEnie for Windows requires Microsoft Windows version 3.1 or better, a 386/16Mhz computer with 4 megabytes of memory, 4 megabytes of free space on your hard disk, and a VGA monitor.

If you've downloaded GEnie for Windows, it will be in your current directory. Using the Windows File Manager, find the file you've just downloaded (called FE101.EXE or something similar). Double-click on it. The file expands itself, creating several other GEnie files.

There should now be a file called SETUP.EXE. Double-click on it. You are asked if you want to create a GEnie directory. Press (ENTER). You may also be asked if you want to create a GEnie program group. Choose Yes. GEnie is now set up, including an icon on your Windows desktop. To run the GEnie software from now on, just double-click its icon.

If you got GEnie in the mail or bought it from a store, place the GEnie disk in your drive and select Run from Windows Program Manager's pull-down File menu. Type in

```
a:setup
```

or

```
b:setup
```

depending on which drive the GEnie disk is in.

GEnie for Macintosh

The Mac version of GEnie requires at least a Mac Plus or Classic, with 4 megabytes of memory, and running System 6.1 or higher.

If you downloaded the GEnie software, double-click its icon. A GEnie folder and all applicable files are automatically created. To run GEnie from now on, just click its icon.

If your GEnie software is on a floppy disk, just place the disk in the drive. Double-click on the disk icon. Double-click on the GEnie Setup icon. That's all!

Aladdin

Aladdin, as its name implies, summons up GEnie and takes control of it. The Aladdin software is available for the Atari ST, DOS, and Macintosh. It has many commands allowing you to decide which forums you want to read, what files you want to download, what e-mail you want to send—all offline. You can then have Aladdin log on for you automatically, perform your tasks quickly, and then log off.

This software is complex to use and only recommended for the seasoned GEnie user. You can download a copy of Aladdin or get more information by typing the keyword

```
aladdin
```

Charges and Surcharges

GEnie costs $8.95 a month, which includes four hours of standard (non-prime) connection time. After that, you are billed an additional $3 per hour.

There are several *premium* services; each has its own extra hourly charge. These services include brokerage, stock quotes, FAX, analyst, and other such business/financial features.

Type

```
bill
```

any time while online to change your billing information or to review your current bill.

GEnie has hefty additional charges if you're not careful. Those who call in using 9600 baud are tagged an extra $6 per hour—however, they are allowed free use of the GEnie 800 phone service.

EXPERT TIP

Only use 9600 baud when you are downloading files. If you're reading messages, chatting, playing most games, or using e-mail, you don't need high speed.

Most area codes have access through GEnie's own network. This is free of additional charges during non-prime time, but costs $9.50 per hour during business hours (from 8 A.M. to 6 P.M., local time, on weekdays). If you use a different local network, such as SprintNet, DataPac, or an international network, you pay extra. Contact GEnie for specifics.

Logging On: Rubbing the Lamp

If you use your own communications software, set it for eight data bits, no parity, and one stop bit (8N1). You must also change your settings to half-duplex (local echo), at 300, 1200, or 2400 baud. See Chapter 4, The Datemobile, for information on how to set up your modem and dial.

Dial your local GEnie access number. When you've connected, type

HHH

Your should see a prompt that looks like

U#=

Without any spaces, type your User ID, a comma, and then your password. For example, if your ID is AAA11111 and your password is "machismo," you'd type

aaa11111,machismo

SOFTWARE TIP

If you have the GEnie software, you can log on automatically. Select the Settings option from the File pull-down menu and then select Logon from the side-menu. Type your User ID number and password in the specified boxes. Click OK. You can now access the Connections option, also in the Settings item under the File pull-down menu. Here you type in your local access number, its baud rate, and the COM port of your modem. Click the OK button when done. You can now select the Logon option from the Online pull-down menu.

In the future, you need only click the Logon button, which appears when you first run your GEnie software.

SOFTWARE TIP

Select the Log Off option under the Online pull-down menu.

You're now online! You are told if you have any mail, and a list of the hottest news, features, and GEnie services is shown. To learn more about a particular announcement, just type its number. Press (ENTER) to leave the announcements and proceed to the Top menu.

Logging Off

To exit GEnie, at any time, just type

`bye`

While chatting, type

`/bye`

Getting Around: The Magic Carpet Ride

There are two ways to navigate GEnie: The easy way, and the not-so. The easy way involves the GEnie *front-end* software and a mouse, the not-so easy way involves your own communications software and your fingers. See The Software section, at the beginning of this chapter, for information on how to get a copy of the GEnie front-end package.

Since the software is in its early stages, it often switches to *terminal mode*. This mode turns the GEnie front-end into just another communications program; you have to navigate by typing in menu selections and commands at the *command line*. This chapter will discuss how to master GEnie using both command-line and front-end navigation techniques. For a comparison, see Figure 11-2.

```
GE Information Services

 1.   About GEnie
 2.   New Members' Information
 3.   Hot & Happening Events On GEnie
 4.   Communications (GE Mail & Chat)
 5.   Computing Services
 6.   Travel Services
 7.   Finance & Investing Services
 8.   Online Shopping Services
 9.   News, Sports & Features
10.   GEnie Games
11.   Career/Professional Services
12.   Business Services
13.   Leisure Pursuits & Hobbies
14.   Education Services
15.   Entertainment Services
16.   Symposiums on Global Issues
17.   Research & Reference Services
18.   Leave GEnie (Logoff)

Enter #. <H>elp?
```

```
Menu Navigator

Pages: 1 · TOP · GE Information Service

About GEnie
New Members' Information
Hot & Happening Events On GEnie
Communications (GE Mail & Chat)
Computing Services
Travel Services
Finance & Investing Services
Online Shopping Services
News, Sports & Features
GEnie Games
Career/Professional Services
Business Services
Leisure Pursuits & Hobbies
Education Services
Entertainment Services
Symposiums on Global Issues
Research & Reference Services
Leave GEnie (Logoff)
```

FIGURE 11-2 A comparison of GEnie's TOP menus: command-line on the left vs. front-end on the right

SOFTWARE TIP

In most cases, the front-end menus are identical to the command-line ones, as in Figure 11-2; the only difference is that GEnie software users double-click on what they need instead of typing in its number. In other words, the software is just an *easier* way of navigating GEnie, not necessarily an alternate way. However, there are some special features available only to GEnie software users. These Software Tips will tell you exactly what to do.

Figure 11-2 shows a comparison of the GEnie command-line menu and the front-end Menu Navigator. The two are essentially duplicate. To access a menu item, command-line users just type in its associated number at the

```
Enter #,<H>elp?
```

prompt and then press (ENTER). For example, to access Communications, you would type

```
4
```

To return to the previous menu, type

```
p
```

Front-end users need only double-click on an item with their mouse to access it. The Menu Navigator window makes it easy to return to previous menus. Just click on the Page box (the box that reads Page 1 - TOP in Figure 11-2). A listing of all the menus you've visited so far appears. Click on the one you wish to return to.

The software has six icons along the top button bar. These icons are, respectively: File Cabinet, To Do List, Read New Mail, Stop Incoming Text, Move To a Page#/Keyword, and Locate User. Each of these commands is described in the following subsections. The seventh icon acts like a traffic light, telling you when GEnie is busy receiving or sending data. Table 11-1 lists the basic GEnie commands, for both the front-end and command-line.

Another big difference between the command-line and the front-end is how information is viewed. With the GEnie software, text appears in a window. You can then use the scroll bar to read through a message. The command-line GEnie, however, displays a page of text and then usually prompts you:

```
Press <RETURN> or <S>croll?
```

Simply press (ENTER) to read the next page.

Moving Through Menus

At the top of each GEnie menu, you should see two things: A *page number* and a one word *keyword*. For example, GEnie's main menu is Page 1, with the keyword TOP. With one of

SOFTWARE TIP

Click on the Move To icon (the picture of the arrow pointing to the pages) or select Move to Page/Keyword under the Online menu. An input box appears. Type in either a keyword or a menu number and you automatically zoom off to the appropriate menu or area.

these bits of information in hand, you can zoom off to any GEnie menu. There are two ways to move:

- The key to navigating GEnie lies in keywords. Every GEnie menu, product, and service has its own logical keyword. All you have to do to access a menu is type its keyword, at any menu prompt.

- If you're a numbers person, you might find it easier to remember the page numbers of your favorite menus. To move to any page number, just type M followed by the number you're interested in. For example, to move to the Family RoundTable, which is page 1235, type

    m 1235

You can get even more specific if you like, using a semicolon. For instance, if you want to access the second menu selection of the Family RoundTable (The Bulletin Board), just type

    m 1235;2

COMMAND-LINE TYPE:	FRONT-END CLICK ON PULL-DOWN MENU:	ACTION:
M <#>	Online, Move to Page/Keyword	Moves to a particular page number.
P	Page Box in Menu Navigator	Returns to the previous menu.
TOP	Online, Move To, TOP	Goes to GEnie's main menu.
CTRL + S	(Use the scroll bar)	Freezes text that is scrolling in too fast.
CTRL + Q	(Use the scroll bar)	Continues displaying text.
CTRL + C	Online, Send Break	Stops incoming text.
H	Help	Describes the current menu and commands.

TABLE 11-1 GEnie's basic navigation commands

Index

To look around GEnie for items that suit your fancy, type

```
index
```

at any prompt.

Select the Keyword Search for Products item. Type in any descriptive word, such as "sex." A list of all applicable GEnie areas—for instance, Family RoundTable or GEnie Personal Ads—appears. You can then select any item that interests you.

GEnie Genres

GEnie's TOP menu offers the following services to get you started:

- *About GEnie.* An index of GEnie services, information on your Bill and Account, help on connecting to and navigating GEnie.
- *New Members Information.* Beginner chat and bulletin boards for those who'd like to give GEnie a test drive.
- *Hot and Happening on GEnie.* Find out about GEnie's latest service, special shopping deals, or quirky news stories.
- *Communications.* Where e-mail, chatting, and other cyberdating essentials come together. See the Mail and Chat sections, later in this chapter.
- *Computing Services.* The latest computer news, help, customer support, and shopping.
- *Travel Services.* Find out where to go, how to get there, and arrange it all.

- *Finance and Investing Services.* Quotes (not by Mr. Shakespeare, but by Mr. Dow and Mr. Jones), investing how-to, and various company profiles.
- *Online Shopping Services.* Welcome to the GEnie mall.
- *News, Sports, & Features.* Up-to-the-minute world, sports, and entertainment news. There are also several amusing syndicated features and columns here, as well as the GEnie newsstand of online magazines.
- *GEnie Games.* Games so darn cool that there's a section later in this chapter devoted especially to them.
- *Career/Professional Services.* Find work, hire employees, and network with other people in your field. Who knows, you might just find the person of your dreams while closing a deal.
- *Business Services.* Where the worlds of small and large business collide. Read the latest news, reference books, and opinions from prominent business people.
- *Leisure Pursuits and Hobbies.* RoundTables for anyone interested in automotive stuff, aviation, pets, needle-arts, modeling (as in building ships in bottles, not in posing before a camera—information about that would be in the Photo and Video RoundTable), Disney, zymurgy, and many other hobby and avocational areas.
- *Education Services.* Homework help, online schools, and help with applying (and getting in) to college, plus handy medical advice.
- *Entertainment Services.* If you're entertained by it, then GEnie discusses it: books, music, sports, games, astrology, and all the latest Hollywood scoop.
- *Symposium on Global Issues.* White House news, international RoundTables, and other places to discuss any discussion-worthy issue.
- *Research and Reference Services.* An online reference library. If you need to look anything up, it's likely to be here, in one form or another.
- *Leave GEnie (Logoff).* Log off GEnie and re-enter the real world.

Downloading

GEnie has over 200,000 different files for your downloading pleasure. Check out the Family RoundTable for several file libraries that may be of interest to cyberdaters. The Family Album category, for instance, has pictures of many of your favorite Family RoundTable personalities. Figure 11-3 shows one example.

EXPERT TIP

If your communications software has the Ymodem or Zmodem protocol, you can download several files at once. Just separate their names or numbers by commas.

FIGURE 11-3 A downloaded photograph of Cuddles, leader of the singles section in the Family and Personal Growth RoundTable

To enter a RoundTable's library, select Library from the menu (or double-click on the icon of the diskettes); this is usually menu item number 3.

Select Set the Software Library to see a list of categories. Type in the number of the category that interests you. Select ALL Libraries if you're interested in the entire shebang.

Select Directory of Files to list all the files in the current library category. The listing includes the file's number, name, type (text files are designated by an *x*), the person who uploaded the software, the date the software was uploaded, the size of the file in bytes, and the number of times it has been downloaded.

You can select Download a File from the main Library menu when you've found a file you're interested in. You are asked:

```
Enter Download Request or <H>elp?
```

Enter the file's number or exact filename, as it appeared in the directory listing.

You get a full description of the file, and then the prompt:

```
Press <RETURN> to skip, <D>ownload, <L>ist, or <Q>uit
```

Type

```
D
```

to begin the download.

If you'd rather see detailed information about *all* of the category's files, select the Browse Through the Files option to see full descriptions. After reading about a file, you can either skip to the next file, list the file (if it's a text file), download it, or quit and return to the Libraries menu. Type

```
D
```

to download.

Any time you download a file you are asked

```
Select Download Protocol
1. XMODEM
2. XMODEM (w/1K blocks)
3. YMODEM
4. ZMODEM
```

Select a protocol and then instruct your communications software to begin downloading, using that protocol. See Chapter 4, The Datemobile, for more details.

SOFTWARE TIP

The front-end software automatically shows you a list of all library areas when you double-click on the Library icon. To see which new files are in a particular area, click on its folder. The folder opens and a list of all the new files appears. To read the full description of a file, double-click on it. You can then click on the Download button to automatically copy it onto your computer. You're asked if you want to download it immediately, or wait until later. Click Download Now. A screen appears, showing you your file's progress.

If you'd like to see all the files in a particular library, select the List All option from the Libraries pull-down menu.

You can also click on the blank space to the left of any file (or library area) to place a check mark next to it. These files are now known as *checked*. You can view the description of all checked files by selecting Browse Checked from the Libraries menu. You can download selected files by checking them and then selecting the Download Checked Files option from the Libraries menu.

Summoning Other GEnies

Your GEnie member profile can be as information-rich or as lean as you like. Spend some time concocting an attention-getting profile: something witty, charming, and detailed. Other people often find out more about you from your profile, helping them decide if they should get friendlier (or not).

To access the GEnie profile menu, type

```
profile
```

You can see what your profile currently looks like by selecting View Your Profile. If you haven't already set a profile, select Enter Your Profile. You get prompts for your real name, your address, your company, your interests, and other personal information. You can also enter a sort of essay about yourself, when prompted for your Text Entry. Type in a few lines, indicative of your wit and wisdom. When you're done, type

```
*s
```

to save your text. You are asked to confirm your entry.

If you'd like to change your profile, select the Change Your Profile. You see a numbered list of your basic information, your optional information, your interests, and your text entry. To change an entry, type in its number, press (ENTER), and then type in the new info.

You can also search the profiles. Select the Search Profiles option. You can search for a particular interest, first name, last name, e-mail address, company, city, and/or state. Select

a search parameter by typing its number and then entering the text you wish to search for. For example, to find people interested in cooking, type

`1`

and then

`cooking`

You can search for several parameters at once. For example, if you want to find Californian cooks only, you could also type

`8`

and then

`CA`

When you're ready, choose the Execute Search option by typing

`9`

A list of all matches appears, listed by GE mail address. You can now type in the number given for each person you're interested in, and the corresponding member profile appears on your screen. You are also given the opportunity to send mail to that person.

Messages

GEnie's bulletin boards have a certain edge to them, making them inherently interesting places to meet other people. The emphasis is on long dialogues, intelligent discussions, and off-kilter points of view. You can find bulletin boards in every RoundTable.

Nights at the Roundtables

A GEnie RoundTable (RT) is where enthusiasts—for most any subject—can read each other's messages, hold impromptu chats, network, or trade software files. Each RoundTable has its own set of leaders, known as sysops. Sysops can give you access to certain restricted areas, if you feel you need it. Select Private Category Request to learn about restricted categories and to find out if you're eligible to join.

Relevant RoundTables can be found in the Business, Issues, Leisure, and Computing menus, or just about anywhere else. Use the GEnie Index to find RoundTables that fit your well-rounded interests. Once you know what they are, you have lots of ways to get to them. For instance, you could access the Family RoundTable by looking under the Global Issues section of the TOP menu, by typing *family*, or by typing the Family RoundTable's page number—*1235*.

Bulletin Boards

When you first enter a RoundTable menu, you should see a Bulletin Board item. Select it—it's usually the first item on the menu.

Bulletin Board messages are organized by category and then by topic. A list of the main bulletin-board commands can be found in Table 11-2.

If you're a regular visitor to the current Bulletin Board, you may want to read all the new messages. To browse through the latest posts, in all categories, type

`bro`

At the conclusion of each topic's messages, you are asked if you want to reply.

If you'd rather select a broad category of messages to read, command-line users should type

`cat`

A listing of categories, similar to Figure 11-4 appears; each category is preceded by a number.

COMMAND	ACTION
BRO	Browses all new items in all categories.
BRO CAT	Browses all new items only in the current category.
CAT	Shows you a list of all the Bulletin Board's categories.
DES <category#>	Describes a particular category.
EXI	Exits the Bulletin Board.
IND	Shows you a descriptive index of all the topics within every category.
NAM	Lets you give yourself a custom pseudonym that appears when you post a message.
REP	Replies to a particular topic.
SEA	Searches all the message topics for a particular word or phrase.
SET <category#>	Changes the current category.
STA	Starts a new topic in the current category.
TOP	Lists all the topics in the current category.

TABLE 11-2 Basic bulletin board commands. Equivalent commands can be found under the GEnie software's Boards pull-down menu

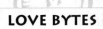

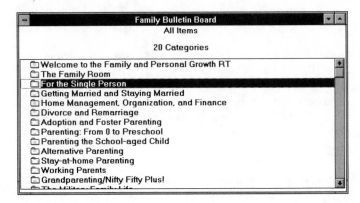

FIGURE 11-4 A bulletin board category listing

You can read the description of a category by typing *des* followed by the category's number. For example, to read about the For the Single Person category, type

`des 3`

To access a category of messages, just type *set* followed by the category's number. For example, to move to 3. For The Single Person, type

`set 3`

To see a listing of all the topics in the current category, type

`top`

Alternatively, you can see a list that tells you how many new messages there are in each topic. Just type

`new`

A listing similar to Figure 11-5 appears; for command-line users, each topic is preceded by a number instead of an icon.

You can then browse through the current category by typing

`bro cat`

At the end of each topic, you get a chance to leave a response of your own.

SOFTWARE TIP

Immediately upon entering a Bulletin Board, front-end users see a list of categories, as in Figure 11-4. To read about a category, click on it once to highlight it and then select Show Category Description from the Board's pull-down menu.

FIGURE 11-5 Topics, topics, topics. Which one appeals?

Reading

Once you've spotted a topic you're interested in, there are several ways to read through the messages. You can browse through all new messages in a particular category by typing

```
bro cat
```

You can also read specific messages by typing *rea* followed by the topic's number. For instance, to see topic number 12, Online and Long Distance Relationships, type

```
rea 12
```

Or you can select a range of topics. For instance, to read topics 10 through 14, type

```
rea 10-14
```

If you like, you can read a specific message number, within a topic. For example, to read starting from message 10 in topic number 12, type

```
rea 12 10
```

Last, you can read *all* the messages (including old ones) in a category by typing

```
rea all
```

SOFTWARE TIP

To see the topics in a particular category, click on that category's folder. The folder opens and a list of topics appears, as in Figure 11-5. Select Show Topic Description from the Boards pull-down menu to read a description of the currently highlighted topic.

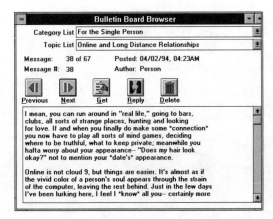

SOFTWARE TIP

To read the new messages in any topic, simply double-click on the topic which interests you. A screen similar to Figure 11-6 appears. You can click on Next to continue reading through the messages, or Previous to review old messages.

If you'd like to read *all* the messages in a topic, select List All from the Boards pull-down menu. Double-click on a category and then double-click on a topic.

You can also select a number of topics to read through. Simply click on the blank space preceding each topic (or category, if you want to read all its topics). A check mark appears. Once you've checked all the areas you're interested in, select Read Checked from the Boards pull-down menu. You can also save all the checked messages to your filing cabinet, for later perusal. Just select Save Checked to Filing Cabinet from the Boards menu.

Replying

Responding on GEnie works a little differently from most other online services—you do not reply to individual messages, but rather, you add a new message onto the end of any particular topic. This gives GEnie topics the feel of ongoing conversations.

Since Bulletin Boards are friendly sorts of places, you may want to give yourself a nickname, which will always appear next to your e-mail name. Just type

```
nam
```

You are asked to enter your pseudonym. Any messages you post will include this new name.

After all new messages for a topic have been displayed, you can add a response to the current topic by typing

```
rep
```

FIGURE 11-6 Reading a GEnie message

While reading any message, click on the Reply icon to add a response to the current topic. You can then enter the message, as in Figure 11-7. If you like, you can use the Paste feature under the Edit pull-down menu to import any text you've previously Cut or Copied from GEnie or other Windows/Mac applications. Click on the Return to Topic icon when your reply is complete. If you decide to abort your message, click on the Delete Reply trash can icon.

See the next section for details on how to write your message.

If you'd like to reply privately through e-mail, you must write down or remember the GE mail address of the message's author. You can then type

    mail

and send a letter to that person as outlined in the Mail section of this chapter.

Writing

If you'd like to start a topic of your very own, first be sure you're in the proper category. Use the

    set

command to get there. You can now type

    sta

and a new topic is started. You are asked

    Enter the topic Subject
    <------ (39 characters maximum)------>

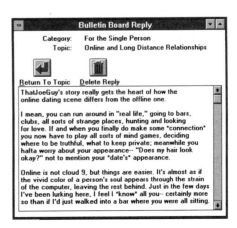

FIGURE 11-7 Writing a message using the GEnie software

Type in a descriptive one-line summary of your topic. For example, you could type in:

> `How To Meet People Online`

You are now asked for additional topic information:

> `Please enter a summary of the Topic (limited to 3 lines). Type`
> `*X to abort. Enter memo text. Type *S to send, *H for help.`
> `1>`

Type in up to three lines describing your topic, pressing (ENTER) at the end of each line. Type

> `*S`

at the beginning of a blank line when you're finished.
    You are now asked

> `Do you want to enter the first message? (Y/N)`

It's polite to kick off the conversation by posting the first message. Press Ⓨ. The following prompt lets you know it's time to begin:

> `Enter memo text. Type *s to send, *h for help.`
> `1>`

Type your message in, line by line, pressing (ENTER) at the end of each line. When your message is complete, type

> `*s`

at the beginning of a blank line. Your message is stored.

EXPERT TIP

If your communications software offers an upload feature, you can upload your message text instead of typing it. At the /> prompt, type

   *u

You can then upload the text file, using a standard ASCII protocol. Once your message has been loaded in, type

   *s

at the beginning of the next line to send the message.

If you decide not to send your message after all, type

   *x

to abort.

There are several other editing commands available, detailed in Table 11-3. For instance, if you want to review your message before you send it, type

   *1

EDITOR COMMAND	ACTION
*D,<#>	Deletes line number <#>.
*I,<#>	Inserts a line after line number <#>.
*L	Lists the entire message with line numbers, allowing you to decide what to edit.
*PRE	Previews the way the message will appear to readers.
*S	Sends the message, posting it.
*X	Exits the message without sending it.
*<#>,<text>	Replaces line number <#> with the specified <text>.
*U	Uploads a text file from your hard disk and places it in the message.

TABLE 11-3 Editor commands

Suppose you spot an error in line number 5, which reads:

```
5> Deer Date:
```

You can either delete the line entirely by typing

```
*d,5
```

or you can type in a new line number 5 by typing

```
*5,Dear Date:
```

All in the Family

The Family and Personal Growth RoundTable is where singles, couples, and anyone in-between can talk about dates. Discuss how to meet dates, how to keep 'em, lose 'em, deal with 'em, marry 'em, divorce 'em, raise families with 'em, and more. Military lifestyles, gay lifestyles, over 50, under 30, teens, single parenting: If it falls anywhere on the wide spectrum of human relationships, it's probably here. If not, why not start a new topic?

To access the RoundTable, just type

```
family
```

A menu similar to Figure 11-8 appears. Select the Family Bulletin Board option.

Also noteworthy is the Romance Writer's RoundTable, for those amateurs and professionals interested in reading, writing, or just hearing about good romantic stories. Move to

```
romance
```

Personal Ads

GEnie has an extensive classified ads service, which includes a category especially suited for cyberdaters: The Personal Ads.

To access the classifieds, move to

```
ads
```

FIGURE 11-8 The Family RoundTable, where dating begins, progresses, and comes to a number of different endings

Select the Place an Ad item and indicate whether or not you want to be *anonymous*—respondents can send you mail, but will not know who you are. Anonymous ads cost $1, other ads are free.

You are then asked to select a main category. You can type

?

for a list. To post in the GEnie personals, type

7

You then have to choose a sub-category. Again, type a question mark (?) for a list. Personal ads only have two sub-categories:

- *300*. GEnie Personals: Standard personal ads.

- *301*. Valentine Personals: Valentine's Day greetings for your special someone, when that time of year rolls around.

  Type

  300

to post a standard ad. You are then asked how long you want your ad to remain posted; select 7, 14, or 30 days. Finally, you can type in your ad, line by line. When you're done, type

*s

LOVE BYTES

You may then enter three keywords, separated by commas, to describe yourself. For example:

```
witty, redhead, female
```

You are shown what the ad will look like and told the charges. If you want to save the ad, press Ⓨ.

If you'd like to browse other people's ads, select Browse an Ad item from the Ads menu. Select a main category of ad (type 7 for personals), and then a sub-category (*300* for standard personal ads). You can then read through each ad, one at a time. At the end of each ad, you are asked if you want to send an e-mail reply. If so, type

```
r
```

otherwise, just press (ENTER).

Mail

When you first sign on to GEnie, you get a message if you have any new mail. To access GEnie's e-mail area, just type

```
mail
```

Remember, your GEnie mail address consists of your first initial, last name, and an identification number. This address is separate from your user ID. Other people's addresses appear in a similar format.

Next to each e-mail address, there's a user description. This can be your name, your favorite nickname, or any other phrase that describes you. This personalizes your messages, making up for your cryptic e-mail address.

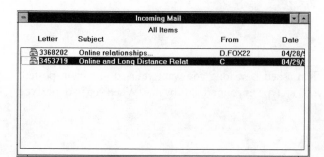

FIGURE 11-9 A handy list of all your GE mail

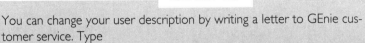

EXPERT TIP

You can change your user description by writing a letter to GEnie customer service. Type

feedback

to write them. You can also have them change your e-mail address, though they charge a fee to do so.

Reading Mail

To read your new mail, type

2

to select Read GEnie Mail. Your letters appear, one after another.

Once you've read your mail, it remains in your mailbox for five days. You can read all your mail—both old and new—by selecting List All Letters in Your Mailbox from the Mail menu.

Replying to a Letter

To reply to a letter, you need to enter a part of GEnie known as the *mail command mode*. Select GE Mail Command Mode from the Mail menu. You should see the prompt:

Command?

Type

list all

to display a list of all your letters, showing who each letter is from, who it was sent to, the date it was mailed, and what its subject is. Each letter also has its own queue number (the order in which the letter arrived).

SOFTWARE TIP

Select List All from the Mail pull-down menu. Double-click on the letter you wish to read and the text will appear, as shown in Figure 11-10.

You can also click on the blank space to the left of any letter, placing a check mark next to it. You can then read the letter by selecting Read Checked from the Mail menu. You can also save the checked mail in your filing cabinet: Choose the Save Checked to Filing Cabinet item from the Mail menu. Erase checked mail by selecting Delete Checked Item from Mail.

When reading a letter, click on Next to read the next available piece of mail.

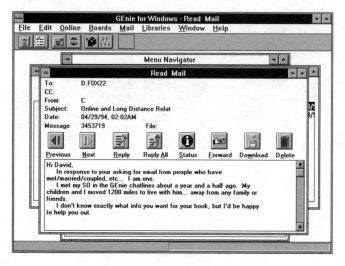

FIGURE 11-10 Message in a bottle: reading your GE mail

To reply to a particular piece of mail, type *rep* followed by that piece of mail's queue number. For instance, to respond to the second letter, type

```
rep 2
```

You may now write your letter, as detailed in the next section.

Sending Mail

To write a letter, select Compose and Send GE Mail Online (item number 6) from the general GE Mail menu. You are asked to whom the letter should be sent:

To:

Type in a valid GE Mail address (remember not to use blank spaces). If the address is not valid, GEnie complains until you fix it.

SOFTWARE TIP

To reply to the current letter, just click on the Reply button. The Mail Composition window appears, and the recipient of your letter and its subject are automatically filled in. You can now enter your mail, as detailed in the next section.

Similarly, you can click on Forward to send the current letter to a different user. You are asked for your recipient's e-mail address and the subject of the message. You are also given a little room to type in a few comments.

If you don't know a person's exact GE mail address, you can easily look it up. Select the Search GE Mail Directory option from the Mail menu. Type in as many letters of the person's last name as you know. Then type in the person's first name (if you don't know it, just press (ENTER)). You are shown a list of possible matches, including each person's e-mail address. You may have to narrow your search further if there are too many names. There are prompts for city, state, and other personal information.

You then get a chance to send out a

Carbon Copy:

If you want several people to receive your letter, type their GE mail addresses here, separated by commas. Otherwise, just press (ENTER). Now type in a short, descriptive subject of your letter at the

Sub:

prompt.

You may now type in your letter, line by line. You should see a

1>

To send mail, select the Create item from the Mail pull-down menu (you may do this online or off). A screen similar to Figure 11-11 appears. Enter your recipient's e-mail address in the TO: box and any additional recipients in the CC: box. You may also click the Address icon to use a name that you have previously stored in your personal address book. Double-click on the name you want to send the letter to. Click on the CC circle and then on an appropriate address, if you'd like to send any carbon copies.

Type an appropriate subject in the Subject: box. You can then enter your text in the text entry box. Alternatively, you can use the Paste command (under the Edit pull-down menu), to paste any text which you have previously Cut or Copied.

Click on Send Now to mail your letter. You may also click on Send Later, storing your letter in your to-do list, which you may access at any time by clicking on the To-Do icon (the checked box).

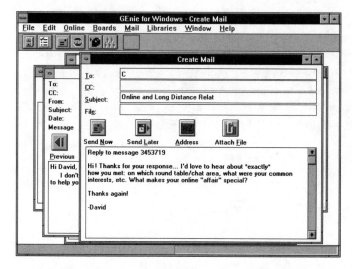

FIGURE 11-11 Composing GE mail in a flash using the front-end software

After you get to the end of the line, press (ENTER). You then see a

> 2>

and so on.

You can edit the letter using the standard editing commands. These can be found in Table 11-3.

When you're done entering your letter, type

> *s

at the beginning of a new line to send it.

Attached Files

Along with letters, you can send any sort of software through GEnie's mail. For instance, you might want to mail someone your digitized photograph, to match a face to your online persona.

If someone sends you a file, you get the news when you look at your new mail. You can then select Receive (Download) Attached File from the Mail menu.

SOFTWARE TIP

GEnie's front-end lets you find out if a given e-mail address is valid. Just select Verify Address from the Mail pull-down menu. Type in the address, and the system tells you if it exists.

SOFTWARE TIP

To attach a file to a letter you write, click the Attach File icon. A list of the files on your hard disk appears. If necessary, click on a directory to view its files. Double-click on the file you want to send. Click on the OK button. That's all there is to it; your specified file is now attached.

If someone sent you a file through GEnie mail, the Download icon appears, bright and shiny. Click on it to download the file.

You can download the file as usual, as described earlier in the Downloading section.

To send somebody a file, select Send (Upload) Attached File. Upload your file at the prompt. It's similar to downloading, only you access the uploading capabilities of your communications software instead. See Chapter 4, The Datemobile, for information on uploading. Once your file is transferred, you can type a GE mail message as usual.

Address Book

You get an address book feature only with GEnie's front-end software. This allows you to store any e-mail addresses you may come across, making it much easier to send those people letters in the future.

To add an address to your book, select Edit Address Book from the Mail pull-down menu. Type the name and description of your friend in the Name box. Type that person's valid e-mail address in the Address box. Click on the Insert button to add the address.

When editing your address book, you can also delete, change, or sort your addresses. Simply click on the appropriate command and then double-click on a name.

Chat

Well, Miles and I had originally met in THE Chatlines, here on GEnie while I was in the midst of flirting. His "handle" gave me an unrealistic impression of him and I didn't pay him much mind. Over the course of months, as we both frequented the chatlines, and I had begun to volunteer there, we said passing "hello's" and not much more. I was in the middle of a nightmarish divorce (still am) and one night we ended up on the same channel. Miles mentioned he was just about to rent a house and needed a roommate and half-jokingly said I could be his roommate if I wanted. I figured this was just a really weird guy and I told him more about myself . . . letting him know that he did NOT want me as a roommate. <G> The information included the fact that I have three children. To my surprise, he said, "So?" So I decided I would go ahead and talk to him on the phone . . . proving to him that his "offer" was incredibly ridiculous . . . he lived 1200 miles away. After we spoke on the phone, I was even more confused. He was one of the nicest men I had ever met . . . and his voice had such a calming effect. Instead of showing HIM how ridiculous it all was, he showed

ME how viable it was. But there was still the problem of not REALLY knowing him . . . it all was really weird. We began talking regularly on the computer and on the phone . . . and I began feeling more and more like I wanted to be with this man. I was hosting a party that was coming up, and he vowed he was going to make it to that party so we could meet. Well, we (he) decided that we (he) couldn't wait 'til the party and he flew over to spend New Year's Weekend with me. It was then that I knew moving was going to be a "risk worth taking." I also carefully examined what would happen if the relationship didn't work out . . . and it was still a good risk. One month later, I was loading all of my belongings and toddlers into a U-Haul (which is a story in and of itself <G>). I am disabled and can't get out much, so it didn't matter much to me what state I lived in . . . although leaving the state I had grown up in was difficult at best. Miles and I have now lived together for 15 months with no plans of breaking up soon. We've had our "moments" as all couples do . . . and now the fact that I "met" him online is merely a fading memory.

GEnie has tons of places to yak it up. In addition to the main Live Wire chat areas, each GEnie RoundTable has its own *real time conference* (RTC). GEnie also specializes in conferences with famous (and not so famous) celebrities, allowing audience members to meet with the greats.

Notify

This feature, allowing you to send brief messages to anyone who is currently online, is available only to users of GEnie's front-end software.

To hail Redhead, for example, you'd need to know her GE mail address. If you don't know it, you can search for it in the GEnie member profiles (see the Summoning Other GEnies section, earlier in this chapter). Assume her address is R.HEAD2. You can then find out if she's currently logged on by selecting Notify from the Online pull-down menu and then selecting the Locate GEnie User option from the side menu.

You are asked to enter a GE mail address. Type

```
r.head2
```

You are told whether or not Redhead is online and, if so, where she's hanging out. You can then click Notify to send her an instant message. Just type the message in the text box and click on the Send button. For example, you may want to invite Redhead to join you in the Chat Lines for a private talk.

SOFTWARE TIP

Currently, the GEnie front-end software has no chat facility built in. If you access a chat area, you enter the terminal mode, which means you have to work with command-line navigation and commands.

If someone notifies you, the Notify alert appears on your screen, showing your that person's message. You can then click on Notify to type your own message back to them; otherwise click on Cancel.

Chat Lines

GEnie's main chat area can be entered by moving to

```
chat
```

Select the fourth menu option, Enter Chat Lines. You are asked to type in a handle—a personalized nickname which other chatters will know you by, such as "Redhead," "SweetTalker," or "Lenny." Your handle can be up to 24 characters long. Press (ENTER) to make your user name your handle.

If you want to change your handle during the conference, use the /han command. For instance, to change from "Lenny Lovelooker" to "Karl Lovelooker," type

```
/han Karl Lovelooker
```

You are then shown a list telling you how many people are in each of the 40 chat channels. You are asked:

```
What CHANNEL (1 to 40)
?
```

Press (ENTER) to join channel 1, otherwise type the number of the channel you're interested in. Different channels may have different topics or moods. Experiment. You should now see the message:

```
** <Lenny Lovelooker> is on.
```

EXPERT TIP

You can set your handle permanently by selecting Change/Reserve Your Handle at the Chat menu. You are asked to type in the handle you wish to use. You can type in any name or phrase, so long as it is less than 24 characters long. When you enter a chat line you will automatically be asked if you want to use your default handle. If you do, just type

```
y
```

to use it. Otherwise type

```
n
```

to enter a new handle.

Each comment starts with the speaker's handle, so the conversation reads like a play script. If you want to say anything, type it and press (ENTER). Your words may be cut off by somebody else's talk. If this happens, just continue typing; your words will appear to others as you intended them. For instance, if your handle is "Lenny Lovelooker" and you type:

`What's up, folks, besides the national debt?`

everyone in your channel sees:

`<Lenny Lovelooker> What's up, folks, besides the national debt?`

See Figure 11-12 to watch Lenny Lovelooker signing in, selecting a channel, and then talking.

If your chat screen becomes too cluttered, you can have GEnie put blank lines between messages. Just type

`/bla`

You can type

`/help`

to see a listing of all the additional chat commands. Some basics are shown in Table 11-4. To find out more about the people on your channel, type

`/sta`

which displays a list of each person's *job number* (a unique ID number assigned to each GEnie chatter), mail address, and state. You can find out about the members of other channels by first typing

`/use`

to see a listing of which channels are active. You can then type *sta* followed by a channel number. For example, to learn about the people on channel 7, type

`/sta 7`

```
Handle of <Lenny Lovelooker> will be used.
Ok (Y/N)?y
Cha/Use   Cha/Use   Cha/Use   Cha/Use
   1   7     3   1     5   2     6   2
   9   4    10   1    11   1    14   2
  22   3    33   3    40   2    44   1
  45   5

What CHANNEL (1 to 45)
?1
Welcome to Channel 1
** <Lenny Lovelooker> is on.
Hi everyone.
<CA Dreamin> a macro
<-Hyposian Elvis-> wow
<Lenny Lovelooker> Hi everyone.
<-Hyposian Elvis-> hi lovelooker
<CA Dreamin> Hi ll
<*smoothy*> hey lenny!
My moustache itches!
<Lenny Lovelooker> My moustache itches!
|
```

FIGURE 11-12 Channel surfing on GEnie

COMMAND	ACTION
/BLA	Inserts a blank line between each person's message.
/CAL <job#>	Calls someone with job number <job#> who's on another channel.
/CHA <#>	Moves to channel number <#>.
/EX	Exits chatting and returns to the previous menu.
/HAN <handle>	Changes your nickname.
/STA <#>	Displays the status of the people on channel <#>.
/SEN <job#> <message>	Sends the person with job number <job#> the message <message>.
/SQU <job#>	Squelches (stops displaying talk from) the person with job number <job#>.
/USE	Shows you how many users are on each currently active channel.
/WHO <job#>	Displays information about the person with job number <job#>.

TABLE 11-4 GEnie's basic chat commands

You may decide to switch to a new channel. If so, type */cha* followed by the channel's number. For example, to move to channel 15, type

    /cha 15

To learn the details about a particular person, type */who* followed by his or her job number. For instance, to learn the handle, GE mail address, channel, and state of job number 99, type

    /who 99

alternatively, if you know a person's handle (i.e. "Redhead"), you can find out more about her by typing

    /sho Redhead

You can then send her GE mail or look up her member profile. See the relevant sections, earlier in this chapter.

To tap someone on the shoulder—whether they're in your channel or anywhere else—use the */cal* command. For instance, to call the person with job number 99, type

    /cal 99

Number 99 sees the message:

    ** <Lenny Lovelooker> is calling.

EXPERT TIP

If you want to hold a private conversation with a date, just use the /pri command. You must find out your date's job number; suppose it is 16. You can then type

`/PRI 16`

Your sweet 16 gets the message:

`** <Lenny Lovelooker>   Job 99 requests you in the private mode.`

and must now type

`/pri 99`

You see the message:

`Job 16 has joined you in private mode.`

You two can now talk to your heart's content, without anyone else overhearing. To exit the private mode, type

`/xpr`

You can also hold a private conversation with *several* people by using the scramble /scr command. Choose a password, such as "Monotone." You can then set up your own scramble channel by typing

`/scr monotone`

You can now use the /send command to tell your friends what your scramble password is. If they type

`/scr monotone`

they enter in a private conversation with you. You can stop a scramble conversation by typing

`/xscr`

You may also whisper a complete message to another user. Just type /sen followed by a person's job number and the message you wish to send. For example, to whisper, "Hey do you want to go to a private chat channel with me?" to number 99, just type:

`/sen 99 Hey do you want to go to a private chat channel with me?`

Number 99 gets the message:

`** <Lenny Lovelooker> [Job 13]  Hey do you want to go to a`
`private chat channel with me?`

If you don't want to receive messages for whatever reason, type

`/nos`

If you only want to avoid messages from a specific harassing user, type /nos followed by that user's job number. For example, if number 13 is bothering you, type

`/nos 13`

To begin receiving messages again, just type

`/xnos`

To stop displaying *anything* a particular user types, type /squ followed by the annoying user's job number. For example,

`/squ 13`

squelches number 13.
When you'd like to exit the chat lines entirely, just type

`/ex`

Real Time Conferences

Each RoundTable has its own Real Time Conference (RTC) for meetings, discussions of major issues, and interviews with topical celebrities. To enter an RTC, just select the Real Time Conference option from any RoundTable menu. For instance, see the Family RoundTable menu in Figure 11-8. The Family RT holds a weekly singles conference that you won't want to miss—check out the schedule of RoundTable events for details.

You get a list of available rooms, with a note of the number of people in each room. You are then asked

`What ROOM (1-3)?`

Type (ENTER) to walk into the first room, otherwise type the room number of the place you want to visit.

When you enter a room, there may be a note posted on the door, telling you about the meeting that's currently being held. If the room is private or a meeting is in progress, the room may be locked, in which case you see the message:

`The door to that room is locked.`
`Please choose another?`

You may either type in a different room number or, if you feel you deserve access to the room, you may knock. To knock on room number 6's door, for instance, type

`/kno 6`

The room's leader may grant you access. Do not knock on a room when the Do Not Disturb sign is displayed.

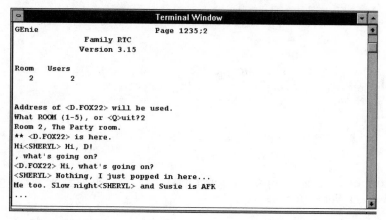

FIGURE 11-13 Real Time Conferencing allows you to chat live with folks about any RoundTable topic

See Figure 11-13 for a sample RTC session. Most of the commands used in the RTC are the same as those used in the standard Chat Lines. Just type what your want to say and press (ENTER). There are a few special commands, however, which are detailed in Table 11-5. These are used primarily during games and celebrity interviews.

GEnie Games

GEnie has devoted itself to bringing its members the snazziest online games available. Many games have their own front-end software, which allows full-color graphics, sound, and animated action—all while battling (or teaming up with) other GEnie members worldwide. Since you can usually chat with your fellow competitors, a GEnie video game may become the dating game.

To access the multi-player games menu, move to

801

COMMAND	ACTION
/RA	Raises your hand. Use it if the room is in Listen Only mode and you'd like to speak. At an appropriate time, you are asked to type in whatever you want to say.
/ROL	Rolls the dice.
/ROOM <#>	Moves to RTC room number <#> (Identical to the Chat Line's /CHA command).

TABLE 11-5 Real Time Conferencing commands, for use during special events

You can then select from one of the following games:

- *CyberStrike.* This game redefined online multi-player combat. You're in control of a CyberPod, a two-legged armored battle-vehicle. With your array of weaponry, you can run, duck, jump, and even climb around the complete CyberCity, defending your team's power towers and blowing up enemies. If you lose too many power towers, your Pod dies of malnutrition. All the while, you can chat with fellow team-mates. (Requires an IBM with 1 Megabyte of Memory and VGA.)

- *Air Warrior.* Choose from 20 different warplanes or 3 different wars. Using the realistic pilot controls, dogfight with your enemies and try to get the last woof. (Versions available for IBM, Mac, Amgia, and the Atari ST.)

- *Hundred Years War.* A detailed military simulation. You control several generations of warriors, leaders, and ladies, interacting with other GEnie users who may be allies, enemies, or lovers. (No graphics; can run on all computers.)

- *Dragon's Gate.* Create a character and explore this medieval fantasy world with magic, mercenaries, and maidens. (Can run on all computers; graphical Mac version available.)

- *Federation II.* Pop culture and sci-fi collide in this wacky space trading game. Pilot your starship around the universe, meeting other traders and exploiting them, killing them, or just chatting with them. (Can run on all computers; graphical IBM version available.)

- *Galaxy I.* Colonize the galaxy. This futuristic military simulation allows you to fight, cheat, bribe, seduce, or con your chunk of an intergalactic monopoly. (No graphics; can run on all computers.)

- *GemStone III.* Enter the realistic town of Kelfour's Landing, where you can visit the shops and go on a shopping spree for food, weapons, or armor. You can then head out to the countryside where you'll run into fellow GEnie thieves, wizards, or fighters. (Can run on all computers; graphical IBM version available.)

- *Multi-Player BattleTech.* Learn to pilot futuristic Mech weaponry, working your way up through the ranks of your team's army. Join armies or work as a mercenary. Either way, you can travel across cities and planets, meeting and battling other soldiers. See Figure 11-14. (Requires an IBM.)

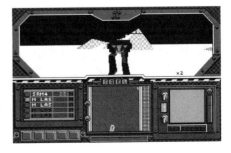

Figure 11-14 Multi-Player BattleTech: Get teched off while blowing up your GEnie friends

SOFTWARE TIP

When downloading front-end game software, you enter terminal mode. You have to type in your commands at the command-line. When you download a file (by typing *d*), the GEnie software does *not* automatically begin the download. You need to access Terminal Mode from the Online pull-down menu and then select the Receive File option from the side menu. Type in the file's name and then click on the OK button.

NTN Trivia. Compete against other trivia-masters in this fast-action game show. Not only do you play against fellow GEnie members, but the NTN network links you up to bars, casinos, and restaurants across North America. You can even build up real prize points which can be redeemed for free GEnie connect time, electronic equipment, and such. See Figure 11-15. (Can run on all computers; graphical IBM, Mac, Amiga, and Atari versions available.)

Orb Wars. Join a team and then compete against other wizards, battling with your wits and magic. (Runs on all computers; graphical versions available for IBM, Mac, Amiga, Atari ST, and Apple IIGS.)

QB1. Predict what the quarterback will do during actual NFL and college football games. Not only can you compete against GEnie members, but against people in taverns, hotels, and casinos all over North America. (Requires an IBM, Atari ST, Amiga, or Mac.)

RSCARDS. Bridge, blackjack, poker, backgammon, checkers, chess, or reversi. (Can run on all computers; graphical IBM, Mac, Atari ST, Apple IIGS, and Commodore 128 versions available.)

Stellar Emperor. Conquer colonies around the universe, becoming the Lord Emperor of All the Galaxies. (Can run on all computers; graphical IBM Windows version available.)

Stellar Warrior. Join an Alliance, step into your starship, and battle the others. (Can run on all computers; graphical version available for IBM, Amiga, and Atari ST.)

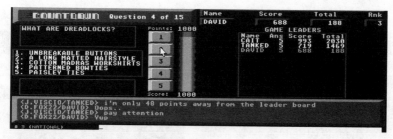

FIGURE 11-15 In pursuit of trivia, online

In addition, you can manage your own football, baseball, or basketball team as part of the fantasy sports playoffs in the Sports RoundTable (move to *Sports*). You can also check out the TSR Online RoundTable (move to *TSR*), where you can play a fantasy role-playing game with other GEnie enthusiasts.

When you enter a game menu, you usually get the option to read about the game. Select the appropriate About Game item for basic information and instructions. If the game uses graphics and sound, you need to download special front-end software to use it. Select Download Front-End Software. Always read the Information About Front-End Software item first before selecting the download option; this lets you know what sort of computer system you need, and how to set the game up.

Typically, you just type

d

when prompted, to begin the download. You may need to select a protocol, if you have not already done so. See the Downloading section of this chapter for more information.

Games usually come in one large file which, when run, automatically extracts itself into several different files. It's a good idea to make a separate folder or directory for each game you download. Copy the downloaded game file to your new directory and then execute the file.

Most GEnie multi-player games work as their own front-end software. This means they automatically dial up GEnie, connect you to the appropriate menus, and get you started shooting and scoring. The first time you run a game you have to enter your GEnie ID number, password, and local access number, when prompted. See the Logging On section at the beginning of the chapter for details.

Getting the hang of a GEnie game may take a little while, due to the new commands and tricky strategies. Don't be afraid to ask other players for help—they once needed it too. Each multi-player game also has its own RoundTable, where relevant questions can be asked.

Corking the Bottle

If your three online wishes are cool multi-player video games, ongoing quirky conversations, and low-end rates (on nights and weekends only, mind you), then sign on to GEnie and consider your wishes granted.

If ease-of-use is high on your wish list, however, you may want to think twice before you uncork the bottle. GEnie's front-end software, at its current stage, leaves a lot—of functionality and speed—to be desired.

DELPHI

800-695-4005
DELPHI INTERNET SERVICES CORPORATION
1030 MASSACHUSETTS AVENUE
CAMBRIDGE MA 02138

STEVE AND I MET ALMOST A YEAR AGO

on a single parents' bulletin board on another online service. I'm a single mom of two kids and a full time graduate student living in Augusta, Georgia. My daughter Kelly is 11 and my son Kristopher is 6. Steve was a widower in Indianapolis raising his almost 16-year-old daughter Mandy. There were about 40 or 50 single parents posting on that bulletin board at the time. We were just friends, along with everyone else. Then in April 1993, that service announced a giant rate increase. Many of the single parents there decided to move together to another online service which was very different from the first one and took a little more computer skills to learn to use. Steve and I are both fairly computer literate, so we found ourselves working together a lot to help our friends learn their way around the new place and get used to it. We began e-mailing each other often as we (and others) helped our single parent friends make the move and adjust. One thing led to another (as they often do!) and before long we found ourselves interested in a lot more than just friendship. One morning, hours before I was to take a major exam, I received yet another e-mail from Steve. But this one was different. It started off with a lot of the technical computer stuff we usually e-mailed back and forth, but at the end of this particular letter, Steve said "I was wondering if you were involved with someone, if you are not wanting to get involved with someone, or if possibly you might want to get involved with me." I e-mailed back the

reply "yes" and included my phone number. After a lot of e-mailing, and a lot of phone calls, we decided we really needed to meet face to face. We only had a weekend, and we live 750 miles apart, so we decided to meet half-way. Steve got out a map, and just picked a town—Jellico, Tennessee. It turned out to be a beautiful little town, nestled in the mountains. And that weekend turned out to be everything we had hoped it would be! Shortly after we became romantically involved with each other, we made our final online service change, to Delphi, where we are co-hosts of The Single Parents Network, a custom forum we created as a support group and a cyberspace "home away from home" for our single parent friends.

We announced our engagement to our online single parent friends in September, and on July 3rd, we will be married in the same little town we met in—Jellico. Many of our single parent friends plan to attend, some of whom we have met face to face, many others we have not (yet!). They will be traveling from all parts of the country: Maryland, Ohio, Illinois, Arizona, New York, and Florida to name just a few. As a group, we are very close and I am looking forward to gathering us all together in one spot.

What It Is

In ancient Greece, Delphi was considered to be the navel of the Earth, the very center of the universe. Delphi's local oracle had a direct connection to the gods, cryptically predicting visitors' fates with ease. In the world of online dating, Delphi Internet Services may not exactly foresee your romantic future, but it can certainly help enhance it. Delphi connects you not to the gods, but to a steady cross-section of other mortals.

Delphi, the United States' fifth largest online service, is a no-frills, menu-driven system. You'll need to log on using your own communications software. You'll have to learn several easy commands and type each one as you need it. There are no cute icons, sounds, or screen layouts. Though it may all seem like Greek to you at first, this chapter will help take the confusing edge off Delphi navigation.

The modest Delphi environment is dressed up with many of the standard online features: business resources, files, entertainment, games, news, reference books, shopping, and travel. Delphi also has complete menu-driven access to the Internet. Indeed, many of Delphi's users head straight for the Internet, never exploring what Delphi itself has to offer.

Delphi has many romantic spots, perfect for meeting, courting, or just getting to know a person. While most other commercial services shy away from advocating online dating of any kind, Delphi all but promotes it. The talk on Delphi also tends to be a bit more risqué than most other areas of pay-cyberspace, which can turn some people on and put some people off.

Minute for minute, Delphi is the cheapest of the online services. If you plan to be online a lot, Delphi's your best bet, at about a buck an hour. If you call Delphi during prime-time business hours, though, you'll accrue Olympian-sized bills; Delphi charges a hefty daytime surcharge for most area codes.

How To Connect

Signing up is a straightforward process. Have your Visa or Mastercard ready and use your modem to call 800-365-4636. Press (ENTER) a few times until it asks you for your

Username:

at which point, you type

JOINDELPHI

(this may be automatically typed for you).

When you are asked for a

Password:

type

SNT94

You are now prompted for your name, address, and telephone number. You are asked to type in a *Membername*. This one-word Membername—also called the username—is how people will recognize you, refer to you, and e-mail you. Choose something fitting your personality, something that grabs attention. Once your Membername is chosen, you cannot change it. You are also given a list of several possible Membernames.

All relevant financial information now scrolls down your screen. Read it carefully, as it supersedes any information printed here. Delphi has it set up so that readers of this book are given a free month of access, including five free hours (additional hours are $1.80). Just use the password indicated above.

You now need to enter your billing information. When prompted, type in the kind of credit card you have, its number, and its expiration date. Though the first month is free, Delphi needs this information in case you exceed your free five hours, access a premium service, or call during prime time.

Then the system asks for your mother's maiden name. This gives you an extra layer of security—it's *not* your password. You type in a temporary password next. It must be one word, between 6 and 12 letters long. The first time you log on to Delphi, the system asks for a new, permanent, password.

Next, the system asks for your area code. Do so and press ENTER. A list similar to the following appears:

```
Choice  City                St  Phone        Speed
  1       New York City      NY  212-741-8100 300/1200
  2       New York City      NY  212-645-0560 2400
  3       New York City      NY  212-741-4950 300/1200
  4       New York City      NY  212-645-0560 2400
  5       New York City      NY  212-620-6000 300/1200
  6       New York City      NY  212-645-0560 2400

Are any of these SPRINT numbers a local call for you? [Y]
```

If the numbers shown are within your local calling area, press ENTER. Otherwise, type

n

and you get a new list of numbers. Type in the choice number of the network in your calling area that runs at your modem speed.

The screen gives step-by-step instructions on how to log on to Delphi. Write these down. You can even go through a simulated practice log on, to make sure you understand the process. Enter the Delphi access number into your terminal software's dialing directory. See the Logging On section of this chapter for more help.

Charges and Surcharges

The basic rates for Delphi fall under two plans:

💲 *The 10/4 Plan:* $10 a month for four hours of use. Beyond that, it's $4 an hour.

EXPERT TIP

If you have a 9600-baud or faster modem, temporarily select a 2400-baud network from the list. Later, online, you can find a 9600-baud local number by typing

go us 9600

EXPERT TIP

To see how long you've been online, type

    /time

§ *The 20/20 Plan:* If you spend a lot of time online, this is one of the best deals in cyberspace. For $20 a month, you get 20 hours of use. Beyond that, it's only $1.80 an hour. There is a one-time $19 enrollment fee.

If you want access to the Internet, you pay an additional $3 a month; the first month you sign up is free. Certain *premium* sections of Delphi also cost extra: much of the finance data, FAX service, and the Librarian (an online research service). Premium items have a dollar sign ($) next to them on the menu. If you choose a premium item, Delphi tells you how much extra you will be charged.

Once you decide on a basic plan, the surcharges can get complicated. If you live in Massachusetts or Missouri, you can use a free local number. Otherwise, you have to use a local-access carrier (see the Public Data Networks section of Chapter 5, Buckling Up). Delphi can be reached through several networks. You get the number closest to you when you sign up.

In the mainland United States, there is no surcharge when using a local-access carrier on holidays, weekends, or during the evenings (from 7 P.M. to 6 A.M., local time, for Tymnet; 6 P.M. to 7 A.M. for SprintNet). If you call during business hours, you generally pay an additional $9 an hour.

Rates for Canada, Hawaii, Puerto Rico, and other countries vary. It's always a good idea—no matter where you're calling from—to check with Delphi in advance to find out exactly how much you'll be paying.

Logging On

Since Delphi has no special software, you need to log on manually. This involves calling a public data network, entering a special series of codes, and then typing in your username (Membername) at the

USERNAME:

EXPERT TIP

If you live in Massachusetts or Missouri, simply call Delphi direct (617-576-0862 or 816-421-6938, respectively), 24 hours a day, free of surcharges.

prompt and your password when when the system asks for

PASSWORD:

Your communications program should already have the correct configuration, by default. Either eight data bits, no parity, one stop bit (8N1), or seven data bits and even parity (7E1) should work. Also check that full-duplex, no auto linefeeds, and XON-XOFF handshaking is enabled. For help with these settings, see Chapter 4, The Datemobile.

You should have learned your local public data number when you first signed on to Delphi. In most cases, this is either a SprintNet or Tymnet number; if you're not sure which, call Delphi member services. If you are calling Delphi directly (in Boston or Kansas City), simply press (ENTER) a few times. You may see the *LOCAL>* prompt, in which case you should type

c

If you already have Internet access, you can connect to Delphi by telneting to *delphi.com*. Otherwise, use your communications software to dial your local number. Wait for the modem to connect and then do the following:

For SprintNet

You see an empty screen. If you are calling at 2400 baud, press (@), (SHIFT)+(D), and (ENTER).
If you are running at 300 or 1200 baud, press (ENTER), (SHIFT)+(D), and (ENTER) again. When you see

TERMINAL=

press (ENTER) once more. You should then see an @. To connect, type

c delphi

and (ENTER).

For Tymnet

After dialing your local number, wait a few seconds. Depending on your baud rate you either see nothing, a string of *X*s, or the message:

PLEASE TYPE YOUR TERMINAL IDENTIFIER

Press the letter (O). When the message

PLEASE LOG IN

appears, type

delphi

and press (ENTER).

Logging Off

To disconnect from Delphi, at any menu prompt, just type

`bye`

If you are in a conference group (chatting), you can exit Delphi by typing

`/bye`

Getting Around

Similar to a basic BBS (see Chapter 6), Delphi works using text menus. You see a list of choices, and you select the one that interests you. See Figure 12-1 for Delphi's main menu.

You need only type the first couple of letters to select an item. For instance, to access the Groups and Clubs menu, you simply type

`gr`

and press (ENTER). You then get a new menu, allowing you to chat with or write messages to people interested in a variety of hobbies.

You can see detailed information about your current menu by typing

`help`

at any time. You get a list of help topics. At the

`Topic?`

```
MAIN Menu:

Business and Finance        News, Weather, and Sports
Computing Groups            Reference and Education
Conference                  Shopping
Entertainment and Games     Travel and Leisure
Groups and Clubs            Using DELPHI
Internet Services           Workspace
Mail                        HELP
Member Directory            EXIT

MAIN>What do you want to do? group

GROUPS and CLUBS Menu:

Aviation SIG                Radio SIG
Business Forum              Science Fiction Sig
Close Encounters            Senior Forum
Golf SIG                    Sports Connection Online
Custom Forums               Theological Network
Environment SIG             TV/Movie Group
GameSig                     USA Gymnastics
Hobby Shop                  WCF - World Community
Languages and Cultures      WIDNet-Disability Network
```

FIGURE 12-1 Delphi's main menu

prompt, type in the topic you need further information on. You may also get a list of sub-topics. Press (ENTER) a few times to exit the help menus.

To return to a previous menu, press (CTRL)+(Z). Alternatively, you can type

```
exit
```

If you ever get stuck or lost, (CTRL)+(Z) helps you back out into more familiar territory. You can return to the main menu by typing

```
main
```

Many other Delphi commands are accomplished using the (CTRL) key. Table 12-1 lists several of the more useful keypresses.

Occasionally, Delphi provides a list of various articles you can read. You see a prompt that looks something like:

```
(Scan, Read, "?", Exit)
```

Type

```
scan
```

to see a list of your choices, such as:

```
1 Learn about Delphi
2 How to get the most out of using Delphi
```

You can then read whatever you're interested by typing *read* and its number. For example, to read the first item, type

```
read 1
```

KEY PRESS	ACTION
(CTRL)+(Z)	If you're typing an article or e-mail letter, this finishes it.
	If you're using the menus, it returns you to the previous screen.
(CTRL)+(O)	When you're reading a message you don't care to read, this skips to its end.
(CTRL)+(C)	Cancels the current activity, in case you choose the wrong operation from the menu.
	If you're in the middle of writing an article or letter, this aborts it.
(CTRL)+(S)	Stops text. If you're reading an article and it scrolls too fast, this puts on the brakes.
(CTRL)+(Q)	Resumes text. Always press this after pressing (CTRL)+(S) to continue reading.

TABLE 12-1 Use (CTRL) to control your trip around Delphi

If you are reading a long message or article on Delphi you may occasionally see the

More?

prompt. If you don't want to read the rest of the text, press Ⓝ, otherwise just press ⏎ENTER to continue.

Delphi has a handy feature that lets you jump to any faraway menu: Go. For example, to access the Close Encounters classified ads area, you would normally have to go through several steps. First, you would need to type

group

to access the Groups and Clubs menu, and then you'd type

close

to enter the Close Encounters special interest group. Finally, you'd have to type

classifieds

But you can do all this in one quick step simply by typing

go gr close clas

Delphi Departments

You can access all of Delphi's features from the main menu.

- *Business and Finance.* Here you can find business news; get commodity, CD, futures, money market fund, or stock quotes; talk to an investment expert; buy and sell commodities; or connect to a foreign-language translation service. Most of these financial features, aptly enough, cost extra money.

- *News, Weather, and Sports.* Complete online newspapers, including business, entertainment, sports, weather, and national news.

- *Computing Groups.* Talk to computer users, purveyors, and experts. If you access a database, you can copy software from Delphi onto your home computer. The forums allow you read or leave a wide variety of computer-related messages.

- *Reference and Education.* A handy area including two encyclopedias, a gourmet recipe helper, a medical advice reference, and access to dozens of specialized databases. Note that using the databases often costs extra. Watch for the ($) symbol.

- *Shopping.* Here's your connection for pricing and buying cars, computers, gourmet coffee, magazines, software, and UNICEF greeting cards. If you meet someone extra-special you can order a dozen long-stemmed roses from here, at the press of a few keys, and have them delivered the next day.

- *Entertainment and Games.* Here's one of the best places to waste your time, including fantasy and adventure games, logic games, Flipit, poker, VT-100 "graphics" games,

trivia, and more. You can play most of these games against other people, online. See the Chat section of this chapter for descriptions of some of Delphi's multi-player games. Slicing people's arms off with your longsword or pirating intergalactic ore from their vessels is often a good way to meet them. You can also get your horoscope here (is love in your stars?), browse movie and book reviews, or write a chapter in a collaborative online novel.

- *Travel and Leisure.* If you meet someone *really* special who lives 1,000 miles away, you can use this area to book an airline reservation, car rental, cruise, or even a hotel.

- *Groups and Clubs.* These special interest groups are where Delphi users discuss fiction, theology, writing, computer art, photography, music, or other hobbies. There are areas specific to adults and/or dating. See the sections on Messages and Chat, later in this chapter.

- *Internet Services.* Welcome to the Internet! Delphi offers complete, menu-driven access. See Chapter 7, The Internet.

- *Member Directory.* A listing of all Delphi users. See the Finding Delphi Dates section.

- *Using Delphi.* This section has all the information you need about accessing Delphi from the United States and overseas, plus special payment plans, latest usage rates, tips on using Delphi, and a list of Delphi's newest features.

- *EXIT.* To finish your Delphi session.

Downloading

Files on Delphi are stored in databases. Many Delphi databases contain digitized photographs. The Close Encounters special interest group (sig), for example, contains two areas: You'll find G-rated portraits in "Sig Members" and steamier snapshots in "Play Ground"— prepare to unfog your monitor. To get access to the adult files, however, you need to download a form, fill it out, and mail it to the Close Encounters staff along with a photocopy of your driver's license to prove that you're 18 years or older.

To access the Close Encounters database, type

```
go gr close data
```

A listing of all the available areas appears (some sections appear only if you have adult access):

Open Forum	Our Place
Close Encounters	Art Gallery
Fantasies	Poetry
Lifestyles	Bare Essence
Noteworthy News	Ramblings
Personal Health Issues	Heritage Searchers
Play Ground	Sig Members

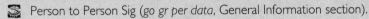

EXPERT TIP

Most Delphi sigs scan your photograph for free, if you send it in to them. Check the Announcements for more information or send e-mail to one of the managers of the sig you'd like to be in. Other areas where you can find mug shots of Delphi users are:

- Person to Person Sig (*go gr per data*, General Information section).
- Computer Graphics Sig (*go com graph data*, Faces of Delphi section).

Most every sig has its own database of text files, software, and graphics. See Chapter 4, The Datemobile, for information on how to view graphics once you download them.

Upon entering any database, you see a list of topics. Type in the name of the topic that interests you. For example, to access the Close Encounters database of member photographs, you would type

```
sig members
```

You can now see a brief listing of all the files by typing

```
dir
```

Continue pressing (ENTER) until the listing is complete.

Since these listings may be quite long, it's a good idea to search for a keyword that describes the type of file you're looking for. For instance, if you only want to download photos of Delphi's male users, you first type

```
search
```

and then, when prompted for a keyword, you type

```
male
```

You are told how many files match your search criterion. If you want to narrow the search, type

```
narrow
```

and then type in a second keyword, such as

```
tall
```

You can continue narrowing down (dark, handsome, and so on) until there are only a few applicable files.

To read a detailed description of each file, type

```
read
```

If the file doesn't sound interesting, press (ENTER) to read about the next available file. If you decide you want to download the file, type

`down`

If you haven't already selected a download protocol, enter one now. Then access the download feature of your communications program. See Chapter 4, The Datemobile, for instructions on how to transfer files.

When you're done searching a topic, you can change the topic of the database by typing

`set`

and then choosing a new topic.

Finding Delphi Dates

The Member Directory is a powerful database, or date-a-base, of Delphi's populace. In addition to the main membership listing, most special interest groups (sigs) have their own directories. This allows you to customize your profile depending on your surroundings; drawing out the technical side of yourself in the computer sigs, talking about the loving side of yourself in the dating sigs.

The directory can easily help you find people with similar interests. To access the main directory, type

`go memb`

At any other sig menu with the Member Directory option, just type

`memb`

To enter or change your personal information, type

`i-am`

You are then grilled with several personal questions, such as your city, state, and birthdate. You can make your profile more interesting by adding keywords—headings that people can search by. You can use keywords to group your attributes or favorite hobbies. Some sample keyword topics are "Sex," "Status," "Accomplishments," "Age," "Hobbies,"

"Religion," and "Occupation." You can describe yourself using as many keywords as you like. To add a keyword onto your profile, type

add

The system asks which keyword you'd like to use. You can type

?

for a list of sample topics. You can either view all the keywords currently in use (a long, long, list), or you can type

recommend

to see a short list of recommended keywords.

The best way to get ideas on how to structure your *I-Am* entry is to browse other people's profiles. If you've met someone on Delphi and want to find out more, type

whois <username>

For instance, if Lenny posted some interesting messages in one of the forums, you can get a closer "glimpse" of him by entering

whois lenny

To search for interesting and appealing Delphi neighbors, you can view every user's profile alphabetically by typing

browse

You are asked at which letter you want to start. Press (ENTER) to start at the beginning.

Since this list tends to be long, you can also view specific people according to their interests. Suppose you're crazy about gardening. To see a list of descriptive keywords, type

list

One of the words that appear is "hobbies." Simply type

search

EXPERT TIP

You can view a Delphi user's main profile at any time (in conferences, at menus, or in forums) by typing

/whois <Membername>

where <Membername> is replaced by the Membername of the person you're interested in finding more about.

to view a list of people who described their hobbies, and then enter

hobbies

You are asked which hobbies to *Search For:*. Type

gardening

A list of eligible green thumbs appears, as in Figure 12-2. You can now send them e-mail and chat about your forget-me-nots. If things go well, *you* may soon become someone's forget-me-not.

Messages

You can exchange messages galore in Delphi's forums. Table 12-2 lists the basic commands you need to master.

Forums can be found in any sig. Delphi's Business and Computing areas have appropriate sigs. The Groups and Clubs area, however, is where the fun is; it contains over a dozen general sigs pertaining to popular hobbies—including dating.

The first time you enter a sig you are generally asked if you want to join. You should see the following menu:

```
Membership Agreement and Features
Join this Group
Enter as a Nonmember
Exit


NONMEMBER>(Member, Join, Enter, Exit)
```

```
I-Am
Who-Is
List-Keywords
Browse
Search
Help
Exit

DIRECTORY>(I-Am,Who-Is,List,Browse,Search): s

What KEYWORD:hobbies

Search for:gardening

Matches found for the following membernames:

DAVID52      LLYR        MCAMPOS     NANC        SIRBARON
KENSAN       JONGEE      APPA        HASZAG      KENNETH2423
BOWEN19894   CORRADETTI

Found 12.

Would you like the complete profiles printed for the selected
membernames?
```

FIGURE 12-2 Harvesting the seeds of love from Delphi's membership directory

COMMAND	ACTION
ADD	Posts a new message.
BACK	Reads the previous message in a thread.
DIR	Displays a list of messages.
DIR /NEW	Displays a list of the latest messages.
FOLLOW	Follows a message's thread.
FORWARD	Sends a copy of the current message over e-mail.
NEXT or (ENTER)	Reads the next message.
READ NEW	Reads only the newest messages.
READ WAITING	Reads all messages addressed to you.
REPLY	Responds to a message.
TOPIC	Sets or shows the current message's topic.
<number>	Reads message number <number>.

TABLE 12-2 Delphi forum message commands

Type

```
member
```

to read all about the sig, its forums, conferences (chat), and file areas. You are told what type of people hang around the sig, and what sort of conduct you're expected to keep. Some sigs are limited to adult usage only. You are also told what time the sig's conferences are held; most sigs hold a weekly "meeting" in the conference area, which you are invited to attend. Last, you are told who the manager or sysop of the sig is. If you ever have problems, send mail to this person.

If the sig interests you, type

```
join
```

You enter the sig. The next time you access the sig, you will automatically be registered as a member. Some sigs may begin with cute opening *banners*, as in Figure 12-3.

Reading Messages

Forum messages are organized by topic. When you first step into a forum, you can simply press (ENTER) to read the first message in the currently set topic. If any messages have been addressed specifically to you, pressing (ENTER) allows you to read those first.

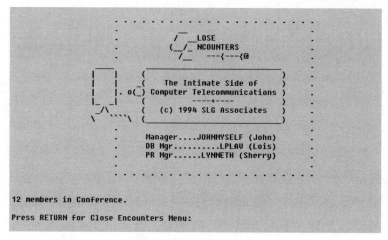

```
                    / __LOSE
                 (__/_ NCOUNTERS
                  /__  ---<---<@
        _____
    | |  (                       )
    | _(      The Intimate Side of  )
    | |. o(_) Computer Telecommunications )
    |_ _|  (      ----+----           )
    _/\....\ (    (c) 1994 SLG Associates )
    \ `..`\ (_____)

            Manager....JOHNMYSELF (John)
            DB Mgr.........LPLAU (Lois)
            PR Mgr......LYNNETH (Sherry)

12 members in Conference.

Press RETURN for Close Encounters Menu:
```

FIGURE 12-3 Getting ready for a Close Encounter

To see a list of topics, type

`topic`

Normally, you see messages pertaining to all the sig's topics. If, for some reason, a topic does not interest you, type

`clear`

and then type in the name of the topic to ignore. For instance, if you're in the Close Encounters sig and want to skip sig members' verse and rhyme, type

`poetry`

To see the topics on your current reading list, type

`show`

To read only the latest messages, type

`read new`

If you only want to read messages addressed specifically to you, type

`read waiting`

There are two different ways you can read through your messages. If you want to read them one by one, chronologically, just continue pressing (ENTER). You can also read messages by their *threads*—each message followed by its responses, like an actual conversation. To follow a particular message's thread, type

`follow`

at the sig prompt. Continue reading along the thread by pressing (ENTER).

Most likely, you want to browse, choosing those messages that interest you. To see a directory of all the subjects, type

dir

A list similar to Figure 12-4 appears, showing you each message's number, the date it was posted, the person who posted it, and its subject. If the directory listing continues beyond one page, you see the prompt:

Press Return to Continue

As suggested, press (ENTER) (or (RETURN)) if you'd like to see the next page. You can return to the previous prompt, as usual, by pressing (CTRL)+(Z).

Since some topics may contain thousands of messages, you might want to see only the more recent subjects. If this is the case, type

dir /new

You can also begin the directory at any particular message number. If you only want to see the subjects of message number 7833 and on, type

dir 7833

When you see a specific message that interests you, just type its number. You can also read a specified number of the latest messages by typing a negative number. For example, to see the last 20 messages posted, type

-20

```
Msg     Date    From        To          Top Subject

3542    1-MAY   THIB        EGME        How RE: The Health Club!
3543    1-MAY   ALOVELACE   THIB        Gen RE:
3544    2-MAY   BIPED       ALOVELACE   Gen RE:
3545    2-MAY   NWCS        LARRY2744   Gen RE: general discussion
3546    2-MAY   NWCS        DDOVERTON   Dat RE: What do you think I should do?
3547    2-MAY   NWCS        WILDTURKEY  Dat RE: What do you think I should do?
3548    2-MAY   DWEST1      DDOVERTON   How RE: The Health Club!
3549    2-MAY   EGME        THIB        How RE: The Health Club!
3550    3-MAY   BRENDADAVIS ALEXANDRAM  Per RE: Penpals wanted
3551    3-MAY   BRENDADAVIS NWCS        Gen RE: No Notes
3552    3-MAY   BRENDADAVIS LARRY2744   Per RE: Penpals wanted
3553    3-MAY   BILGETT     LFOUSSARD   Gen RE: WELCOME!
3554    3-MAY   LARRY2744   BRENDADAVIS Per RE: Penpals wanted
3555    3-MAY   EGME        NWCS        Dat RE: What do you think I should do?
3556    3-MAY   EGME        LARRY2744   Per RE: Penpals wanted
3557    3-MAY   EGME        BRENDADAVIS Per RE: Penpals wanted
3558    4-MAY   THIB        EGME        How RE: The Health Club!
3559    4-MAY   JOEYLUV     ALL         Gen new kid on the forum

Press RETURN for More.

FORUM>Reply, Add, Read, "?" or Exit>
```

FIGURE 12-4 A directory of Delphi messages

Replying or Forwarding

To respond to a message you've just read, simply type

`reply`

Delphi also has a useful feature that allows you to forward any message you've just read to someone via e-mail. Simply type

`forward`

You are asked to enter the Delphi user's Membername. See the Mail section of this chapter for more details on how to send a letter.

Writing a New Message

To post a new message, type

`add`

As in Figure 12-5, you have to assign your message to a topic. If you're not sure what topics there are, press (ENTER).

You also have to say who you want to send the message to. Press (ENTER) if the message is for everybody, otherwise type in a particular Membername. When asked for

`Subject:`

enter a short summary of your message.

You can now type in your message, line by line. Type carefully; once you get to the end of a line and press (ENTER), it's a hassle to change it.

```
FORUM>Reply, Add, Read, "?" or Exit> add
To: [ALL]
Subj: Luau
Topic?
Please select one of the available topics.

Topics set:

General Discussion    Florida Singles
I Hate It When...     Dating
How To Meet           Personals
Suddenly Single       The NUG

Topic? Personals
Please enter your message below.  Control-Z when Complete.  /HELP for Help.
I'm a 29 year old travel agent in Florida. I like working out, adventure,
and good classic books like _Wuthering Heights_. I'm posting because I'm
planning on visiting Hawaii next month and I'd rather not travel alone. If
anyone, male or female, shares my interests and wants to spend this Christmas
on a beach, I'd love to hear your Aloha.

Thanks!
```

FIGURE 12-5 Adding a Delphi message

EXPERT TIP

If you'd like to reply privately to someone, you can easily access Delphi mail by typing

```
mail
```

Send the person e-mail, as usual (see the Mail section, later in this chapter). When your mail is sent, press (CTRL)+(Z) to return to the forum and continue reading messages.

If you finish typing a line but then spot an error, you can erase it entirely and begin typing anew. Just type

```
/delete
```

at the beginning of the next line. To review your final message, type

```
/list
```

When you finish entering the text, press (CTRL)+(Z) to post it. If you change your mind, you can cancel your message by pressing (CTRL)+(C) instead.

Dateworthy Forums

Delphi has two main sigs where cyberdating is the rage:

- *Person to Person (go gr pers)*. This is where teens and young adults meet, discuss relationships, and shoot the breeze. The "Relationships" topic is a good place to discuss dating dilemmas.

- *Close Encounters (go gr close)*. The "mature" area, where Delphi users can achieve a close encounter of the kindest kind. This forum is for users 18 and over. There are many love-related topics, such as "Personal Health Issues," "Poetry," "Rambling," "Bare Essence," and more.

Custom Forums

The custom forums are where things get wild. Created and maintained by Delphi users themselves, there are over 100 custom forums pertaining to topics you may or may not have ever heard of. Enter the custom forums area by typing

```
go custom
```

You can then type

```
dir
```

to see a listing of available topics.

To start listing them all, as shown in Figure 12-6, type

scan

Some forums are designated as *(open)*, which means anyone can wander in and browse around. Other *(application only)* forums require an application. Still others are *(closed)* to the public altogether. To find out more about a forum, type its number (the number in its directory listing, not the forum number itself). You may be asked if you want to join the forum. If an application is required, your request is e-mailed to the manager of the forum. He or she will let you know, within a few days, if you have been granted access. In some cases, you may need to send in proof of age through U.S. snail mail.

Some of the following forums may interest you:

- *Callahan's Saloon (006).* Ye olde Irish pub, where problems are solved, drinks are bought one-for-one, and a friendly ear is always apt to be found. Along with an ear, you may also find a mouth, eyes . . . who knows?

- *Single Parents Network (007).* If you're acting as both mommy and daddy, here's the place to talk with others who are familiar with your special set of challenges.

- *In Full View (022).* The gay forum, for support, friendship, issues, and more.

- *The Edge (028).* The counterculture meets here to discuss counters, culture, and general revolutionary fun stuff.

- *The Bonding Place (029).* This is where those interested in sexual bondage can tie themselves up and knock themselves out.

- *Singles Forum (057).* The place where the unspoken-for can roam. Topics here include everything from "How to meet" to "Dating" to "Single again."

```
More?(Y, N, "?" or Number)
  22  FORUM 033 - STATUESQUE AND RUBENESQUE (OPEN)
  23  FORUM 034 - THE FURRY FORUM (APPLICATION ONLY)
  24  FORUM 035 - SCADIANS ON DELPHI (OPEN)
  25  FORUM 036 - COMEDY CLUB ONLINE (OPEN)
  26  FORUM 037 - PROGRAMMING FORUM (OPEN)
  27  FORUM 038 - TEEN/YOUTH FORUM (OPEN)
  28  FORUM 039 - HEARTH AND HOME (OPEN)
  29  FORUM 040 - PARROTHEAD MADNESS (OPEN)
  30  FORUM 041 - OS/2 (OPEN)
  31  FORUM 042 - CHAT AND CHAT GAMES FORUM (OPEN)
  32  FORUM 043 - ADVENTURE AND RECREATIONAL SPORTS (OPEN)
  33  FORUM 044 - GO PLAYERS' FORUM (OPEN)
  34  FORUM 047 - PET LOVERS' FORUM (OPEN)
  35  FORUM 048 - MULTIMEDIA FORUM (OPEN)
  36  FORUM 050 - ROISSY  - LE MAISON DE PLAISIR (APPLICATION ONLY)
  37  FORUM 055 - THE TEACHERS LOUNGE (OPEN)
  38  FORUM 056 - DIVORCE-BEFORE,DURING AND AFTER SUPPORTBOARD (OPEN)
  39  FORUM 057 - THE SINGLES FORUM (OPEN)
  40  FORUM 060 - BUILDING COMMUNITY (OPEN)
  41  FORUM 061 - DEPT. 56 COLLECTIBLES (OPEN)
  42  FORUM 064 - SEAGEAR SAILING FORUM (OPEN)
  43  FORUM 065 - THE YELLOW SUBMARINE (APPLICATION ONLY)
  44  FORUM 068 - SEARCHING FOR ROOTS (OPEN)
More?(Y, N, "?" or Number)
```

FIGURE 12-6 One of many screenfuls of Delphi's user-created custom forums

Interested in something, but there's no forum for it? For $29.95 and a $5 monthly maintenance fee, you can be the manager of your very own forum. For information and an application, type

```
start
```

at the *CUSTOM FORUM>* prompt.

Book and Candle Pub (080). A largely literary saloon geared toward lovers of arts, culture, and books.

Pen Pals (099). Hook up with people around the world who are interested in exchanging mail, whether it be electronic or paper.

12-Step Sex/Love Addicts (142). If you're a lovaholic, here's where you can turn for help.

To access a custom forum, you must know its three-digit number. For instance, to jump to the Singles Forum, you would type

```
go custom #057
```

Classified Ads

Many sigs, including Person to Person and Close Encounters, have their own classified ads sections. To access the classified ads, simply type

```
class
```

at any sig menu prompt.

You get a menu of topics. For example, in the Close Encounters classifieds section the topics range from "Dating" to "Naughty but Nice" to "Personals" to "Group Sex" to "Friends Only." Type in the first few letters of the topic that interests you. Alternatively, you can type

```
search
```

to search all the topics for a particular piece of text. Type in a keyword, a descriptive adjective or attribute such as "Colorado" or "intelligent."

You can now browse through the topic. To post an ad of your own, type

```
post
```

You may then select the *form* your ad can take. Usually, just type

```
2
```

to post a standard ad.

You are now asked for the headline of your ad. Type something eye-catching, such as:

`your life (love life) depends on reading this`

You can now type in your message, line by line. Since you are not charged for classified ads, be as long-winded and descriptive as you want; no need for cryptic acronyms (of course if your ad is *too* long, people may skip it altogether). Press (CTRL)+(Z) when you're done. You see a list of categories. If your ad fits in one of the categories, type it in. If not, most classifieds have an "other" section, where you can specify a category of your own.

You can now designate up to four descriptive keywords. This allows people to search for your ad more easily. If you want to see a list of common words, type

`y`

and then select from the list or pick a keyword of your own.

Finally, you may post your ad by pressing (ENTER) at the *ENTRY COMPLETE>* prompt.

Mail

> My three previous relationships have been with people I've met online. My present wife is an "off-liner." Just luck that we even met. Also good luck that she isn't online— we only have the one computer and the one phone line (so far). She is resigned to my going upstairs to get online. She sorta sighs, and about every three months she asks me if I'm writing to a girlfriend or anything, just to be sure. I tell her I have too many, more important things to do online . . . . What tends to bore me about off-liners is that they really don't understand what is so great about being here online. They don't understand the community of it all, even though we are all <usually> separated by hundreds, even thousands of miles. What bores off-liners about me is that most of them are simply not interested in this "non-traditional" method of socializing . . . . What I most like in a relationship is a person or persons who share some of my interests. Online, I can find like-minded people easily. I just search Delphi Forums. This is where the community of "my people" will be located. And they communicate in a way that is convenient for me—electronically . . . . . I think I'll stop there. I'm beginning to sound like my standard joke—a telecomm-evangelist <grin>.

If someone has sent you new mail, you get a message when you log on to Delphi:

`You have 1 New mail message(s).`

You may also hear a beep while online, and receive the message:

`New mail from BOS::Redhead.`

If you're not sure if you have new mail, you can check at any menu prompt by typing

`scan`

There are many ways to enter Delphi's mail area. At any menu prompt, just type

`/mail`

You can also access mail directly from a forum. Suppose you read a message and want to send its author some private e-mail, simply type

```
mail
```

and send a letter as detailed later in this chapter. When you're done sending mail, you can type (CTRL)+(Z) to return to the forum, continuing to read where you left off.

In a conference, you can send somebody mail by typing

```
/mail
```

Again, pressing (CTRL)+(Z) returns you to the conference.

When you are working with your mailbox, you should always see the prompt:

```
MAIL>
```

Table 12-4 lists the basic mail commands you need to know.

Reading Your Mail

Type

```
dir
```

to see a listing of the messages in your mailbox. Figure 12-7 shows a typical directory listing. If you have new letters, only they are shown; otherwise, you are shown a listing of

COMMAND	ACTION
(ENTER)	Reads the next available letter.
BACK	Reads the previous letter.
DEL	Deletes the letter you just read.
DEL <number>	Deletes letter number <number>.
DELETE/ALL	Erases all the letters in your mailbox.
DIR ⁄	Lists the subjects of all your letters.
FORWARD <Membername>	Forwards the current message to <Membername>'s mailbox.
READ/NEW	Reads all your new mail
REPLY	Replies to the sender of the message you just read.
SEND	Sends a letter.

TABLE 12-4 Delphi e-mail commands

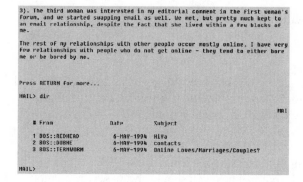

FIGURE 12-7 A list of all the new mail

all the old mail you haven't yet deleted. The directory listing includes each letter's number, the Membername of the person who sent it, the date it was sent, and its subject.

If the directory list is long, press (ENTER) to read the next page. To read a letter, simply type in its number. In most cases, you want to start reading your first letter. Type

    1

and then continue pressing (ENTER) to read through all your mail.

A typical letter is shown in Figure 12-8. The first line tells you the Membername of the person who sent you the letter. It may also contain that person's real name.

The message also includes the date and time (Eastern Standard Time) it was sent.

When you're done reading a letter, it's a good idea to delete it. This saves space and keeps your mailbox organized. To erase a letter, type

    del

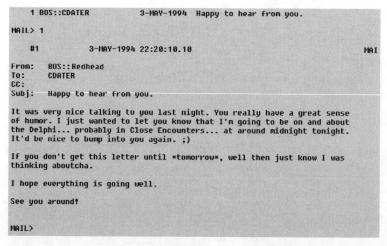

FIGURE 12-8 Reading a typical letter

If you want to get rid of a specific message, type

`del <number>`

where <number> is the letter's number, as shown in the directory listing. For instance, to delete Redhead's message, type

`del 2`

Answering or Forwarding a Letter

To respond to the sender of the letter you've just read, type

`reply`

EXPERT TIP

If you accidentally delete a letter, don't panic. All "deleted" messages are actually moved to a temporary folder called the *wastebasket.* Switch to the wastebasket folder, while in the mail system, by typing

```
select wastebasket
```

View the directory. Your message is there, good as new, and you can read it or pull it out. As soon as you exit mail, however, Delphi dumps your wastebasket, and whatever you deleted turns into digital dust.

Replying to a letter is just like sending one, except the letter is automatically addressed. The subject of your response is also filled in for you—the letter's original subject preceded by "*RE:*". For example, if you are replying to a letter with the subject "Is online love possible?" Your response letter's subject is

```
SUBJECT: RE: Is online love possible?
```

If you want to forward a copy of the current letter to another Delphi member, type

```
forward
```

EXPERT TIP

If you have a text file on your hard drive, you can send it as a letter. First you need to upload the file to your workspace. Enter the workspace by typing

```
go work
```

and then type

```
upload
```

to upload the file. See the Download section of this chapter for more information. Suppose you upload a file called REDHEAD.TXT. Type

```
mail
```

to enter your mailbox. Finally, send the file by typing

```
send redhead.txt
```

Type in your letter's address and subject, as usual. The file REDHEAD.TXT becomes the body of the letter.

Type in the name of the recipient. You can also type in a new subject. See the next section for more details on how to send a letter.

Writing a Letter

At the *MAIL>* prompt, type

send

to compose a letter to another Delphi member. The next prompt asks to whom the letter should be sent:

TO:

Type in the Membername. You can enter several Membernames if you wish, separated by commas. The system then asks for a

SUBJECT:

You can now type in your letter, line by line. Be sure to press (ENTER) at the end of each line; words do not automatically wrap onto the next line. Review your line carefully; once you press (ENTER) you cannot go back. When you're ready to zip your letter away, press (CTRL)+(Z). To abort, you can press (CTRL)+(C) instead, and the letter is not sent. The letter-writing process is shown in Figure 12-9.

```
MAIL> send

To:     david

Subj:   Hoping to hear from you.

Enter your message below. Press CTRL/Z when complete, or CTRL/C to quit:
I read you personal ad/message in the Singles custom forum and I'm excited
to "meet" you. We share a lot of interests, such as amateur tag-team wrestling,
ice cream vending, and ballot box stuffing.

I'm going to be online at around midnight tonight-- in the main Conference
area. My nickname will be Redhead. It'd be great to see you around!

In any case, welcome to Delphi; I look forward to reading your posts, e-mail,
and maybe even bumping  into you in a conference.

Just out of curiosity; how old are you? I'm 31 (though I don't look a day
over 30 <grin>).

-Redhead
```

FIGURE 12-9 Writing a Delphi letter

Chat

Myself> the very features that make this such a great way to meet people are also a liability in that dishonesty can lead to problems very quickly

Perry> I think that we have to be skeptical of people online . . . since it's so easy to be deceived. (a hard lesson learned)

Lj Storm> but you never really know if you are getting to know a person, or the person's image of what he wants others to perceive

Myself> one reason this can happen so easily is that it is easy to forget . . .

Perry> But I don't know that there are any more basically dishonest people online than there are anywhere else.

Myself> . . .that while you are separated by computer hardware and wires . . .

TCOMJMH> i have nothing to hide

Myself> . . .you are actually dealing with real people

JOHNJERSEY> Don't you also think that 90% of online chats are bull because people just don't trust one another?

Perry> I don't.

TCOMJMH> i don't

Perry> Most of the online chats I've had with people have been real.

Larry> the mystery is what attracts people.

TCOMJMH> why should i be afraid of my keyboard

Myself> it isn't the keyboard - it is the person at the other end of the line

Delphi patriots are crazy about their conferences. Normally, you find a cozy number of people hanging out in the main conference, which can be accessed by typing

```
go conf
```

There are usually round-the-clock Scrabble games and other general chat areas.

Most every sig also has its own conference. When you first access a sig, you are told how many members are currently conferencing. Most conferences give you the option to type

```
ann
```

at any sig's menu to access the Announcements. This lets you know when the sig members typically hold their "meetings," and what the topics of discussion will be. To enter a sig's conference, just type

```
conf
```

Those who have entered a conference but have not yet selected a conference group are known as *idlers*. To see a list of fellow idlers, type

```
who i
```

If you're an idle worshipper, you can invite one of the idlers to join you in a conference. Type

page <name>

where <name> is replaced by an valid Delphi Membername. If you have other Delphi friends, you can page any user who is currently logged on. If your name is Cyberdater and you are in the Close Encounters forum, the person you page sees the following message:

Cyberdater invites you to join him in the Close Encounters conference.

Your date has to make his or her way to the

CONFERENCE>

prompt. At that point your date sees the message:

Would you like to talk to Cyberdater?

Your date can then join you by typing

y

If you have already entered a group, your date will join you there. Otherwise, a new group will be created and you and your sweetie will automatically be placed inside.

Joining a Chat Group

When you are ready to chat, you have two options: You can join a group where people are already conversing, or you can start a new group. In either case, type

join

at the *Conference>* prompt.

You are asked what group you want to join. To see descriptions of the current groups, type

/who n

EXPERT TIP

If you want some one-on-one conferencing, you can create a private group. If you and your date have already entered a group, just type

/gprivate

The *n* designates non-private groups; no point listing private groups, as you can enter one only if you know its password. You see the number and name of each group, with the names of that group's members. Something like this appears:

```
43)  Dating Talk!
        Redhead, Lenny.Lovelooker, CyberDater,
```

To see more information about a specific person, you can use the /whois command. For instance, to find out about Redhead, type

```
/whois redhead
```

You see Redhead's complete member profile, if she has filled one out. (See the Finding Delphi Dates section of this chapter to learn how to fill out a profile of your own.)

If one of the conference groups sounds appealing, type in its number and press (ENTER).

To create a group of your own, just type in a descriptive name. The group is created, and you are its only member. You can now wait for people to join you or—if patience isn't your forte—you can page members, inviting them to swing on by.

Once you enter a group, you should hear a beep. All the group members see a message similar to the following:

```
** Cyberdater has entered group "Looking for Love" **
```

If you created a group (or were the first person to enter an existing group), you are known as its *manager*. The group is at your command. You can change the name of the group by typing

```
/gname <name>
```

where <name> is replaced by the new name of your group.

In a Group

Once you've joined a group, you see each member's comments prefaced by his or her Membername, and the discussion reads like a play script. See Figure 12-10 for a sample screen.

You can create a private group too, if you desire. Create a group, as usual. It's polite to use the word "Private" as part of the group name so that others know not to join you. For instance, create a group called "Private Cyberdating." Once you and your date have entered the group, make it officially private by typing

```
/gprivate
```

If your date has not yet arrived in the conference area, or if you want to invite a third person, you can create a key that will unlock your group's door—set a password. If you want the word to be "redux," type

```
/gpass redux
```

You can now page your date, inviting him or her to join you. Send a polite message including the name (or number) of the room you're in and its password. For instance, to invite Redhead:

```
/send Redhead Hi, I'm in the Private Cyberdating group in
the Close Encounters sig, and the password is redux if you'd
like to join me.
```

Redhead would then have to make her way to the appropriate conference. When she gets there she would need to type

```
/pass redux
```

and then

```
/join Private Cyberdating
```

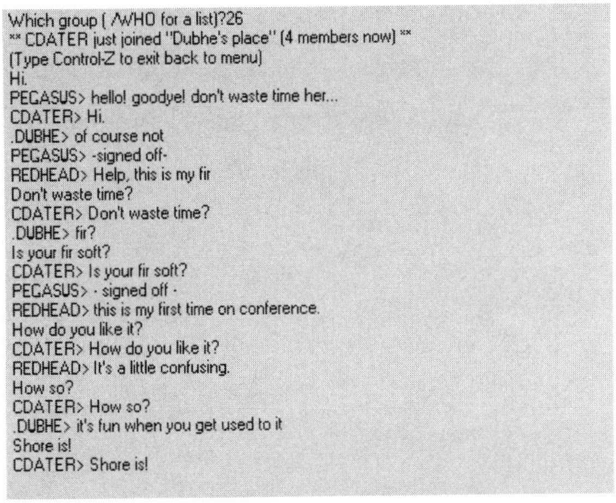

```
Which group ( /WHO for a list)?26
** CDATER just joined "Dubhe's place" (4 members now) **
(Type Control-Z to exit back to menu)
Hi.
PEGASUS> hello! goodye! don't waste time her...
CDATER> Hi.
.DUBHE> of course not
PEGASUS> -signed off-
REDHEAD> Help, this is my fir
Don't waste time?
CDATER> Don't waste time?
.DUBHE> fir?
Is your fir soft?
CDATER> Is your fir soft?
PEGASUS> - signed off -
REDHEAD> this is my first time on conference.
How do you like it?
CDATER> How do you like it?
REDHEAD> It's a little confusing.
How so?
CDATER> How so?
.DUBHE> it's fun when you get used to it
Shore is!
CDATER> Shore is!
```

FIGURE 12-10 Decoding the conversation in a Delphi conference

EXPERT TIP

If your screen gets too cluttered and you'd prefer not to see what you type as you type it, use the

`/norepeat`

command. If you decide you want to see your words after all, type

`/repeat`

If you'd like to speak up, just type and press (ENTER). For example, if your Membername is Cyberdater and you type

`Hi, how's everyone doing this fine evening?`

and then press (ENTER), everyone in your conference sees:

`.Cyberdater> Hi, how's everyone doing this fine evening?`

At times, what you type may become spliced by somebody else's words. If this happens, do not worry and do not backspace. Just keep on typing and press (ENTER) when you're done; your comment will appear as you intended.

Beyond mere talking, the Delphi conferences contain several powerful functions. Table 12-5 lists the main chat commands you need to be familiar with. To see a full list of commands, type

`/help`

Use the /action command if you want to *do* something, not just say it. For example, type

`/action throws his hands up in despair.`

and the people in your conference group see:

`Cyberdater throws his hands up in despair.`

Remember, if you ever want to see a person's complete member profile, just type

`/whois <name>`

where <name> is replaced by a valid Membername. If all you know is a nickname, you may not be able to see the person's member profile.

To change *your* nickname, just use the /name command. For example, if you want to be known as Lenny, just type

`/name Lenny`

COMMAND	ACTION
/ACTION <*action name*>	Performs an action, as opposed to speaking.
/CANCEL	Stops paging somebody you've been trying to reach.
/EXIT	Leaves the current conference group.
/JOIN <*name*>	Joins an existing conference group (or creates a new one).
/MAIL	Enters e-mail; returns to the current chat conference by pressing (CTRL)+(Z).
/NAME <*name*>	Changes your nickname.
/PAGE <*name*>	Invites another user into group.
/REJECT	Returns a polite "No thank you" if you are paged.
/SEND <*name*>	Sends a private message to another member, anywhere on Delphi.
/SQUELCH <*name*>	Ignores whatever <*name*> types, and does not allow <*name*> to page you.
/WHO	Lists all the conference groups and tells you who's in them.
/WHOIS <*name*>	Displays profile from member directory.

TABLE 12-5 Delphi conference chat commands

When you do this, however, people can't find out more about you by viewing your user profile. When you /*page* someone or /*send* a private message, however, you are designated by your real Membername.

If you want to invite someone to join you in the conference—whether they are idle, in another conference group, or on another section of Delphi altogether—use the /*page* command. For example, if you know that Redhead is online, just type

```
/page Redhead
```

She receives a message telling her that she's cordially invited to join you, similar to

```
Cyberdater invites you to join him in the Close Encounters
conference.
```

This page continues until she either answers or rejects it. If you want to stop paging Redhead just type

```
/cancel
```

If *you* receive a page while in a conference, you can return the page by typing

```
/answer
```

EXPERT TIP

If you don't want to be interrupted by people paging you and sending you online messages, you can type

`/busy`

at any Delphi menu (not only in the conference). To receive pages again, type

`/nobusy`

If you're busy you can tell the pager, by answering with a polite "No thank you." To brush someone off, type

`/reject`

To whisper something to somebody privately, you can use the */send* command. You can issue this command to anyone who is currently logged on to Delphi. For example, if you want to invite Redhead into a private conference group, just type

`/send redhead I'm thinking of starting a private conference group. Interested?`

Redhead then sees the message:

`Cyberdater>> I'm thinking of starting a private conference group. Interested?`

The double arrows (>>) always indicate a private message.

Unfortunately, the online world contains a few persistent sour apples—people who will keep trying to */page* you even after you've */rejected* them, or people who'll */send* you a barrage of lewd messages. If you want to drop a particular person completely—ignoring all pages, sends, and even conference talk—use the */squelch* command. For example, to ignore CyberPutz, type

`/squelch cyberputz`

If you'd like to move to another conference group, first type

`/who n`

to see a list of the non-private groups available. You can then use the */join* command to enter the group. For instance, if the group's name is "Marathon Daters," type

`/join marathon daters`

When you're ready to leave the conference area for good, just press (CTRL)+(Z) as many times as you need, backing out to previous menus.

Fun and Games

The *Entertainment and Games* section of Delphi has quite a few primitive but nonetheless addictive multi-player games. Some of these include:

- *Poker.* Type *go ent pok,* then type *enter* to begin playing. You start off with $1,000 in your account; you can buy up to 1,000 one-dollar chips. You then see a listing of available poker tables. Select a table by typing the first two letters of its name. Get ready to bite down on your cigar, fix your visor, and put on your poker face. The system deals you a hand. When it's time to bet, you are given your options. Meanwhile, you can type anything you like, chatting with the other poker people. See Figure 12-11 for a typical round.

- *FlipIt.* Type *go ent flip* to play Delphi's version of Othello. You can play against the computer or against other flippers.

- *Scramble Word Game.* Type *go ent scra.* You see a matrix of letters. Try to make up as many words as you can using adjacent letters. Several people can play against each other at once.

- *TQ Trivia Tournament.* Type *go ent tq.* Try to answer the boggling multiple-choice questions. Meanwhile, you can type anything you like, chatting with other trivia-meisters. There are weekly tournaments where you can really play against the pros.

- *Quest.* Type *go ent quest.* This fantasy role-playing game brings you back in time to a land of warriors, assassins, dwarves, dragons, and, of course, gold. Fight and cheat and steal and try to make your fortune (kind of like real life!). You can talk to other users in the meantime.

```
Jubes wins and takes the pot of 9701, for a total of 35995 chips.
6 Page> wtg!
4 Jubes> tq
4 Jubes> GO 4
Starting 7 Card Stud
Ante up - 32 each.
5 CDATER>  sits out
(You don't have enough chips.  To play at this table, you need a minimum of
   1280.  You may be able to buy more with BUY 200)
2 Mr. Me>  sits out
Pot now has 128 chips.
Maximum stake is 35995.  Pot limit on raises.  (Jubes)
4 Jubes is dealer.  Shuffling... (44 card deck - no 2s or 3s)
1 Tiger          shows 7S (Seven High)
3 Passin         shows 6S (6 High)
4 Jubes          shows 6C (6 High)
6 Page           shows KD (King High)


6 Page shows the high hand - Open, please.
6 Page, you must open.
2 Mr. Me> bartender...a gin and tylenol...dont skimp on the cherry
Wow
5 CDATER> Wow
```

FIGURE 12-11 Ante up, boys and girls

    Stellar Conquest. Type *go ent stell.* Run an interstellar tramp freighter, trading goods all over the galaxy. While battling other starships, trading ore, and taking care of your spaceship's mechanics, try to make some new friends (or make a date).

Divining Delphi's Future

It's cheap. That's the main thing to remember about Delphi Internet Services. Once you get used to the Delphi commands, it's not too hard to navigate; Delphi is well organized and its menus are clear. Unfortunately, due to Delphi's popular Internet access, many Delphi users never stop to say hello at the conferences or forums. The chat areas are often deserted. There are indeed Delphi folk looking for dates, but you'll have to hunt to find 'em.

If text menus don't daunt you, if cryptic commands don't haunt you, Delphi provides all your meat-and-potato cyberdating needs. Delphi can be thought of as a nostalgic online service, reminding old-time users of the way cyberspace *used* to be before anyone knew what an "icon" was. If you're a fan of simplicity, Delphi may charm you. If you're looking to catch a look of the telecommunications future, look elsewhere.

SHOUTING OVER THE WALL

N THE PRECEDING CHAPTERS,

you learned how to join an online service and send e-mail to fellow cyberdaters. But what if you need to reach somebody who belongs to a *different* service? For instance, your best CompuServe friend may have suddenly decided to switch to Delphi. Have you two lost contact forever? Or suppose you meet someone at a party and (being the hip dude you are) mention you frequent cyberspace. Suppose further that she (this woman of your dreams) says, "Oh me too! Here's my address, write me sometime, willya?" Suppose even further that she gives you an America Online screen name, and you belong to GEnie. Should you just sigh, crumple up the address, and throw it away?

Thanks to the intensive Internet, most every online service can communicate with any other one. The Internet acts as a messenger: It will crawl over the walls of one online service, trek across cyberspace in marathon time, and deliver your message to a foreign service. To send mail from one network to another, follow these two steps:

1. See the section of this chapter named From <your service>. This will tell you how to mail a message to the Internet.

2. See the From the Internet section of this chapter. This will tell you how to address the letter so that it will be sent from the Internet to the appropriate destination.

For instance, to send a letter from CompuServe to user ABC1234 at PRODIGY, you would look in the From CompuServe section. Here you're told how to send a message to the Internet (by prefixing it with *INTERNET:* at the To: prompt. Next, look in the From the Internet section under PRODIGY—this tells you to use an address in the form *<user-ID>@prodigy.com*. Thus your complete address for mailing to Lenny at PRODIGY from CompuServe is:

```
INTERNET: abc1234@prodigy.com
```

Read the Your Address section of Chapter 7, The Internet, for details on Internet addressing. Also note that since you can send mail through the Internet, resources such as mailing lists (see the section in Chapter 7) are available on *any* commercial online service. You should note, however, that some services may charge a slight "postage" fee for each Internet letter your send or receive.

Each of the following sections will also tell you how to send FAXes and regular U.S. Postal mail, if such a service is available.

From a Fidonet BBS

To send mail to the Internet, address your letter to *<name>@<location>* ON *1:1/31*. For example to send to lenny@banana.com, type

```
lenny@banana.com ON 1:1/31
```

You can also send mail directly to a WWIV brand of BBS. Simply address your mail to *#<number>@<location>* ON *1:100/215*. For example, to send to 12345@bananas, type

```
#12345 @bananas ON 1:100/215
```

From a WWIV BBS

You can send mail through the Internet by addressing it to *<name>#<location>@506*. For example, to send mail to lenny@banana.com, send to

```
lenny#banana.com@506
```

If the recipient's Internet address begins with digits, as in the case of CompuServe, begin the address with a quote.

You may also write directly to people who are on a Fidonet system. You'll need to know the zone, node, and Fidonet number of the BBS you want to reach. For example, if you want to mail Lenny Lovelooker at zone 1, node 2, number 3 (1:2/3) you'd type

```
Lenny Lovelooker ON 1:2/3 @656
```

From the Internet

This is the grand gateway of inter-network communications. Chapter 7, The Internet, will tell you exactly how to send mail. In a nutshell, every Internet address is in the form *<name>@<location>*. Following are the formats of addresses to various online services.

- To A Fidonet BBS: Every Fidonet BBS is listed by its zone, node, and number, such as *1:2/3.4*. To reach Lenny Lovelooker at 1:2/3.4, send to:

  lenny.lovelooker@p4.f3.n2.z1.fidonet.org

- To WWIV-Net: To send to user number 1234 at WWIV net number 9999 you would type

  1234-9999@wwiv.tfsquad.mn.org

- To America Online: Send to *<screenname>@aol.com*. Remove spaces, if the screen name has any. So, for example, to send a message to LENNY 34, send to:

  lenny34@aol.com

  Note that long messages are automatically split up into several different letters.

- To CompuServe: To send mail to a CompuServe user, replace the comma in the ID number by a period. For instance, to contact user ID 71234,1234 is at:

  71234.1234@compuserve.com

- To PRODIGY: Send to *<user ID>@prodigy.com*. For example, to reach abcd12a, type

  abcd12a@prodigy.com

- To GEnie: Send to *<GE mail address>@genie.geis.com*. For instance, to reach L.LOVELOOKER, type

  l.lovelooker@genie.geis.com

- To Delphi: Send to *<membername>@delphi.com*. For example, to reach LLOVELOOKER, type

  llovelooker@delphi.com

- To Applelink: Send to *<user>@applelink.apple.com*.
- To AT&T Mail: Send to *<user>@attmail.com*.
- To Bitnet: Send to *<user>%<location>.bitnet@mitvma.mit.edu*.
- To BIX: Send to *<membername>@bix.com*.
- To MCI-Mail: Send to *<usernumber>@mcimail.com*. If the user's number is 123-4567, remove the dash and send to *1234567@mcimail.com*.

To other BBSs: Many BBSs have their own Internet addresses. For example, ECHO users can be reached at *<username>@echonyc.com,* and you can reach WELL people by e-mailing to *<username>@well.sf.ca.us.* If you know somebody who has an account on an Internet-hooked BBS, call up that BBS to find out its host address.

From America Online

To send mail to the Internet, simply send to *<user>@<location>.* AOL will automatically figure out that you're interested in sending through the Internet. For instance, to send to lenny@banana.com, just type in his address in the *To:* box:

```
lenny@banana.com
```

For a nominal charge, you can send FAXes or standard U.S. Postal mail on AOL by selecting the Fax/Paper Mail item from the Mail pull-down menu. To send a FAX, type the name, the at sign (@), and the full FAX number of the person you're trying to reach in the *To:* box. For instance, to send a FAX to Lenny Lovelooker at 111-222-3333, type

```
Lenny Lovelooker@111-222-3333
```

You can now type in the rest of your message as usual. You'll be told how much the FAX will cost. AOL will send off the FAX immediately. When the FAX arrives, you'll be notified via e-mail.

If you'd like to send standard snail mail, type *<recipient's name>@usmail.* For example, to send a letter to Lenny Lovelooker type

```
Lenny Lovelooker@usmail
```

Type in your letter, as usual, and then click on the *Send* button. You'll be asked to type in Lenny's address as well as your own return address. Your letter will be sent within 24 hours.

From CompuServe

To send mail to the Internet, type the word *INTERNET:* before a valid Internet address. For example, to send to lenny@banana.com, just type

```
INTERNET:lenny@banana.com
```

in the *Send To:* box.

For a nominal charge, CompuServe allows you to FAX messages to any machine worldwide. All you have to do is type the word *FAX:* before the number. For example, if you want to send a FAX to 111-222-3333, send to:

```
Lenny Lovelooker: FAX:1112223333
```

You can send standard U.S. Postal mail by *Going* to *ASCIIMAIL.* Type in your message (up to four print-pages long). At the *Send ($) to (Name or User ID):* prompt, type

```
postal
```

You'll be asked for the recipient's name and address, one line at a time.

You can also send telexes by preceding the telex number by the *TELEX:* flag. You can send MCI mail, as well, again by preceding the user's number by the *MCIMAIL:* flag.

From **PRODIGY**

PRODIGY itself has no facility to send mail to the Internet. However, if you Jump to *mail manager,* you can download the Mail Manager software (for $4.95). Mail Manager lets you compose your letters offline and then send them to the Internet, over U.S. Postal mail, or to a FAX machine. Simply select the Method of Delivery option; you'll be prompted for the remaining information.

From **GEnie**

To send a GE Mail letter through the Internet, send it to *<name>@<location>@INET#.* For example, to send to lenny@banana.com, type

```
lenny@banana.com@INET#
```

Alternatively, you can be automatically prompted for each piece of information by using GEnie's Internet area. Just type

```
internet
```

and then select Send an Internet Message. You'll be guided through all the steps.

You can send FAX letters, as well, by addressing your letters to *<name>/<FAX#>@FAX#.* For example, to reach Lenny Lovelooker at 111-222-3333, send mail to:

```
Lenny Lovelooker/1-111-222-3333@FAX#
```

Again, if you'd like to be guided through the FAX process, you can just type

```
FAX
```

and then select Send a Fax Message.

From **Delphi**

To send mail through the Internet, just surround the Internet address in quotes and precede it by the *internet* marker. For example, to send to lenny@banana.com, type

```
internet"lenny@banana.com"
```

ECLECTIC BBS LIST

A list of the most dateworthy BBSs in most every area code follows. Note that most of the BBSs allow adult access only, though there may be areas for minors to mine, as well. These numbers are in working order as of print time; however, like any great galaxy, the stars in the BBS sky may fizzle away into black dial-tone holes. Check out Chapter 6 for the scoop on BBSs.

Toll Free

800-874-2937 Online With Hayes
800-564-4686 Starship][(call 800-521-2733 for access)

United States

201-791-8850 Chat Chalet (adult)
201-798-0065 Computer Connections
201-935-1485 Starship II (multi-player games, friendly chat)
203-583-0715 Adults 'R' Us
203-627-8088 Over Exposed
203-667-3068 First Impressions
206-754-4878 The Sceptic Tank (adult only system)

206-588-3792 Grownup's Playhouse
206-756-5160 Tacoma Adult Party
206-838-7908 Bangkok Express
206-838-7908 Seattle Net
206-946-4554 Night Moves
210-533-3882 Godfather's Palace
210-623-1395 Danse Macabre
210-648-3874 X-Factor

212-248-8039 Midnight Caller (adult, match-maker)

212-233-4328 CybErotiComm BBS (great chatting in a club-like atmosphere)

213-933-4050 Metro Online (mainly date/chat, 60 lines)

213-484-0260 The Downtown

213-933-4050 The West Side (over forty marriages so far!)

214-497-9100 Texas Talk (like the name says; come on y'all)

214-235-5288 Lunatic Fringe

215-860-9724 The Newtown Express Inc. (dating/adult chat)

215-368-1162 Naughty Bits

215-724-5324 The Swinger's Connection

216-381-3320 PC-Ohio (large chat board, 300 conference areas)

216-726-2620 Rusty n' Edie's (124 lines of chat power)

216-741-5888 Bill n' Bob's Place (adult chat/swingers)

216-749-1020 Swingles

217-792-3663 Sexy Modem (free adult meeting place)

217-398-4450 GIBBS (adult originality)

218-879-8721 Sensual BBS (erosnet)

219-744-4908 Play Board

301-843-5247 Crow's Nest

301-990-7565 Apples of Eve

302-324-8091 The DVUG

303-233-1316 Fred's (large chat board)

303-375-1263 NIX*PIX (huge adult board, graphics and chat)

303-426-1942 Telepeople (adult and FidoNet)

303-933-0701 Eagle's Nest (large chat board)

303-940-7357 Colorado Connection

305-321-2410 Isles of Shae (many lines of chat/games)

305-473-2314 Misty Moonlight

305-594-4526 Adults Only Mansion

309-382-2410 Daffy's Dementia (erosnet)

310-376-9567 Beach Cities (erosnet)

310-391-1351 MicroSource (erosnet)

310-434-0401 Q Continuum

310-823-5979 Compu-Net (erosnet)

310-986-9705 69 Fantasy Line (erosnet)

312-581-1111 Villiage Information Systems

312-902-3599 CompuErotica

313-289-2659 Adult Computer Alley

313-379-4729 Outer Limits

313-562-0051 Bruce's Place

314-772-1014 Roman Empire

314-893-6099 Doc in the Box

314-965-5296 Cheswick's

316-522-6412 The Silver Eagle

317-447-9653 First Amendment

319-235-0772 The Missing Link

401-732-5292 Eagle's Nest Communications (many message bases)

403-299-9923 Logical Solutions (erosnet)

404-244-7059 Intimate Visions (sensual awareness)

404-642-9516 Power Systems (erosnet)

404-924-8472 Index System (chat)

404-962-5116 Showcom Online (erosnet)

404-992-5345 Hotlanta (adult multiline chat)

405-376-1610 Citadel

405-391-6604 Oracle

405-670-3925 Digital Encounters (dating)

405-672-5538 WildSide

407-795-6549 Warped Vector (erosnet)

408-263-3393 Amateur Action

409-693-0549 The NO-NAME (erosnet)

410-836-3072 The Whiplash Fantasy

412-856-6322 The Open Door

413-527-7360 Shangrila

414-289-0145 GLINN Super System

414-375-2088 Wizard of Oz (erosnet)

414-728-8554 Farmer's Daughter

414-789-4210 EXEC-PC (one of USA's largest BBSs)

415-703-8200 Eye Contact (32 lines of chat; also try 415-255-5972)
415-365-4194 California Space
415-323-4191 Space BBS
415-323-4193 Computer Exchange
415-495-2929 Studs
417-683-5534 Laura's Lair (adult spice, fantasy fulfillment)

501-562-7399 The Moonman
501-663-1547 Wet Dream
502-361-4225 Electronic Mafia
502-893-8102 The Improv
503-297-0278 1st Choice Communications
503-386-2903 T&E Verbal Abuse Network
503-640-4321 Hide Away
504-888-6515 Silver Streak
508-228-6500 Why I
508-760-2147 Nightsoft Videotext
513-752-8248 C.C.C.
515-256-0402 Twisted Sister (erosnet)
515-285-1190 Alternatives (erosnet)
515-945-6227 Heat In The Night (a free chat-line)
515-981-0926 The Psycho Ward (erosnet)
516-689-5390 Lifestyle (where all lifestyles clash)
518-383-2282 Fantasy Land

601-342-5680 Purgatory
601-392-6114 Gulf Coast Adult Lifestyles (erosnet)
602-458-8206 Duke's Doghouse
602-936-3892 Rusty's WildKat
602-955-9338 Boardwalk Hotel
602-966-5155 Georgia (plenty of chatter, y'all)
603-298-9872 The Night Owls
603-672-8123 Funny Farm
606-836-1267 Penal Colony
608-257-0486 Boardwalk BBS (general chat)
608-654-7678 Other Women (erosnet)
608-784-4679 Rosie's BBS
608-788-8086 Le Cross Roads

609-772-0895 MRC*Net (adult action)
609-884-6286 Viking (erosnet)
609-371-0828 Fast's Raceshop
612-566-5726 The Friendship
615-227-6155 The Third Eye (adult)
615-361-5956 Cheyenne Social Club
615-383-0727 The Nashville Exchange (many message areas)
615-452-4098 City of Brass (erosnet)
615-499-6449 Adult Mail Drop
615-675-6994 Data World (many files, discussions)
615-893-4616 Woody's World
616-725-7548 Playboard
617-862-9373 Argus Com (65 lines of chat; also try 617-674-2345)
617-354-5776 Channel One
617-828-0868 American Playhouse
617-383-2978 South Shore Secrets
619-264-8412 Christ, She's At It Again!
619-281-8616 The General
619-452-8137 Mushin (erosnet)
619-584-8456 San Diego Connection (adult multiline chat)

702-435-0786 Rebel (erosnet)
702-438-3625 The Other BBS
702-644-1537 Nighthawk
703-352-2945 Adult Fantasy
703-667-3530 Another Dimension
708-827-3619 Lambda Zone (adult, alternate lifestyles)
708-934-3045 Intimate Mansion
713-575-1050 Houston Chat Channel
713-937-0504 After Hours
714-455-2790 The Chateau
714-539-9374 The Black Pines
714-871-4018 Boot Hill
714-952-8910 Pleasure Island (10 chat lines)
715-445-6000 Global Gallery (the world online)
717-394-7451 The Covenant (erosnet)
718-241-9007 Paradise Network

718-251-9346 Modem Operated Remote
   Exchange (misc. goodies)
718-357-0501 Midnight Connection (general
   board, matchmaker)
718-428-6123 The Windup (exclusive adult
   board, deluxe matchmaking system)
718-547-4210 After Hours
718-547-4210 David's Girls
718-782-1586 Brooklyn After Dark

803-294-9657 Blackbeard's Tavern
804-490-5878 Pleasure Dome (adult discussions)
808-521-2359 The In-Touch (aloha, adults)
812-479-1310 Digicom
813-275-1746 Diver Down (erosnet)
815-895-6608 The Insomniacs
816-363-4673 The Gore Zone
816-468-6900 Pizazz
816-380-3480 Gabby's Lounge (adult chat)
818-358-6968 Odyssey (large nationwide
   multiline chat system)
818-886-0872 KBBS (32 lines of networking)
818-982-7271 Prime Time (nationwide chat)
818-709-4275 Lace (online adult magazine
   and meeting place)

903-534-1918 Texas Open Forum
904-387-4269 Ranchouse (erosnet)
904-476-1270 Titan Software Solutions (adult
   files/games)
904-744-8596 Night Time BBS
904-765-9663 Rompus Room (erosnet)
904-768-3854 Eros Se Star (erosnet)
904-829-1442 Starlight Acres (erosnet)
905-722-1484 Apple-Wize (erosnet)

908-446-0774 Swinging Door (adult lifestyles)
908-671-2528 Wild Bill's
912-788-9952 Wild & Dangerous
914-426-0729 Node 66 East
914-723-3397 Sex on the Beach
914-961-7032 Data Shack (a good, general
   BBS)
916-668-9453 Bigtime's Woodland Exchange
   (erosnet)
918-660-0745 Darwin's Theory (erosnet)
918-663-1249 Cat-Tastrophe Center
   (erosnet)
918-838-0816 Night Watchman (ersonet)
919-535-4239 The Pyramid
919-735-9406 Wag Tongue Alley

International

+0923-213372 Softels Monster BBS—Great
   Britain
+33-148020821 Slatch2—France
+34-1-519-46-45 Icaro BBS—Spain
+351-1-4919755 B-Link BBS—Portugal
+3861-218-663 ABM-BBS—Slovenia
+44-724-858-241 Ultima!—United Kingdom
   (erosnet)
+46-431-70909 Buller BBS—Sweden
+49-6233-55087 Kurpfalz BBS—Germany
+662-255-5981 War On Virus BBS—Thailand
+81-3-3255-8856 Janis II—Tokyo
+852-414-9393 iLink Information Service
   Multi-User Chat—Hong Kong
+886-2-703-5180 DaemonWorld BBS—
   Taiwan
+972-52-503801 Channel V—Israel

INTERNET PUBLIC
ACCESS PROVIDERS

Many of the following networks provide much more than Internet access. Echo, MindVox, NovaLink, and the WELL, for example, have such features as rowdy online chatting, personal ads, eclectic message areas, and dating sections. Check out a few places before settling on one.

Prices vary depending on calling area and whether you call during peak or off-peak hours. Also, prices listed here may no longer be in effect.

A2I Communications (rahul.net)
price: $20/month
modem: 408-293-9010 or 408-293-9020; log
on as *guest*

Achilles Organization (achilles.org)
price: $60–$300/year
modem: 613-824-2706, 613-824-6807, or
613-874-0524

Agora RainDrop Laboratories
(agora.rain.com)
price: $6/month
modem: 503-293-1772; log on as *apply*

Alaska, University Tundra Services
(acad1.alaska.edu)
price: $20/month
modem: 907-789-1314
voice: 907-465-6453

Anomaly (anomaly.sbs.risc.net)
price: $200/year
modem: 401-331-3706 or 401-455-0347
voice: 401-273-4669

Ariadne Greek Academic and Research
(leon.nrcps.ariadne-t.gr)
price: DR 5900/quarter
modem: +301 65-48-800
voice: +301 65-13-392 (Athens, Greece)

Black Box (blkbox.com)
price: $108.25/6 months
modem: 713-480-2686
voice: 713-480-2684

CAM Communications Accessibles Montreal
  (cam.org)
price: Can$25/month
modem: 514-931-2333
voice: 514-931-0749 (Montreal, Canada)

Cg57: E & S Systems Public Access
  (cg57.esnet.com)
price: $30/3 months, $50/6 months, $80/9
  months, $100/year
modem: 619-278-8267
voice: 619-278-4641

ClarkNet Internet Services, Inc. (clark.net)
price: $23/month
modem: 410-730-9786, 410-995-0271, 301-
  596-1626, 301-854-0446, 301-621-5216;
  log on as *guest*
voice: 800-735-2258 then give 410-730-9764

CNS: Community News Service (cscns.com)
price: $2.75/hour; $10/month minimum; $35
  signup
modem: 719-520-1700; log on as *new*,
  password *newuser*
voice: 719-592-1240

Connect (connect.com.au)
price: A$2000/year
voice: +61 3 5282239 (Melbourne, Australia)

CRIS (cris.com)
price: $2/hour
modem: 800-877-5045; select option 5
voice: 800-745-CRIS

CR Laboratories Dialup Internet Access
  (crl.com)
price: $17.50–$19.50/month
modem: 415-389-UNIX; log on as *newuser*
voice: 415-381-2800

CSN—Colorado SuperNet (csn.org)
local price: $1–$2/hour; $15/month minimum
long distance: $8/hour additional
voice: 303-273-3471

CTS Network Services (crash.cts.com)
price: $10–$23/month; $15 signup
modem: 619-637-3640; log on as *help*
voice: 619-637-3637

Cyber—The Cyberspace Station (cyber.net)
price: $15/month; $10 signup or $60/6
  months
modem: 619-634-1376; log on as *guest*

CyberGate (gate.ne)
price: $17.50/month
modem: 305-425-0200
voice: 305-428-GATE

Data Basix (data.basix.com)
price: $25/month or $180/year
modem: 602-721-5887
voice: 602-721-1988

Demon Internet Systems (demon.co.uk)
price: £10/month; £132.50/year
modem: +44 (0)81 343 4848
voice: +44 (0)81 349 0063 (London area,
  United Kingdom)

Dial 'n Cerf (cerf.net)
local price: $3–$5/hour; $20/month; $50
  signup
long distance: $8–$10/hour; $20/month
voice: 800-876-2373 or 619-455-3900

Dircon: The Direct Connection
    (dircon.co.uk)
price: £10/month; £7.50 signup
modem: +44 (0)81 317 2222
voice: +44 (0)81 317 0100 (London area,
    United Kingdom)

Echo Communications (echo.com)
price: $19.95/month; $9/month Internet
    access; $40 signup
modem: 212-989-8411; log on as *newuser*
voice: 212-255-3839

EiNet (einet.com)
price: $18–$30/month
voice: 505-343-1060

Eskimo North (eskimo.com)
price: $13/month to $96/year
modem: 206-367-3837
voice: 206-367-7457

Evergreen Communications (libre.com)
price: $239/year
modem: 602-955-8444
voice: 602-955-8315

Express Access (digex.net)
price: $25/month or $250/year
modem: 301-220-0462, 410-766-1855, 703-
    281-7997, 714-377-9784, 908-937-9481;
    log on as *new*
voice: 800-969-9090, 301-220-2020

FSP: Freelance Systems Programming
    (fsp.com)
price: $1/hour; $20 signup
modem: 513-258-7745
voice: 513-254-7246

Glaids Net (Homosexual Network)
    (glaids.wa.com)
price: $10/month

modem: 206-322-0621
voice: 206-323-7483

Halcyon (halcyon.com)
price: $200/year; $10 signup
modem: 206-382-6245; log on as *new*
voice: 206-955-1050

HoloNet (holonet.net)
local price: $2–$4/hour
long distance: $.50–$7.50/hour additional
modem: 510-704-1058
voice: 510-704-0160

HookUp Communication Corporation
    (hookup.net)
price: Can$14.95/month to Can$300.00/yr
voice: 519-747-4110 (London (Ontario),
    Canada)

IAC: Internet Access Cincinnati (iac.net)
price: $8.95/month
modem: 513-887-8855
voice: 513-887-8877

IBMPCUG UK PC User Group
    (ibmpcug.co.uk)
price: £15.50/month or £160/year; £10 signup
modem: +44 (0)81 863 6646
voice: +44 (0)81 863 6646 (London area,
    United Kingdom)

IDS World Network (ids.net)
price: $10/month or $100/year
modem: 401-884-9002 or 401-785-1067
voice: 401-884-7856

IEunet: Ireland's Internet Services Supplier
    (ieunet.ie)
price: Ir£25/month
modem: +353 1 6790830, +353 1 6798600
voice: +353 1 6790832 (Dublin, Ireland)

IGC: Institute for Global Communications
(igc.apc.org)
voice: 415-442-0220

Individual Network - Rhein-Main (in-rhein-main.de)
price: DM 15–DM 40/month
modem: +49 (0)69 39048414, +49 (0)69 6312934
voice: +49 (0)69 39048413 (Frankfurt, Germany)

InterAccess (interaccess.com)
price: $23/month
modem: 708-671-0237
voice: 800-967-1580

Internet Direct, Inc. (indirect.com)
price: $20/month
modem: 602-274-9600 or 602-321-9600; log on as *guest*
voice: 602-274-0100 or 602-324-0100

KAIWAN Public Access Internet Online Services (kaiwan.com)
price: $11/month; $15 signup
modem: 714-539-5726 or 310-527-7358
voice: 714-638-2139

Maestro (maestro.com)
price: $15/month or $150/year
modem: 212-240-9700; log on as *newuser*
voice: 212-240-9600

MBnet (access.mbnet.mb.ca)
price: $50/year; $25 signup
modem: 204-275-6150; Cass name is *mbnet*, userid is *guest*
voice: 204-474-9727

MCSNet (genesis.mcs.com)
price: $10–$25/month

modem: 312-248-0900
voice: 312-248-UNIX

The Meta Network (tmn.com)
price: $20/month; $15 signup
long distance: $6.75/hour
voice: 703-243-6622

Metronet: Texas Metronet (metronet.com)
price: $5–$45/month; $10–$30 signup
modem: 214-705-2917 or 817-261-7687; log on as *signup*
voice: 214-705-2900 or 817-543-8756

Michnet Merit Network, Inc. (merit.edu)
price: $35/month; $40 signup
voice: 313-764-9430

Millennium Online (mill.com)
price: $10/month; $.10–$.30/minute
voice: 800-736-0122

MindVOX (phantom.com)
price: $15–$20/month
modem: 212-989-4141; log on as *mindvox*
voice: 212-989-2418

MRNet (mr.net)
price: $50/month; $65 signup
voice: 612-342-2570

MSen (msen.com)
price: $20/month; $20 signup
voice: 313-998-4562

MV Communications (mv.com)
price: $5/month minimum
voice: 603-429-2223

NBNet: NBTel's Internet Connection Service (nbnet.nb)
price: $.16/minute; $17.50 signup
voice: 800-561-4459

NeoSoft's Sugar Land Unix
price: $29.95/month
modem: 713-684-5900

Netcom Online Communication Services
(netcom.com)
price: $19.50/month; $20.00 signup
modem: 206-547-5992, 214-753-0045, 303-758-0101, 310-842-8835, 312-380-0340, 404-303-9765, 408-241-9760, 408-459-9851, 415-328-9940, 415-985-5650, 503-626-6833, 510-274-2900, 510-426-6610, 510-865-9004, 617-237-8600, 619-234-0524, 703-255-5951, 714-708-3800, 818-585-3400, 916-965-1371
voice: 800-501-UNIX, 408-554-UNIX

netIOWA (netiowa.net)
local price: $30/month
long distance: $.10/minute
voice: 800-546-6587

North Shore Access
(northshore.ecosoft.com)
price: $9/month includes 10 hours connect, $1/hour thereafter
modem: 617-593-4557; log on as *new*
voice: 617-593-3110

Northwest Nexus (nwnexus.wa.com)
price: $10/month for first 10 hours; $3/hour; $20 signup
voice: 206-455-3505

NSTN Inc.(nstn.ns.ca)
price: $1–$6/hour; $35 signup
voice: 902-468-NSTN

Novalink (novalink.com)
local price: $9.95/month; $1.80/hour (beyond 5 hours)

long distance: $1.80/hour
modem: 800-937-7644; log on as *new*
voice: 800-274-2814

Nuance Network (nuance.com)
price: $25/month; $35 signup
voice: 205-533-4296

Nuchat: South Coast Computing Services, Inc. (sccsi.com)
price: $3/hour
modem: 713-661-8593
voice: 713-661-3301

OARnet (oar.net)
local price: $2–$4/hour
long distance: $5–$12/hour additional
voice: 614-292-8100

Old Colorado City Communications
price: $25/month
modem: 719-632-4111; log on as *newuser*
voice: 719-632-4848

Olympus (pt.olympus.net)
price: $25/month; $10 signup
voice: 206-385-0464

PANIX Public Access Unix (panix.com)
price: $19/month or $208/year; $40 signup
modem: 212-787-3100; log on as *newuser*

PEINet Inc. (peinet.pe.ca)
price: $20/month
modem: 902-892-5600
voice: 902-892-7346

The Pipeline (pipeline.com)
price: $15–$35/month
modem: 212-267-8606; log on as *guest*
voice: 212-267-3636

The Portal System (portal.com)
local price: $19.95/month; $19.95 signup
long distance: $2.50–$13/hour additional
modem: 408-725-0561; log on as *info*
voice: 408-973-9111

PSILink: Personal Internet Access (psi.com)
long distance: $1.25–$18/hour; $9–$29/month
voice: 703-620-6651

PUCnet Computer Connections
(PUCnet.com)
price: Can$6.25–Can$25/month; Can$10
signup
modem: 403-484-5640; log on as *guest*
voice: 403-448-1901 (Alberta, Canada)

RealTime Communication (wixer.bga.com)
price: $75/year
modem: 512-459-4391; log on as *new*
voice: 512-451-0046

Resudox Online Services (resudox.net)
price: $19/month (10 free hours); $2/hour
modem: 613-567-1714
voice: 613-567-6925

SkyPoint Communications, Inc.
(skypoint.com)
modem: 612-458-3889
voice: 612-475-2959

SSnet: Systems Solutions (marlin.ssnet.com)
price: $25/month; $20 signup
voice: 302-378-1386 or 800-331-1386

Teleport (teleport.com)
price: $10/month
modem: 503-220-0636; log on as *new*
voice: 503-223-4245

Telerama Public Access Internet
(telerama.pgh.pa.us)
price: $.66–$1.32/hour; $6/month minimum
modem: 412-481-5302; log on as *new*
voice: 412-481-3505

Tyrell On-line Communications (tyrell.net)
price: $10/month to $90/year
modem: 816-45-INPUT; ID is *cu,* password is
5-3
voice: 816-459-PLUG

UUNet Canada (uunet.ca)
price: Can$6/hour
voice: 416-368-6621 (Toronto, Canada)

UUNorth (uunorth.north.net)
price: Can$25/20 hours; Can$20 signup
voice: 416-225-8649 (Toronto, Canada)

Vnet (char.vnet.net)
local price: $25/month
long distance: $3.95/hour
modem: 704-347-8839, 919-406-1544, or
919-851-1526; log on as *new*
voice: 704-374-0779

Wariat: APK—Public Access UNI* Site
(wariat.org)
price: $15/20 hours, $35/month, $20 signup
modem: 216-481-9436
voice: 216-481-9428

WELL: The Whole Earth 'Lectronic Link
(well.sf.ca.us)
local: $15/month; $2/hour
long distance: $4/hour additional
modem: 415-332-6106; log on as *newuser*
voice: 415-332-4335

Winternet (icicle.winternet.mpls.mn.us)
price: $19.95/month to $215.40/year
voice: 612-941-9177

The World (world.std.com)
local price: $5/month plus $2/hour or $20/
month for 20 hours
long distance: up to $5.60/hour additional
modem: 617-739-9753; log on as *new*
voice: 617-739-0202

Wyvern Technologies (wyvern.com)
price: $15/month or $144/year, $10 signup
modem: 804-627-1828
voice: 804-622-4289

XMission (xmission.com)
price: $19/month
modem: 801-539-0900
voice: 801-539-0852

XNet Information Systems (xnet.com)
price: $75/6 months
modem: 708-983-6435
voice: 708-983-6064

INDEX

Books have a substantial influence on the destruction of the forests of the Earth. For example, it takes 17 trees to produce one ton of paper. A first printing of 30,000 copies of a typical 480-page book consumes 108,000 pounds of paper which will require 918 trees!

Waite Group Press™ is against the clear-cutting of forests and supports reforestation of the Pacific Northwest of the United States and Canada, where most of this paper comes from. As a publisher with several hundred thousand books sold each year, we feel an obligation to give back to the planet.

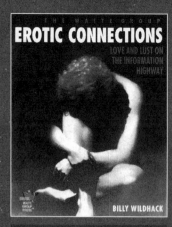

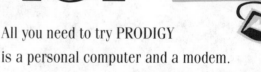

SATISFACTION REPORT CARD

Please fill out this card if you wish to know of updates to
Love Bytes: The Online Dating Handbook, or to receive our catalog.

Company Name:

Division/Department: **Mail Stop:**

Last Name: **First Name:**   **Middle Initial:**

Street Address:

City: **State:**   **Zip:**

Daytime telephone: (   )

Date product was acquired: Month   Day   Year   Your Occupation:

Overall, how would you rate *Love Bytes: The Online Dating Handbook*?

- ☐ Excellent
- ☐ Very Good
- ☐ Good
- ☐ Fair
- ☐ Below Average
- ☐ Poor

What did you like MOST about this book?

What did you like LEAST about this book?

How did you use this book (problem-solver, tutorial, reference...)?

How did you find the pace of this book?

What version of C++ are you using?

What computer languages are you familiar with?

What is your level of computer expertise?
- ☐ New
- ☐ Dabbler
- ☐ Hacker
- ☐ Power User
- ☐ Programmer
- ☐ Experienced Professional

Where did you buy this book?
- ☐ Bookstore (name):
- ☐ Discount store (name):
- ☐ Computer store (name):
- ☐ Catalog (name):
- ☐ Direct from WGP   ☐ Other

What price did you pay for this book?

What influenced your purchase of this book?
- ☐ Recommendation
- ☐ Advertisement
- ☐ Magazine review
- ☐ Store display
- ☐ Mailing
- ☐ Book's format
- ☐ Reputation of Waite Group Press
- ☐ Other

How many computer books do you buy each year?

How many other Waite Group books do you own?

What is your favorite Waite Group book?

Is there any program or subject you would like to see Waite Group Press cover in a similar approach?

Additional comments?

Please send to: Waite Group Press
Attn: *Love Bytes: The Online Dating Handbook*
200 Tamal Plaza
Corte Madera, CA 94925

☐ **Check here for a free Waite Group catalog**   *Love Bytes: The Online Dating Handbook*

EXPLORE the INTERNET
— FREE! —

Delphi Internet™ offers you full access to the Internet and now you can explore this incredible resource with no risk. You get 5 hours of evening and weekend access to try it out for free!*

Use Delphi Internet's mail to exchange messages with over 30 million people throughout the world. Download programs and files using "**FTP**" and connect in real-time to other networks using "**Telnet**." Meet people from around the world with "**Internet Relay Chat**" and check out "**Usenet News**," the world's largest bulletin board with over 10,000 topics.

now supporting **9,600** *and* **14,400 bps** *at no extra charge!**

If you're not familiar with these terms, don't worry; DELPHI has expert **online assistants** and a large collection of help files, books, and other resources to help you get started. After the free trial you can choose from two low-cost membership plans. With rates as low as $1 per hour, no other online service offers so much for so little.

5-Hour Free Trial!*
Dial by modem, 1-800-365-4636
Press return a few times
At *Password*, enter DH994

DELPHI
I N T E R N E T™

Send e-mail to INFO@delphi.com
Questions? Call 1-800-695-4005 (voice)